G000167854

Finding the Real Jesus

Goff Butler

Editor - Kathy Butler

"It is hard to seriously consider Jesus; his birth; his life: his teaching; his cross; and come to any conclusion other than that Jesus is a king, even if his kingdom is one we have not experienced, even if his kingdom seems a Utopia beyond our dreams."   *G. Butler*

Rosebush Publishing

First Published April 2012.

Scripture taken from the HOLY BIBLE, NEW INTERNATIONAL VERSION NIV Copyright 1973, 1978, 1984, 2011 by Biblica. Inc. TM. Used by permission. All rights reserved worldwide.

Scriptures and materials quoted are from the Good News Bible copyright 1994 published by the Bible Societies/Harper Collins Publishers Ltd UK, Good News Bible copyright American Bible Society 1966, 1971, 1976, 1992. Used with permission.

The Revised Standard Version of the Bible, Apocrypha, copyright 1957, Division of Christian Education of the National Council of Churches of Christ in the United States of America. Used by permission. All rights reserved.

Extracts from The Authorized Version of the Bible (The King James Bible), the rights in which are invested in the Crown, are reproduced by permission of the Crown's Patentee, Cambridge University Press.

Copyright Kathy Butler.
No part of this publication is to be reproduced without the permission of the editor, Kathy Butler.

Printed and bound by CPI Group (UK) Ltd, Croydon. CR0 4YY

ISBN 978-0-9572064-0-3

FINDING THE REAL JESUS

Who was Jesus?

Why did he come?

The Reverend Godfrey Butler
Edited by Kathy Butler

DEDICATON

This book is dedicated to my dear husband Godfrey Butler, whose work it is. He was passionate that ordinary people should learn about God, about Jesus, about the real meaning of life. He spent many hours researching backgrounds of places and people, so that he could give a full and accurate account of events.

I believe he would be pleased to know that through this book his work is still serving its purpose.

Kathy Butler

ACKNOWLEDGMENTS

I would like to say a big thank you to my granddaughter Katja Cross for her ideas and production of the covers.

I am grateful to my three daughters, Karen, Jackie and Debra for their advice and opinions especially on the format of the book. They have been invaluable 'sounding boards' for my thoughts. I want also to thank my friend Rosemary Dark for reading the talks, marking errors and making suggestions. Gratitude also goes to Janet Hancock and Jenny Eden for their time reading and correcting, and to Betty Dauncey for her encouragement, ideas and practical help towards launching and marketing this book. Thank you too, to Rosemary Turner, who took the photo of us 'under the rainbow' on the day of our retirement, 26th March 2004.

Kathy Butler

CONTENTS

BIBLE VERSIONS
The New International Version (NIV) is used for most talks.
Others versions used:
The Authorised King James Version of 1611, (AV or KJV).
The Good News Bible (GNB).
The Revised Standard Version of the Apocrypha.
Quotations from Scripture are in Italics.

LIST OF POEMS

Some of these poems were read during services
where appropriate.

The poems are by Kathy Butler

Godfrey Butler was born in 1937 in Brighton, the son of a Merchant Seaman. He was sent to Sunday School at St Bartholomew's Church and later confirmed. In his teenage years he made his decision for God while camping on the Isle of Wight with a local Crusader group. As a young man Goff was an enthusiastic member of Holland Road Baptist Church in Hove, where Rev. George Rudman was the minister. His National Service was spent as a Coder in the Navy.

I was born and grew up in Midsomer Norton in Somerset and became a Christian at High Street Methodist Church. I met Goff at Bognor Regis College of Education where we both trained to be teachers. Goff gained Distinction in Biology and Maths. We married in 1962 and lived for our first five years in Brighton, attending his church in Holland Road. We have three daughters. We moved to New Milton and then to Oxfordshire, where Goff was Senior Master at Berinsfield and became Deputy Headmaster at the Ickneild School in Watlington. While we lived in Wallingford, and while secretary of our Baptist Church, Goff was busy preaching in the nearby Methodist circuit and in our own and other fellowships. It was after he took a memorial service for one of his school colleagues that another said to him, "You should be doing this full time."

It took a few years of prayer, advice and struggle for Goff to balance his duty to provide for his family with the definite call he felt from God. Eventually, with my whole-hearted backing, he applied for early retirement and for acceptance for ministerial training by the Baptist Union.

He undertook three years of study at Regent's Park College in Oxford, while student minister of Boyn Hill Baptist Church in Maidenhead. With great vigour he threw himself into his new life. He worked hard at his studies and early on was found re-tiling the church baptistry for his first baptisms. A building project rebuilt the front of the church and added rooms. Under his leadership and guidance the church grew. In October during his third year, he suffered a serious heart attack.

I sat in bed alone that night wondering why God had led us this way. "What church will ever want him now?" I thought. In my Bible God showed me the passage in Isaiah 42: *I will lead the blind by ways they have not known.* Just then we were blind.

After his by-pass surgery, to my surprise there were three churches requesting him. We accepted the call to Romsey Baptist Church in Hampshire, where we spent six busy and fulfilling years. Goff's preaching built up the fellowship, the church was refurbished and there were many who came to know Christ and were baptised. In 1996 we moved across the New Forest to Ferndown United Church. Here we had eight happy years during which a new children's work was established, many folk were baptised and the church grew substantially, due at least in part to God's word speaking through Goff's biblical teaching.

We retired in 2004 when Goff was sixty-six. He carried on preaching, moderating at other churches and mentoring new ministers until his sudden death in May 2006.

He died whilst still a busy preacher and many people said how they would love to be able to hear him again. Two years later, while redecorating his study I realised I had files of all his talks and sermons typed out in full, each dated with its news-sheet. His sermons prior to 1992 were in school exercise books

I have felt God prompting me to use this resource. Reading through Goff's work I have been moved and my faith deepened, hence this small selection about the life of Jesus. Goff's mission was to show how important it is to know Jesus. As you read this book may the real Jesus shine through to you.

Kathy Butler

The Coming

A path of light through cumulus clouds,
A candle of hope in a devastated city,
A kind word in a land of thorns,
A drop of warm blood on virgin snow,
God in a broken world.

Ferndown United Church April 7th 2002. This was the Baptismal Service for Samantha Yeates and Allan Green.

1. Called to Follow
Luke 4.16-41, Matthew 4.18-25

I want to ask you two questions. They are quite straightforward, no tricks, but I believe it is my responsibility to make you think about them and answer them.

Question One – Have you ever seriously thought about Jesus, who he is, and the claims he may have on your life?

Question Two – Have you ever become a follower of Jesus?
Jesus said, "Come, follow me, and I will make you fishers of men." At once they left their nets and followed him. (Matthew 4.20)

This command of Jesus seems very blunt. Four fishermen are working on the sea shore. Along comes Jesus and calls them to follow him. At once they drop everything and, apparently without a thought for their families, they mindlessly follow him.

I want to suggest to you that if that was what happened, even though it may have worked out well and been the right action to take, it would not have been sensible or a course of action that I would

13

recommend.

But just as it would have been crazy to follow Jesus without first finding out about him, it surely is equally crazy to reject Jesus out of hand, without giving any serious thought as to whether his claim are true or false? Yet that is what so many people do. Perhaps that is what you have done so far in life. Jesus has made no particular impact on you. You have pushed him to one side, ignoring or rejecting him without considering the implications of your actions. If he really is the Son of God, the only Saviour of the world, shouldn't you be taking him seriously?

Simon Peter, Andrew, James and John were not unthinking idiots. They were hard-headed, worldly-wise Galilean business men, with careers bound up in the thriving fishing industry. There is nothing to suggest that they were not doing very nicely. Yet at the call of Jesus they gave it all up to become his followers. They became so sure of him that they were prepared to stake their lives on his claims.

During the persecutions of the emperor Nero in about A.D. 64 Simon Peter was crucified, head down, in Rome. Andrew was crucified in a spread-eagled position in Achaia in southern Greece. James was beheaded by Herod Agrippa 1 in A.D. 44.   John died a natural death but spent many years of his life in exile on Patmos, one of the Greek prison islands in the Aegean Sea.

What must there have been about Jesus to cause men to go that far for their faith? What evidence did they have to entrust the whole of their lives to him?

Jesus was a young man of about thirty. He had newly taken on the role of rabbi, or roving teacher. Simon Peter and Andrew came from Bethsaida and had set up business in Capernaum, a fishing port at the northern end of Lake Galilee. They may well have been in some sort of co-operative with Zebedee and his sons James and John. It wasn't always easy, for Simon was a strong character and James and John were such hotheads that they were known to all the locals as "Sons of Thunder."

Jesus had also set up home, in so far as rabbis had a home, in

Capernaum. Natural curiosity, in such a small community, would lead these men and others to seek out the background of this newcomer. Who was he? Where did he come from? How does he have the audacity to call himself a rabbi, a holy man, a teacher of the ways of God?

As they asked questions they must have discovered that he came from Nazareth, the city over the hill, and was the son of a carpenter; though it was rumoured that he was illegitimate, conceived before Joseph and Mary were married.

Nazareth had a bad reputation. It was known that there were so many cheats and liars there that a local saying went, "Did any good thing ever come out of Nazareth!"

The suggestion was that Jesus had run away to Capernaum because of some trouble he had caused in the synagogue in Nazareth.

The story was that he had been into the synagogue on a particular Saturday; the Sabbath day, and had been invited to read from the Jewish scriptures. They handed him the scroll of the prophet Isaiah and it may well have been that he read the set passage for the day. Turning to the place where it spoke about the Messiah whom they expected God would send, he read:

"The Spirit of the Lord is upon me, because he has chosen me to bring good news to the poor. He has sent me to proclaim liberty to the captives and recovery of sight to the blind; to set free the oppressed and announce that the time has come when the Lord will save his people."(Luke 4.18-21)

Jesus rolled up the scroll and gave it back to the attendant, but instead of then simply going back to his place, he stood his ground and boldly proclaimed:

"Today this scripture has been fulfilled in your hearing."

It was as if he said, "This passage of scripture has come true today – that's me."

The people in the synagogue were furious. They dragged him up to the top of the hill above Nazareth, and were about to throw him down the cliff when somehow, as if by divine protection, he simply walked through the middle of the crowd and slipped away.

That is what had caused him to leave Nazareth and arrive in Capernaum.

There was another strange story about Jesus. It was said he had been out to the river Jordan, the river which flowed south out of the Lake of Galilee and down to the Dead Sea. He had been to see another preacher who was making a great impact. This was John, who some said was a cousin of Jesus. John was calling people to clean up their lives, to repent, and as a sign that they had repented, to be baptised in the river Jordan. Baptism was a sign that they wanted their sins to be washed away and that they wanted to live new lives.

It was said that when John saw Jesus approaching he gave him an extraordinary greeting. He called to the crowds:

"Look, the Lamb of God who takes away the sin of the world!" (John 1.29)

When Jesus asked to be baptised John at first refused, saying he was not worthy to unlace his sandals and appealing to Jesus to baptise him instead. Jesus, however, insisted, saying that by being baptised we do all that God requires. When John baptised him something strange happened. As Jesus came up out of the water a dove fluttered down from the sky and hovered over him. Those who were there were sure they had heard a voice saying:

"This is my Son, whom I love: with him I am well pleased." (Matthew 3.17)

These amazing stories were repeated about Jesus in Capernaum. What did the locals think? Either he was someone very special indeed, or he was a cheat and a liar, someone to steer well clear of.

I have no doubt that Simon Peter, Andrew, James and John, along with all the rest of the locals in Capernaum, were busy checking out this Jesus fellow.

Everyone went to the synagogue in Capernaum. It was expected of every good Jew. What better opportunity to examine this new rabbi than to give him the chance to speak one Sabbath.

The occasion arose. Jesus was invited to speak and settled down to talk to the people about God. Everyone was amazed. He was certainly different. He didn't trot out the same old clap-trap as the usual preachers. There was something vital and real, thought provoking, stimulating, in what he said. Instead of the normal nodding off, everyone was listening when it happened.

There was a man in the synagogue; a well-known oddity. Everyone said he was demon-possessed. Suddenly, as Jesus was speaking, this man stood up and screamed out in a loud voice:

"Ah! What do you want with us, Jesus of Nazareth? Have you come to destroy us? I know who you are; the Holy One of God!"

This poor fellow had often shouted out in the synagogue, but never before had he said anything like this! It sounded real, prophetic. However what really astounded the people was the way Jesus dealt with him. Jesus simply spoke to the spirit:

"Be quiet," Jesus said sternly. "Come out of him!"

The man was thrown to the floor and lay there quietly, unharmed. They realised he had been cured. The evil spirit had left him calm and completely sane, as much in his right mind as anyone else. Everyone was stunned. Now they were convinced that Jesus was someone different, someone special.

Simon Peter was so convinced that he asked Jesus if he would come home with him. His mother-in-law was ill, really ill. She had the kind of high fever which normally ended in death. Simon was very concerned for her. Would Jesus come home with him and say a prayer for her?

Jesus did more than that: *He bent over her and rebuked the fever, and it left her.*

Not only was her temperature down to normal at that moment, but instead of feeling the weakness common to us all after a severe illness, she got up from her sick bed and cooked a meal for them.

Lots of folk had followed Jesus from the synagogue. They had seen what had happened to the man who had been possessed. Now they witnessed Simon Peter's mother-in-law being healed. As the sun set, marking the end of the Sabbath and freedom from its laws, they all wanted to bring their sick friends and relatives to Jesus.

As the sick were brought to him, Jesus was pleased to place his hands on them, and when he prayed, they were all healed.

It is little wonder then, when Jesus came along and met up again with Simon Peter and his brother Andrew, and with James and John, that they were ready to follow him. They had seen plenty of evidence. They knew in their hearts that Jesus was someone very important.

You could make plenty of money catching fish, but it wasn't especially fulfilling. It didn't revolutionise peoples' lives for good. It didn't build the kingdom of God.

So when Jesus came down to the shore and called:

"Come, follow me, and I will make you fishers of men,"

- it was a done deal. What a wonderful privilege it was to be chosen! What a great opportunity! How could they refuse?

Friends, there is so much evidence out there about Jesus, if you will stop and examine it. Jesus does change lives. Jesus does forgive sins and clean up lives. Jesus brings direction and purpose to life. Jesus is alive. Jesus is God's only Son. Jesus died in your place. Jesus does have a claim on your life.

Most wonderful of all – Jesus still calls. His call to you today is probably a sort of burning inside. You know it is true and you sense that he is saying to you:

"Follow me."

The decision is yours. He will not force you to come to him. Countless thousands over the generations have responded. They have come to Jesus and not one of them has been given cause to regret their decision.

What about you? Have you been led to think more seriously about Jesus; who he is and the claims he may have on your life?

As Allan and Samantha are coming to commit their lives to Jesus, he invites you. What will you do?

PART 1

HOW
IT ALL BEGAN

Shepherd

I was there that night
when the air shone
in a sky of spilled wine
red as blood.

I heard in the dazzle
the anthem of birth,
deeper than man's dreaming,
though the sheep slept on.

I knelt where the stars
formed the shape of a cross,
holding my lamb
as an offering.

2. The Beginning of New Hope
Luke 1.26-56

Christmas is nearly with us once again. Are you excited? Does Christmas fill you with hope? The danger is that with all the commercial hype, and with all the work that it entails, we miss the true wonder of God's intervention in our history.

In an endeavour to recapture that hope afresh, I want us this morning to spend a little while looking at the announcement of the news to Mary that she is to have a baby.

Who is this virgin named Mary?
In the sixth month God sent the angel Gabriel to Nazareth, a town in Galilee, to a virgin pledged to be married to a man named Joseph, a descendant of David. The virgin's name was Mary.

The more I study these opening verses, the more improbable God's intervention in human history appears, and therefore if it is true, all the more wonderful.

Firstly I want to remind you of the unique nature of Luke Chapters One and Two. Luke has undertaken to draw up a most careful account for Theophilus concerning the life and teaching of Jesus, and this makes up his gospel. He is also committed to an accurate record of the early days of the church, and this becomes The Acts of the Apostles. Luke always places his narrative in time so that it can be thoroughly checked. We know (verse 5) that this was in the time of Herod king of Judea and that Jesus was born at the time of the census ordered by the Emperor Caesar Augustus. He points out that his was the first census that took place when Quirinius was governor of Syria (2.1-2). The visit of the angel to Mary and the birth of Jesus have a place in history which can be verified by events in Rome, Judea and in Syria.

Throughout the two books written by Luke the language and style is consistent except for the passage Luke 1.5 to 2.52. Though Luke has incorporated these verses into his gospel they originate from someone else, and we believe the original source must have been Mary the mother of Jesus, for only she could have had all these intimate personal insights.

"The sixth month" is the sixth month of Elizabeth's pregnancy. God's plan is already beginning to unfold when God sends the angel Gabriel to Nazareth. Recent Bible translations are correct to call it a town rather than a city, for Nazareth was a small hill town, not in Judea where previous kings had been born, but in Galilee. Galileans were not necessarily irreligious but they were a great deal more lax concerning the application of the law than the Judeans were. They were not concerned, for example, that their food should be strictly kosher. Nazareth, though not inaccessible, was not on any trade route and would have been unknown, had it not been for the pugnacious and rebellious nature of its residents, which gave it a reputation which caused Nathanael to ask, "Did any good thing ever come out of Nazareth?"

Do angels think like us? If they do, I wonder what Gabriel thought when he was asked to go to Nazareth: - "I don't mind going to the temple in Jerusalem to visit Zechariah, a priest of the priestly line of Abijah, that's very acceptable – but to Nazareth in Galilee! Excuse me Lord, are you sure there hasn't been some dreadful mistake?"

But no – God hasn't got it wrong. Gabriel is to go to Mary who is espoused, engaged to be married, to Joseph.

Have you ever realised how little we know about Mary? Joseph, we know, was not the biological father of Jesus. His ancestry is traced back by both Matthew and Luke, and the differences in the records suggest that they did independent research. But of Mary we know nothing, other than that she was a relative, perhaps a cousin of Elizabeth. We know her family was not rich for she was betrothed to an artisan carpenter. All sorts of guesses about her have been made. She must somehow have been of the line of David, and her parents of priestly stock. We think she was somewhere between fourteen and sixteen years of age, and that she must have been a very devout young woman, but we don't know any of these things for sure.

We know that she was a virgin; she had not had sex with any man. And we know that God in his sovereign power and wisdom had chosen her as the vehicle through which his only begotten son Jesus might be born.

I find that amazing. It is something which fills me with hope – because I realise that just as God chose Mary as someone through whom he could do something wonderful, he has chosen me – and he has chosen you.

You did not choose me, but I chose you and appointed you to go and bear fruit, fruit that will last. (John 15.16)

But you are a chosen people, a royal priesthood, a holy nation, a people belonging to God, that you may declare the praises of him who called you out of darkness into his wonderful light. (1 Peter 2.9)

Like you, I am just an ordinary person from ordinary stock – born in a very ordinary town in a country where belief in God is in decline – and yet God has a plan and a purpose, a divine plan and purpose, for my life. He longs to bless me and make me a blessing. I am part of his church, part of his kingdom. The impact he wants me to make is not insignificant. He has appointed me and you – to go and bear fruit that will last! The very thought is empowering. This Christmas will you take hold of that? There could be no greater Christmas gift – than to move into all that God intends for your life.

A Challenging and Disturbing Call

The angel went to her and said, "Greetings, you who are highly favoured! The Lord is with you." Mary was greatly troubled at his words and wondered what kind of greeting this might be. But the angel said to her, "Do not be afraid Mary, you have found favour with God. You will be with child and give birth to a son, and you are to give him the name Jesus. He will be great and will be called the Son of the Most High. The Lord God will give him the throne of his father David, and he will reign over the house of Jacob forever; his kingdom will never end."

Do we have any understanding of what God asks of Mary? In the temple in Jerusalem the priest Zechariah, husband of Elizabeth, was troubled by the appearance of the angel. Mary is troubled by Gabriel's words, *"Greetings you who are highly favoured! The Lord is with you."* Try to remember this is a teenage girl from a small town, who finds herself face to face with the archangel Gabriel! How did you feel in front of your headmaster or headmistress? How would you feel summoned to meet the Queen? "You are highly favoured," means, "You are a recipient of God's glorious grace!" It's no surprise that Mary wonders what is coming.

Gabriel makes the extraordinary announcement, "You are going to have a baby, a son; and you are to call him Jesus." Initially Mary must have thought this was wonderful news. Every girl hoped one day to marry and have children. Every girl prayed to have at least one son. Jewish girls were also taught that they might pray that if they found exceptional favour with God, they might be chosen to bear the Messiah. Suddenly the immediacy of this dawns on Mary. The angel is telling her, that beyond every Jewish girl's wildest dreams, she is actually going to conceive the Christ Child!

The divine announcement continues:

"He will be great."

The language means; "He will be the greatest there has ever been." This greatness contrasts not only with the rest of normal humanity, but also with the greatness of John the Baptist, who would be great in the sight of the Lord:

"He will be called the Son of the Most High."

John was to be the prophet of the Most High; Mary's child has a much higher designation; he is to be the very Son of God.

"The Lord will give him the throne of his father David."

This is a clear affirmation that Jesus will be the promised Messiah. And it is all about to happen now!

The Beginning of New Hope – Luke 1.26-56

Zechariah the priest simply didn't believe the angel who told him that Elizabeth his wife was to bear a son in her old age. To him it was impossible. Mary too is overwhelmed, but her question is not one of disbelief. Her question is how? She knows how babies are conceived, and that she has never slept with Joseph or any other man, and has no intention of doing so until they are given to one another in marriage, so she asks,

"How will this be," Mary asked the angel, "since I am a virgin?"

I want you to see that Mary, though scared by the prospect of what God is calling her to be, is thrilled to the root of her being. I want you to see Mary's faith. Who would believe that God could or would do such a thing as this, and that he would use a little maiden from Nazareth to fulfil his Messianic purposes? Surely at least he would choose some princess in one of Herod's royal palaces. But as Mary thinks about it, she understands that God has chosen her. She is the recipient of the grace of God.

Now as you see the incredible challenge that comes to Mary – does it not put God's call on your life into some sort of perspective?

God seeks a great act of submissiveness from Mary. You too are a recipient of God's grace. You and I are called to be part of his perfect plan. God calls us to step out in faith and to trust him, perhaps in areas where he has been challenging us for years. Like you and me, Mary was just one of the ordinary people. Like you she was weak and ill equipped. I am sure she felt totally inadequate for what God was asking her to be – so listen to God's words to Paul.

But he said to me, "My grace is sufficient for you, for my power is made perfect in weakness." (2 Corinthians 12.9)

When God calls, he makes the impossible happen

"How will this be, "Mary asked the angel, "since I am a virgin?" The angel answered, "The Holy Spirit will come upon you, and the power of the Most High will overshadow you. So the holy one to be born will be called the Son of God. Even Elizabeth your relative is going to have a child in her old age, and she who was said to be barren is in her sixth month. For nothing is impossible with God."

Many years ago someone remarked to me that the two most impossible parts of the Bible are the virgin birth and the resurrection of Jesus. I wonder if that person would change their opinion concerning the virgin birth in the light of current advances in genetics and fertility treatment. I am told that there is nothing now, except ethics, to prevent the cloning of human beings. We can clone sheep – we can clone pigs. Cloning pigs may even be the way forward for obtaining a supply of organs for transplant into humans.

Now in no way am I suggesting that Jesus was a clone, for if cells from Mary were cloned, then Jesus would have been female. But if the incredible things that we see being done biologically in our day and age are possible to man, why should it be too difficult, when God is in charge, for a virgin to conceive a child?

But what about Mary? She did not live in the twentieth or twenty-first centuries. As far as men and women were concerned in her day, children were only conceived when a woman lay with a man. It is all very well for the angel to talk of the Holy Spirit coming upon her, and the power of the Most High overshadowing her. However will she explain it to Joseph – to her parents – and to all the wagging tongues in Nazareth? At best she will be sneered at and ostracised from her community. In all probability Joseph will write her a letter of divorce, and he would even be within his rights to ask that she should be stoned to death! What is Mary to do? What would you do?

At that moment in time, some two thousand years ago, the whole of human destiny hung in the balance, dependent on the willingness of a teenage girl to say, "Yes," to what appeared to be a dangerous and outrageously audacious plan.

Suppose she had said "No!" Did God have a plan B? We just don't know.

It is at this time of decision that Gabriel tells her the news about her cousin Elizabeth – and somehow that is just what Mary needs to help her to go through with the matter. I expect she had often heard about Zechariah and Elizabeth. Perhaps the families had visited. She would have known about their longing for a child, and the hopelessness of it all because she was barren. I imagine Mary realising, – "If God can undertake for them, then he'll see me through too, however great an adventure this is that I am undertaking for him."

"I am the Lord's servant," Mary answered. "May it be to me as you have said." Then the angel left her.

What a wonderful display of confidence in God!

I want you to see this morning that it was no accident of fate, or random chance, or even human supposition that Mary of Nazareth bore Jesus, as was prophesied by Isaiah:

A virgin will be with child and will give birth to a son. (Isaiah 7.14)

It was God's redemptive plan to send his son Jesus to be Immanuel – God with us. Praise God that Jesus really is Christ the Lord.

Many, I believe, have entered into only a fraction of the blessing that God intends for their lives. God longs to do so much more – in you and through you and for you. Maybe he has even given you a vision, a dream, but until now you have not been able to trust him for it.

God's plan was worked through Elizabeth and Zechariah, and through Mary and Joseph. Today God may be challenging you to follow him in some new way. Can you trust him for the future as we pass into a new millennium? God will not let you down, for nothing is too difficult for the Lord.

"Blessed is the person who has believed that what the Lord has said will be accomplished!"

3. Shepherds, Wise Men, and You
Luke 2.1-20, Matthew 2.1-12 KJV

"Fear not; for behold I bring you good tidings of great joy which shall be to all people."

Tonight I've got good news to share with you. If you are prepared to be honest with yourself, this Christmas can be a time of Great Joy!

Imagine being one of those Bethlehem shepherds. Most shepherds worked for their families. Shepherding would be the job of the youngest son. There was no trusting cash to a bank or building society and there would not be much capital appreciation on your typical 'one up, one down' house; so you invested your money in a flock of sheep. However in Bethlehem shepherds were employed by the High Priest to raise sheep for sacrifices, especially for Passover.

It would be the same old routine every day: herding the flocks round the Bethlehem fields and sleeping with them at night in case of wolves or robbers. Endlessly you had to count your sheep because the value of a lost one would be docked from your already paltry wages. Sometimes you had hardly enough food for your family.

At Passover time poor families brought a lamb from their own small flock to the temple for sacrifice, only for it to be rejected by the inspectors. The family was ripped off as one of the Bethlehem lambs was sold to them for an exorbitant price. There was much discontent among the poor.

Now on the surface being a Magi – a Wise Man, was a much better prospect. You have plenty of inherited wealth; you are well educated and considered one of the clever people. You have time to play being "Patrick Moore." All day long you can keep your telescope trained on the skies, looking, watching, calculating and doing some astrology on the side. You are hoping for something exciting and new.

To a shepherd the prospect of becoming a Magi was probably like the car park attendant becoming an airline pilot – but in reality both were hoping for something better.

The sketch we saw was written by Vellum Pitts when he was ninety-two. He had seen that every one of us is like a shepherd or a wise man, whether we are at school, college, office, factory, shop floor or home. We are trapped in our situations. We all need to find a new purpose, a new joy in our lives.

In the back of their minds both the shepherds and the wise men had a deep rooted vision of a better way. This way involved God, who was going to break through and do a new thing which would be good and would bring great joy. For the shepherds, their scriptures spoke about a Messiah or Christ, a man anointed by God, who would take away all the hopelessness and who would establish a kingdom of peace. Strangely their great prophet Isaiah had pictured this Messiah as a lamb who would be sacrificed just like their lambs being reared for the temple sacrifices. Isaiah said the Messiah would:

bear our griefs and carry our sorrows,

be wounded for our transgressions, bruised for our iniquities,

be lashed, and with his stripes we would be healed.

be brought before those who would put him to death.

as he was killed, give himself as an offering for sin.

(Isaiah 53)

The wise men had an idea that one day a great deliverer and King would come. He would be a Jew and his birth would be dramatically heralded by a star.

Put yourself in the sandals of the shepherds, out on the hillside on a chilly night, watching the humps of sleeping sheep

29

under the pale moonlight – when suddenly the night sky becomes a blaze of glory, filled with a dazzling light! You hear voices praising God and telling you not to fear. This is the good news, the Christ has been born!

Now imagine being one of the Magi that same Christmas night. You see that same glory in the sky, but for you it is the bursting into life of a bright new star. You leap up with excitement to tell the others. This is what you have been waiting for: the new King has come!

What do you do? You have no doubt, no hesitation. Whatever the risk, whatever the cost; here is hope, here is joy. You must find the Christ.

If you have the riches of the Magi you can bring costly gifts: gold, frankincense and myrrh. If you are a shepherd perhaps you bring a lamb. You hurry to find him, and realise he is all your faith and hope said he would be. You kneel to worship.

Whether you are shepherd or Magi you are changed. You are turned around. You have found purpose. You now have a relationship with the living God. Your new world order has begun.

I want you to be honest with yourself. Are you searching for something? Do you need to find that God is real? Do you long for the faith that some people seem to have? Have you a God-shaped hole deep in your very being which craves the satisfaction which only God can fill?

God wants you to find Jesus. The angels said that the good news of great joy was for all people. Jesus himself said:

"For God so loved the world that he gave his only Son, that whoever believeth in him should not perish but have everlasting life." (John 3.16)

The apostle John wrote:

"But as many as received him, to them he gave the power to become the sons of God, even to them that believe on his name." (John 1.12)

If you can believe in him, then come, confess your sins. Come to the Christ. Worship and adore your Saviour. Your new world order can begin right now.

PART 2

MIRACLES

OF JESUS

Wind

I lash the waves, I whip the rocks,
I fling the flotsam craft,
the spindly fishing smacks,
I crush the harbour walls to dust.

Few have the fists to face my power
when I rip roots of pine and ash.
When I mock man's imaginings,
his towers and painted palaces,
all his glass houses fall!

The night that He was in the boat
I whistled whirlpools, rushed the keeling boards,
pierced skin and eyes with blinding rain
until they begged,
Master, we're going to drown!

I swaggered in my nimbus crown
across the bursting sky, until He stood;
looked sternly at my bit of fun,
Be still! I lay down.

The Lord of all creation spoke to me -
then came a shining silence on the sea.

Ferndown United Church April 28th 2002
Loch Road Baptist Church April 3rd 2005

4. The First Great Sign about Jesus
John 2.1-11

This the first of his miraculous signs Jesus performed at Cana in Galilee. He thus revealed his glory, and the disciples put their faith in him.

This first miracle of Jesus seems to be an extravagant luxury. To be short of wine at a wedding may have been a terrible embarrassment – but it was hardly a life or death crisis. Then to provide about one hundred and thirty-two gallons, (which is about eight hundred and sixty bottles) of the very choicest wine – we ask what is going on? Yet in that very point we learn an important lesson. None of Jesus' miracles were only kind actions to alleviate distress; they were all signs revealing Jesus for who he was – The Messiah, the Saviour of the world. Each one was to bring glory to God.

Cana is some eight miles north of Nazareth, towards Galilee. It is visible from the hills above Nazareth. Even today it is a poor area with stony soil which supports a few sheep or goats and produces a limited crop of olives or grapes. Any prosperity then and now comes principally from the limestone quarries and the labours of skilled masons who carve the stone. It is a very ordinary place – yet it is chosen by God for Christ's first great sign or miracle.

Grasp hold of this fact for it is important. Jesus works in and with the ordinary. Jesus is still willing, however ordinary you are, at any time, in any place, to bring about a miracle for you; to meet your need, as long as it is for the glory of God the Father.

On the third day a wedding took place at Cana in Galilee. Jesus' mother was there, and Jesus and his disciples had also been invited to the wedding.

This is all the information we have from John: the place and that Jesus, his mother and his disciples were there.

There are other very early writings which tell this same story. They are not scripture so we must not make for them the assumptions we make concerning the truth of scripture. Some were put forward as scripture but were rejected in A.D.170 when the Muratorian Canon met to determine which records should be adopted as Holy Scripture.

Firstly the Coptic Church has a gospel in which Mary's sister is said to be the groom's mother. I think that makes Jesus a cousin of the bridegroom.

Secondly a collection known as the Monarchian Prefaces tells of "The Wedding of John, son of Salome, the sister of Mary." This is consistent with the Coptic gospel, and seems to suggest that John could even be recording an event which occurred at his own wedding.

There are two other background points to note as we get into the story. Firstly, for a Jew the cost of the wedding is the responsibility of the groom's family. Secondly, Mary clearly has responsibilities at this wedding. She is the one worrying and giving orders, so it almost certainly is a family affair.

In Jewish weddings it was expected that the bride would be a virgin. I don't want today to go into the Old Testament scriptures concerning that, but let me remind you how Joseph was concerned, when he discovered Mary was pregnant, not to make her a public example, but to have her put away privately. He would have every right if she was not a virgin, not only to end the betrothal, but even to have her stoned because of her infidelity. Young people, be prepared to go against the culture of your day. Prize your virginity as something precious to be given only to your partner in marriage.

Provided the bride was a virgin, the wedding always took

place on a Wednesday, to allow three full days of feasting before the Sabbath, though feasting would normally carry on for longer than that – at least a week and often two weeks. If she was not a virgin she must be married on a Thursday or a Friday – the message was clear for all.

The day began with festivities – there were traditional customs at both houses and the great game was; when would the groom arrive at the bride's home to take his wife? Part of the suspense of the day was for him not to announce the time he planned to arrive, though it was nearly always evening. The bride and bridesmaids were expected to be ready. The groom would put on his best robe and with a garland round his head would set out with his groomsman and a band of musicians and torch bearers. The bride would be collected. Then, when it was dark, there would be the wedding procession. Lit by flaming torches the bride and groom would walk under a canopy supported on poles held by four close friends. They would take a circuitous route round all the streets in the village. As they passed, well-wishers would come out, call their greetings and strew flowers in front of the couple making their way to the groom's home where the ceremony would take place. Promises were made between families, concerning friendship, loyalty to one another and affirming any property arrangements that had been agreed.

It was not primarily a religious affair. At many weddings a priest was not involved. If the priest took part it would be to pray that God would bless the couple with many children, especially sons. After the promises the husband-to-be would declare, "She is my wife and I am her husband from this day forward." He would then retire to the bridal chamber and the bride's father would lead in the bride, completely veiled, and give her to her husband in the bridal chamber.

Because of this custom of the bride being fully veiled as she was led into the bridal chamber, Laban in the Old Testament was able to pass off Leah rather than Rachel to Jacob on their wedding night.

The marriage would be consummated through sexual union while the guests waited. Though much wine may have been drunk during the day, only then did the feasting proper begin.

There was no going away on honeymoon, but for a week the bride and groom were given simple crowns. For a week they were to be royal and to do no work. A marriage was a great celebration! There was no way of keeping it quiet. The whole village or town would know about it.

Everybody knew because there was so much rejoicing! I have deliberately made much of this because the scriptures tell me that the Church is the Bride of Christ. Does everyone know that we are his? The greatest event in our lives was when Jesus called us and we responded and committed our lives to him. Do we live as if it is great? Is our Christian life a celebration?

I must not trivialise, for there are great trials, pains, difficulties and temptations that face us through life, but the Christian life is not just for the future. It is not simply about a home in glory and some future bliss. The Christian life is about beginning eternal life here and now – a life of joy and peace, with direction and purpose, a life that is shared with others, a life that is appealing.

Have you held back from saying "yes" to Jesus, to putting your life under his control, to allowing him to deal with the sin and hurt and shame in your life?

Whenever the Lord deals with a person, be it a miracle or a searching interview, such as with Nicodemus or Peter, he aims at restoring that person to wholeness. The aim of Jesus is to bring you to wholeness, to build you, to change your situation for good, ultimately to bring you deep joy.

When the wine was gone, Jesus' mother said to him, "They have no more wine."

This miracle presents problems to many Christians, especially those who strongly advocate total abstinence from alcoholic drink. We must all respect this position. We need to see the problems which alcohol can present; the money which is wasted; the harm that is done to individuals and families when alcohol changes the personality of the drinker. Indeed there are many reasons to recommend soft drinks over alcohol.

But wherever we stand over this matter; here we deal with the culture of Jesus' day; a culture where drunkenness was a disgrace; but also where wine was the symbol of joy. The rabbis had a saying, "Without wine there is no joy." Remember the vine was the national symbol of the Jews. It appeared on their coinage. A great golden ornamental vine decorated the Holy of Holies in the Temple.

Wine was important. The cups of wine drunk at the Passover toasted freedom and what God had done for the nation. The Good Samaritan poured oil and wine on the wounds of the injured man. In the East hospitality was a sacred duty, so wine always needed to be available.

For wine to fail at a wedding was the greatest embarrassment. Some would even construe it as an insult to the bride's family. Being poor was no excuse for not having adequate supplies, even if some of the wine you served later in the feast was of an inferior quality.

A disaster happens at this wedding in Cana. It is not just the best wine that has gone, but the "plonk" has gone as well! Mary comes to Jesus. Many say, what a remarkable act of faith, but perhaps there was simply nothing else she could do. I find the love of God absolutely amazing. How often I only come to him when other sources have failed. When will I learn? Because he loves me so much, because he is full of grace towards me – he abundantly supplies my every need!

"Dear woman, why do you involve me?" Jesus replied. "My time has not yet come."

This is a difficult verse. It is so difficult that most translators can't believe it to be Jesus' words and they seek to soften it. Literally translated from the Greek it says, "What have we to do with one another, woman? My hour has not yet arrived." Even though this may seem a very brusque treatment of his mother, Mary senses that all will be well and gives one of the most profound pieces of advice in all of scripture.

His mother said to the servants, "Do whatever he tells you."

That is a gem for Christian living. If God tells you, if Jesus tells you – then you are a fool if you ignore it. Remember God only wants the very best for you.

Jesus said to the servants, "Fill the jars with water," so they filled them to the brim.

Each jar held between twenty to thirty gallons. They were

used to hold water for ceremonial washing; foot washing when guests arrived and hand washing before and after a meal. It was not water for drinking. The water jars were normally filled when the level in the wells was high. They were required by the religious law and so were symbols of a religion in which formal rules had to be obeyed. Men were trapped by a religious system which offered no joy, only bondage.

The men do as Jesus instructed them, having no idea why they are doing it. They obey because Mary has told them to do whatever Jesus tells them. When they have filled the jars with water, Jesus tells them to draw some off and take it to the master of the banquet.

We know what Jesus had done. He had turned it into the very best wine. It was no longer ceremonial water; a sign of the law, but wine; a symbol of freedom, of celebration and of joy.

Which symbolises you today – the ceremonial water, or the wine? If the water, what is it that grips you, that keeps you back from joy? What do you need – forgiveness, healing, purpose, peace?

Just look at the abundance of wine which Jesus supplies. The very minimum was one hundred and twenty gallons but it may have been more like one hundred and thirty-two gallons. God's grace is just like that, super-abundant! A past generation used the term, "Full Salvation," a term that meant that when Jesus comes into your life, he fills you with a joy that is running over.

Let Paul capture the picture for us:

"Now to Him who is able to do immeasurably more than we ask or imagine, according to His power that is at work in us..." *(Ephesians 3.20)*

Think about it - **Jesus turned water into wine**. I want you to remember that John probably wrote his gospel originally for a Greek readership. Like Jews, Greeks held wine as a symbol of joy and rejoicing. Greeks were not as restrained as Jews concerning drunkenness. Greeks had various gods of wine, including Bacchus who was associated with excess of wine, and Dionysus whose temple was at Thyia near Corinth. Each year at Thyia they held the ceremony of "The Three Kettles."

One evening at a great ceremony, the three kettles would be

filled with water in front of the whole congregation, and placed on the altar. The congregation then filed out of the temple and visitors were invited to seal the doors. The next morning the congregation would return. The seals would be broken; the kettles would be taken from the altar and poured out. Year after year a wonderful miracle would have occurred – the water would have become wine!

But the people had been fooled; a great deception was going on. There was a back door and the responsibility of the duty priests to Dionysus was to make sure that during the night the water was exchanged for wine. Many of the locals knew of course, but they kept quiet. Promulgating the deception was wonderful for business. Year by year it brought thousand upon thousand to visit the shrine!

The water put into those foot washing jars at Cana was just water, and if it had stayed there, before many days it would have become stale and flat.

For many of us that is a picture of life – dull, stale and flat. The Devil deceives us into believing that this is all there is to life. We pretend that life is vital, sparkling and exciting, and we seek to sustain the pretence from day to day with tawdry, temporary stimulations. Yet the gospel is that water can be turned into the very best wine. Jesus says there is another way. Jesus says, "I am the way, the truth and the life."

Jesus is no deceiver. Jesus really does turn water into wine. Jesus really does offer a New Way of Living.

What about you? At Cana today they have rejected Jesus. A run-down church marks the site of the miracle, and the village is run-down too. It is dirty and poor, as if to say, "Life is always poor without Jesus."

God offers you a new way of living. Come, taste the wine – and live!

NB Since our visit to Cana in 1975, it has grown and spread considerably. In 2010 I found it more prosperous, with a "Wedding Church" and a shop opposite selling Cana Wine.

5. Sheep without a Shepherd
Mark 6.30-44

When Jesus landed and saw a large crowd, he had compassion on them, because they were like sheep without a shepherd. So he began teaching them many things.

We have two miracles, and in each one Jesus shows his care and compassion for ordinary people, and also for his disciples.

Because we are eager to witness the miracles, it is easy to pass over the early verses in this passage, and so miss some vital insights concerning our spiritual lives.

The apostles gathered around Jesus, and reported to him all they had done and taught.

That is an important exercise for me as pastor, and for you as fellow disciples. Jesus' disciples are checking out with him all they have been doing. We won't go far wrong in our Christian walk, if we check out with Jesus. We must do it in prayer. Jesus is concerned to hear all about our struggles and our successes. He is the one who can give advice, encouragement, strength and help. If we fail to spend this time, we may waste much effort in unproductive labours.

Notice in verse 31: *Then, because so many people were coming and going that they did not even have a chance to eat, he said to them, "Come with me by yourselves to a quiet place and get some rest."*

I've recently bought J.C. Ryles commentary, written in 1857, on Mark's gospel. Looking at this verse he writes, "Sadly there are few in the church of Christ who need these admonitions. There are but few in danger of overworking themselves and injuring their own bodies and souls by excessive attention to others. The vast majority of professing Christians are indolent and slothful, and do nothing for the world around them. There are comparatively few who need the bridle nearly so much as the spur." Wow!

The danger I see today, is of too much activity without reflection - of giving out without taking in - of being concerned to speak for Jesus without first letting him speak to us - of going on doing a thing because we have always done it, rather than being certain it is still the way God wants us to spend our energy. We can only do God's work in God's strength. To be spiritually effective we need the Spirit's filling. To be fresh for God, we need times of refreshment with God.

"Come with me by yourselves to a quiet place and get some rest."

Jesus knows and counsels that we should have time apart, not to remain withdrawn, but to be re-empowered to re-engage in the task of spreading the good news.

He had compassion on them, because they were like sheep without a shepherd. So he began teaching them many things.

He had compassion. His whole being was stirred. This verse really challenges me. What a description of our country today. We have this week heard the Labour Party demanding an apology because a churchman has criticised them for not having a declared policy concerning abortion. When sheep are deprived of a shepherd in open country, the first thing they do is to wander and get hopelessly lost. We are all called to be shepherds. Can we wonder at the state of our nation when the shepherds are failing to go after the lost sheep!

London City Missioner Andrew Hill tells us that when

running a holiday bible club in Custom House he was interrupted by a boy, "Excuse me, who is Jesus?" The boy had never heard and knew nothing at all about Jesus. Does that move me, does that not produce compassion?

A prime role of the Middle Eastern shepherd was to find pasture for his sheep. Without a shepherd they would starve to death. There is a vast spiritual hunger even in Ferndown today. People are looking to alternative foods: New Age teaching, Spiritism, Humanism. They are getting junk food, rather than the Bread of Life.

The other role of the Middle Eastern shepherd was to protect the sheep from danger; wolves, bears and robbers. Friends, with Jesus we are safe. Without him we are defenceless. The vast majority of our community are defenceless against all the wiles of Satan.

Do we have compassion? See what Jesus does, although he and all the disciples were really hoping for a time of retreat.

When Jesus landed and saw a large crowd, he had compassion on them, because they were like sheep without a shepherd. So he began teaching them many things.

Lost people matter to God. They must matter to us too.

The traditional way of looking at this miracle, is that however little we have, it becomes much in the hands of Jesus, but I wonder if God wouldn't have us look just slightly differently at the passage tonight. Could this in fact be an action parable for the disciples?

Look at some contrasting attitudes. The disciples are tired. Jesus is tired. They all thoroughly deserve a break, but their responses are different.

By this time it was late in the day, so his disciples came to him. "This is a remote place," they said, "and it's already very late. Send the people away so they can go to the surrounding countryside and villages and buy themselves something to eat."

"Jesus, for goodness sake, send them home. It will soon be getting dark – people are afraid of the dark. It's not that late? Well at least send them off into the villages so that they can get some food!"

But he answered, "You give them something to eat."

Sheep without a Shepherd – Mark 6.30-44

What a challenge! Here are five thousand men, as well as women and children. "Jesus you are asking the impossible, we just haven't the resources!"

They said to him, "That would take eight months of a man's wages! Are we to go and spend that much on bread and give it to them to eat?"

I can almost hear them add, "No Jesus, send them home!"
Sadly isn't that the classic response of the church through the ages? When Jesus presents us with a challenge, we cannot do it. We haven't got the resources, the people, the money, the talent, the gifts, the training or the time. We've done our bit in the past. We are not risk takers. We don't want to be laughed at. We do not really have compassion for sheep without a shepherd.

Friends, let me tell you again - **Lost people matter to God.** He died for them, and his command to those who would be his disciples, is that we tell those lost people about the Bread of Life, about the Salvation that is only to be found in Jesus.

Jesus turns to his disciples.

"How many loaves do you have?" he asked them. "Go and see." When they found out, they said, "Five - and two fish."

What have you got? No mention of the young boy in this account. Their collective resources are five barley loaves and two small fish. Barley bread was the cheapest and coarsest of all bread. It was the food of the poorest of the poor. The word used for fish is *tarichaea*. This is a salt fish, a little bigger than sardines and named after the little town on the shore of Galilee where they were salted in salt brought from the Dead Sea. They were not especially filling, but they were spicy and would brighten up the barley bread.

Then Jesus directed them to have all the people sit down in groups on the green grass. So they sat down in groups of hundreds and fifties.

The rest of the story we know. Something wonderful, beyond human reasoning or explanation, happened. It was no optical illusion. It was no sharing round of the food that they all had brought but were keeping to themselves. Just as he provided manna in the wilderness, God provides bread and fish sufficient for all.

What an idiot Jesus would have looked if the Father had let him down! But Jesus doesn't even consider that. When God calls – he equips. He didn't need much, just the little that the disciples were able to gather up; the picnic of one young boy from a poor and humble family. Everyone is fed.

And the disciples picked up twelve basketfuls of broken pieces of bread and fish.

Every Jew used to carry a basket. It was called *kophinos, a* wicker basket with a narrow neck, widening towards the base. The original purpose of such a basket was as a picnic box. The Jew was supposed to ensure that all the food he ate was ceremonially clean and pure. By preparing and carrying his own he could be certain of that. However, the Romans used to mock the Jews because of their baskets, and it seems that not too many Jews were concerned about their food being kosher, rather that they were renowned for their skill at scrounging. The smart Jew, it was said, would go out with his basket empty and return home with it full.

There were twelve disciples. They have taken the risk with Jesus. They end up with full baskets. The need of the crowd has been met and they too are fully satisfied.

Do you see what I mean about this being an action parable? The only way to be satisfied is to be a risk taker with Jesus. He will not only use you in a wonderful way. You too will end up wonderfully satisfied.

WALKING ON WATER - Mark 6.45-52

Immediately Jesus made his disciples get into the boat and go on ahead of him to Bethsaida, while he dismissed the crowd. (Mark 6.45)

The final section of our scripture passage concerns disciples who are doing what Jesus has asked, but who find themselves in trouble. At Jesus' word, they obediently get into the boat and set off on the four mile trip back across the lake to Bethsaida.

Notice what Jesus does.

After leaving them, he went up on a mountain to pray.

If Jesus needed communion with his father, how much more do we? The temptation is when things are going well, to become slack in prayer, our time with God.

It was four miles across the lake compared with ten miles round the shore. If the wind was with you an hour would see you across; but if contrary, or if a storm blew up, you would have to take down the sail and depend on the oars and row.

When evening came, the boat was in the middle of the lake, and he was alone on land. He saw the disciples straining at the oars, because the wind was against them. About the fourth watch of the night he went out to them, walking on the lake. He was about to pass by them.

Let us notice: He kept an eye on them. He was aware when they got into difficulty. He took the initiative and went to them. It seemed impossible for him to help in their predicament in the middle of the lake, but Jesus walked on the water!

When they saw him walking on the lake, they thought he was a ghost. They cried out, because they all saw him and were terrified.

I'm sure they were scared stiff, but his purpose was to bring them peace.

Immediately he spoke to them and said, "Take courage! It is I. Don't be afraid!" Then he climbed into the boat with them, and the wind died down. They were completely amazed.

Jesus may put us into some situations where we feel completely out of our depth. He may take us into areas where we have never been before and are afraid, but if we do it because he sends and he commands, he will see us through and we too will be amazed beyond measure.

6. The Storm
Luke 8.22-25

This morning we were thinking about the storm recorded by Mark, where Jesus had sent his disciples on in the boat while he prayed, and later came to them in the middle of the night, walking on the water.

This evening it is another occasion recorded by Mark and also Luke, when in the evening Jesus sets out with his disciples for the region of the Gerasenes where he must minister healing the following morning.

One day Jesus said to his disciples, "Let's go over to the other side of the lake." So they got into a boat and set out.

Many folk would have hesitated to set sail in the evening, but Peter and the other fishermen disciples would have been well used to fishing at night, so for them the darkness held no special fear. But the fact that they leave in the evening indicates to me something of the urgency of the mission Jesus is undertaking. If they are setting out from Capernaum, and everything suggests they are, I would have been all for having a good night's rest in my own bed before setting out in the morning. But Jesus sees that as wasting a good part of the next day. His attitude seems to be, "Let's get there, let us be ready for what tomorrow holds."

As they sailed, he fell asleep.

I am sure you will have heard about the construction of a

The Storm – Luke 8.22-25

Galilean fishing boat – how it would have a low bench in the stern with a leather covered cushion, where it was customary for one of the crew to be allowed to rest while the others kept watch or sailed the boat. After a day with the crowds, doubtless teaching and healing, Jesus would rightly be the one to occupy the bunk and soon he is fast asleep.

A squall came down on the lake, so that the boat was being swamped, and they were in great danger.

I spoke this morning of the winds which would, on occasion, blow down the Jordan valley from the Golan Heights and stir up the lake. While the Sea of Galilee is at first appearance rather like the lakes in our own Lake District and normally placid, it is not unknown for these winds to cause waves up to twenty feet high. Luke tells us this is a sudden occurrence. I feel sure the disciples would not have set out had they suspected such a storm was coming. The boat can scarcely cope and is soon shipping water. There is real danger of the boat going down and all hands being lost, and yet Jesus remains asleep!

The disciples went and woke him saying, "Master, Master, we're going to drown!"

One cannot help but wonder their exact motive in waking Jesus. Was it to warn him, or did they expect him to be able to do something about the situation? What had they learnt? Did they realise he was able to save whatever the predicament?

He got up and rebuked the wind and the raging waters; the storm subsided, and all was calm.

Jesus rebuked the waves. Some have suggested that this indicates that there was an evil force behind the storm rather than a natural happening, that Satan sought to destroy Jesus and the disciples. These folk, I suspect, would see the devil behind every difficulty that comes our way. Whilst I have no doubt that Satan is sometimes involved in our times of trouble, these times are often just unfortunate events – part, yes, of a fallen world. Usually our troubles are not specific attacks on us, and often our problems are of our own making because of our negligence to some matter or other.

Mark says Jesus gave the command:
"Quiet! Be still!" (Mark 4.39)

I think this phrase holds the key. Jesus probably knew all about the coming storm, and he knew the outcome. This is a time of learning for his disciples. He wants them to learn that he is sufficient for every situation, even when their very lives are threatened. Jesus has complete power, even over the forces of nature, and with that simple command he demonstrated his power to his frightened disciples.

"Where is your faith?" he asked his disciples.

Why does he rebuke his disciples? I suggest this is because, like you and me, they are slow to learn. They have been with him for some time now. They have seen him heal; they have seen him work miracles; they have heard his teaching; they have speculated that he is the Messiah, but they have not yet fully learned to trust him.

In fear and amazement they asked one another, "Who is this? He commands even the winds and the water, and they obey him."

It is easy to criticise the disciples and say that by now they should have learnt, but have we? Crises do come in life; if you are not facing any at the moment, be sure the time will come. Is my faith; is your faith ready for the storm? Will you trust Jesus or will you be afraid? This miracle is all about us learning that Jesus is sufficient for our every need. There is no reason to be afraid. You need not be afraid. Cast all your cares upon him! He cares for you.

PART 3

THE GREAT

"I AM"

SAYINGS OF JESUS

I met a Man who Was

After the black time, all the paths were grey:
after the wasting climb; the wilderness
of sky. I clawed through air, searching a way
forward; some bread to fill my emptiness.
Standing on that bare hill, staring at stones,
I knew my hollow need,
                              my starving bones.

Then in the misery of scars, my grief,
a man clothed as a shepherd called my name.
He was the ancient Word; the Way to life.
His eyes knew suffering, and held no blame.
His hand was warm; through thorns I struggled on
and in the dawn
                              He was the risen Son.

7. I am the Bread of Life
John 6.25-59 GNB

"I am the bread of life." Jesus told them. "Those who come to me will never be hungry; those who believe in me will never be thirsty."(John 6.35)

Do you make bread at home? Perhaps you visit a baker's shop where bread is made. If you can recall the delicious smell of baking bread you will know the anticipation it engenders. If you are hungry, you know you will soon be satisfied. You know it will be good.

Jesus says, "I am the bread of life." This morning we have sung about feeding on the living bread, yet sadly, all too often we don't feed on the living bread. Instead of Jesus being our staple diet, he is just the icing on the cake. He is not the basis of our life. He is an extra, and we find that we are not satisfied. Spiritually we hunger and thirst and are unfulfilled.

Let us, this morning, look at and behind our passage of scripture to see if it can help us come to a deeper understanding of Jesus as the Bread of Life. We want to increase our confidence, to fully put our trust in him.

The children dramatised for us the story of the miracle of the feeding of the five thousand with the five barley loaves and two small fishes. This miracle is recorded in all the gospels. Luke gives us the extra little bit of information that it takes place at Bethsaida, a small town, the home of Philip, on the eastern shore of the Sea of Galilee, towards the northern end of the lake.

Now, I want you to recall that the miracles which John recorded were chosen, he tells us, not simply because they were accounts of wonderful acts that brought relief to people, but because they were signs which pointed to Jesus being the Messiah – signs which brought glory to God. So firstly I want to draw out some significant points concerning the miracle of the feeding of the five thousand.

1. The Jewish Passover Feast was near.

Verse 4 tells us that: *The time of the Jewish Passover was near.*

According to Jewish Messianic tradition the Messiah would be revealed at Passover time. It was quite remarkable that the Romans allowed the Jews to continue to celebrate their religious feasts during the occupation, especially the feast of Passover, since at this time of year it would serve as a rallying point, a time of greatly increased nationalistic zeal. The Jews would remember and celebrate freedom from slavery in Egypt and would look for a new deliverer to free them from Rome. There were many pretenders; the Zealots, remember Barabbas, were a particularly dedicated group who caused a lot of trouble at Passover time. So our first point to remember is that it is a sign at Passover time.

2. Concerning the Messiah

One expectation of the Messiah was that he would be a prophet and leader, at least equal in status to Moses, the greatest Jew who had ever lived. God had said in the days of Moses:

"I will send them a prophet like you from among their own people; I will tell him what to say, and he will tell the people everything I command. He will speak in my name, and I will punish anyone who refuses to obey him."(Deuteronomy 18.18)

Knowing this passage, the people are looking for someone with parallels to Moses.

3. Concerning Manna

Listen to the voice of the people:

I am the Bread of Life – John 6.25-29

'Our ancestors ate manna in the desert, just as the scripture says, "He gave them bread from heaven to eat."'

Listen to the voice of Jesus:

"Your ancestors ate manna in the desert, but they died. I am the living bread that came down from heaven. If anyone eats this bread, he will live for ever."

Why is there this discourse concerning manna? At the Passover the Jews remembered how manna had sustained them in the wilderness, but with the passing of time the remembrance had got a bit mixed up. They had forgotten that the manna was provided by God and attributed it as the supreme work in the life of Moses. Moses was their first deliverer, their first redeemer, and the belief had grown up that when the supreme redeemer, the Messiah came, one of the signs that he was the Messiah would be that he would provide fresh manna - bread from heaven.

There was also another tradition. In the Exodus story the Jews were told to preserve some manna as a lasting memorial.

Moses said, "The Lord has commanded us to save some manna, to be kept for our descendants, so that they can see the food which he gave us to eat in the desert when he brought us out of Egypt." Moses said to Aaron, "Take a jar, put two litres of manna in it and place it in the Lord's presence to be kept for our descendants." As the Lord commanded Moses, Aaron put it in front of the Covenant Box, so that it could be kept. (Exodus 16.32-34)

This gold jar of manna had eventually been placed in the Ark in the Temple, but had been lost when the temple was destroyed in the days of Jeremiah. Tradition said that Jeremiah had hidden it, and when the Messiah came it would be revealed again, and the people would be miraculously fed as a sign that the Messiah had come.

Now, put all those ideas together, and you begin to see the tremendous significance of this miracle, this sign, when the five thousand are miraculously fed with bread from five barley loaves. No wonder the people reacted as they did:

Seeing this miracle that Jesus had performed, the people there said, "Surely this is the Prophet who was to come into the world!" Jesus knew that they were about to come and seize him in order to make him king by force.

It could have been a very nasty incident indeed. The Romans would have been on high alert because it was Passover, and here was a potentially rebellious force of five thousand people. Jesus had to leave them to avoid any trouble, so he went off again to the hills by himself.

A Miracle Transformed

Have you caught the drama of this miracle? Perhaps it is the first time you have seen it in this light. This is not a gentle, ethical story of a boy who gives his lunch to Jesus, with its teaching – "Look at what Jesus can do; we must do likewise." Oh, it may include that, but it is a dramatic declaration, a great sign from Jesus – "I am the Christ. I am the Messiah. I alone am the one sufficient to meet your every need!"

Now if the miracle reveals Jesus as the Messiah, what is its special relevance for us today? I think this is what comes out in the second part of the passage. Can you imagine the overnight discussions in the village inns and pilgrim camps? "Has the Messiah come? Will Rome be overthrown? What will this Jesus do next? How did he multiply the bread and fishes?"

The next day the crowds assemble again at Bethsaida. Some have come across the lake from Tiberias. To their surprise there is no Jesus. He had not left in the boat with his disciples, so where is he? They go off in search of him.

When the crowd saw that Jesus was not there, nor his disciples, they got into boats and went to Capernaum, looking for him.

This verse evokes a mixture of thoughts and feelings in me. Partly I'm taken up with the excitement of it all. I realise what a profitable time it must have been for anyone who owned a boat, ferrying people across the lake! I visualise the people who can't find a boat, hurrying along the poorly made roads so that they don't miss what is going on. But another part of me is sad. Why are they following Jesus? It is not because they want to be committed to him.

No! – they want to be entertained. They want to see the next sign, the next wonder.

Some go to Capernaum which Jesus has made his base in the Galilee region. Here they find him, but are mystified as to how or when he arrived there.

When the people found Jesus on the other side of the lake, they said to him, "Teacher, when did you get here?"

Jesus doesn't give them a direct answer, but listen to his reply:

Jesus answered, "I am telling you the truth: you are looking for me because you ate the bread and had all you wanted, not because you understood my miracles."

Now in the Authorised Version this is one of the *"Verily, verily,"* statements of Jesus, one of those statements which Jesus intends they should take full notice of because it is very important. He continues:

"Do not work for food that goes bad; instead, work for the food that lasts for eternal life. This is the food which the Son of Man will give you."

Jesus is saying, "You've followed me today for all the wrong reasons. You followed me not because your minds are on the things of God, but because you ate all that you wanted. You had your bellies filled. You are coming here today because you hope for a bigger and better miracle. All the time your mind is fixed on earthly things, you will go on being hungry. It will be just like the manna that rotted overnight – you will not be satisfied."

This is a theme which runs through all the teaching of Jesus. It is folly to have our eyes fixed on earth rather than on heaven. Remember the Sermon on the Mount:

"Do not store up riches for yourselves here on earth, where moths and rust destroy, and robbers break in and steal. Instead, store up riches for yourselves in heaven, where moths and rust cannot destroy, and robbers cannot break in and steal. For your heart will always be where your riches are. Instead, be concerned above everything else with the Kingdom of God and with what he

*requires of you, and he will provide you with all these other things."
(Matthew 6.19-21 and 33)*

Also in the Parable of the Rich Fool:

*But God said, "You fool!" This very night you will have to
give up your life; then who will get all these things you have kept for
yourself?"(Luke 12.20)*

*"Will a person gain anything if he wins the whole world but
is himself lost or defeated? Of course not!" (Luke 9.25)*

*"For what shall it profit a man, if he shall gain the whole
world, and lose his own soul?" (Mark 8.26 AV)*

I believe Jesus hits the nail on the head. We all go around
spending too much of our time going after things which perish. How
easy it is to get our priorities wrong! It is not wrong to have a nice
home; to fight for fair pay; to campaign for more money to be spent
on the health services; to save for old age; to have a good holiday; to
give time to the family – but these things must never be allowed to
become of greater importance than God!

*"Do not work for food that goes bad; instead work for the
food that lasts for eternal life."*

It seems, at first in our passage, that the crowd has taken the
point.

*So they asked him, "What can we do in order to do what
God wants us to do?"*

Jesus gives them a straightforward answer.

*Jesus answered, "What God wants you to do is to believe in
the one he sent."*

What about your life today? Are you hungry, thirsty, empty?
Can you believe in the one God sent to transform your life, to give
you a new and abundant life, filled with his love and grace?

*"I am the bread of life," Jesus told them. "Those who come
to me will never be hungry; those who believe in me will never be
thirsty."*

8. Jesus the Word, Jesus the Light
John 1.1-14 AV

In the beginning was the Word, and the Word was with God, and the Word was God. .. In him was life, and the life was the light of men, the true Light, which lighteth every man that cometh into the world.

Did this morning's scripture reading make you think of Christmas? For me, that reading is a vital part of a Service of Lessons and Carols. It comes right at the climax and is a powerful passage, full of imagery. That is why I read it from the Authorised Version, so that we captured the full power of the traditional language. Each time I hear it read it shows me something fresh about the greatness of God, yet it is a passage rarely used by preachers. I want this morning to develop two of the images – Jesus is the Word - Jesus is the Light.

I don't doubt that John's gospel is the work of John the Apostle, the son of Zebedee, the beloved disciple, one who was especially close to the Lord. He was privileged with many special experiences, and was given the care of the Lord's mother Mary, a special trust from the cross. John probably wrote his gospel quite late in his life.

He tells us exactly why he wrote it:

"But these are written that you may believe that Jesus is the

Christ, the Son of God, and that by believing you may have life in his name." (John 20.31)

When John was writing the church was rapidly spreading throughout the countries of the Mediterranean. There was a real need for a clearly argued gospel that would satisfy both Jews and Greeks. It needed perhaps more theology than the straightforward narrative of the other gospels, but like the other gospels it is the word of God preserved for us, and as God's word it is eternally relevant.

Let us get into our first image:
Jesus Christ the Word.
In the beginning was the Word, and the Word was with God, and the Word was God.

Those of you who write know the importance of opening sentences. I shall always remember the application for a teaching post which began; "Most men say I am of a stunning appearance." Whatever her qualifications, this lady was assured of an interview!
John's opening is brilliant – inspired!

In the beginning was the Word.

Why is that brilliant? To the Jew, words were especially powerful. They needed to be carefully chosen. There were only ten thousand words in Hebrew compared with two hundred thousand in Greek. Hebrew words could be full of meaning, but there is something more important than that. The Jew believed that words, once spoken, could never be retracted or taken back. They had an authority, a power all of their own. It was important for the Jew to engage his brain before opening his mouth.

What a pity we don't take that to heart today. Damage is done because people do not realise the power of words. "Sticks and stones may break my bones – but words can do lasting damage!" The teaching in James about the tongue is there for a real purpose. He realises just how many people are brought down, who fall into sin, because they can't control their tongue. But let me develop this thought that "Words have Power" to see why John's opening is brilliant for the Jew.

Think for a moment about the Creation story in Genesis.

And God SAID let there be light, and there was light.

Jesus the Word, Jesus the Light (John 1.1-14)

(Genesis 1.3)

> *And God SAID let there be a firmament. (Genesis 1.6)*
>
> *And God SAID let the earth bring forth vegetation, and it was so. (Genesis 1.11)*
>
> *By the WORD of the Lord are the heavens made. (Psalm 33.6)*
>
> *He sent forth His WORD and healed them. (Psalm 107.20)*
>
> *My WORD shall not return unto me void – it shall accomplish that which I please. (Isaiah 55.11)*
>
> *Is not my WORD like a fire, saith the Lord and like a hammer that breaketh the rock in pieces? (Jeremiah 23.29)*

As John opens his gospel, he is saying to the Jews, "I am about to write about Jesus, and I'm telling you about the Word of God. Their Old Testament scriptures began:

In the beginning God –

John's gospel begins:

In the beginning, the Word –

John is saying, "Look, the two are one. Jesus the Word was there before creation with God – without him was not anything made which was made. He was not only with God – He is God." The gospel starts with a shout. "Jewish people wherever you are – be aware, JESUS IS GOD!"

I want us to see the relevance of this for today. Modern thinkers will go so far. They will say Jesus was a good man. Jesus was a man inspired by God. Jesus was undoubtedly a saint. Jesus was a god among many gods.

John hits you with a sledge-hammer. THE WORD WAS GOD – ALL THINGS WERE MADE BY HIM – IN HIM WAS LIFE – JESUS IS GOD.

Once you come to terms with that, you realise that you have to come to terms with Jesus. You cannot go on ignoring him. He must make a dramatic impact in your life. He must be Master, Saviour and Lord.

If this opening is brilliant as far as the Jews are concerned, it is equally brilliant as far as the Greeks are concerned. The Word, in Greek, is The Logos. It is from logos that we get our word logic.

Things which are logical are reasoned and orderly. The Greeks recognised that there is a magnificent, dependable order in creation. Day follows night; season follows season; stars and planets have regularity in their orbits; there are wonderful patterns in creation; there is order in mathematics. Greek thinkers, despite their polytheism – the many gods of the Greek faith – said that at the back of it all there was a single great mind controlling all creation. They called it – the LOGOS.

John in his gospel says, "You are taken up by the idea of this great, guiding, controlling, reasoning, logical mind, the LOGOS. The mind of God has come to earth in Jesus." Plato used to teach that everything on earth is imperfect, but somewhere behind the universe is a perfect pattern. This is an idea that emerges in other cultures too. For example the Persian carpet weaver always makes sure to weave a mistake into his pattern, for there is none perfect except God. John says, "You want the perfect pattern – the standard for life – look at Jesus – the WORD – the LOGOS – GOD."

Once again this is relevant for today. We live in a society which refuses to offer absolute standards. It suggests to young people and older alike, "make up your own mind about sex outside marriage, about drugs, about abortion, about honesty, about covetousness, about responsibility to others, about euthanasia, about race relations, about the use of your money." John says, "You need to know the mind of God. He has revealed it. Look at the perfect pattern. Look at the LOGOS. Look at Jesus."

So the opening is brilliant for the Jew and brilliant for the Greek. It is also brilliant for twenty-first century man to describe Jesus as the WORD. Words are vital tools in communication. Think of the care taken in some circles concerning words. The advertiser, alongside the graphic designer, who spends hours pondering which typeface and style of layout will suit his needs and who chooses just a few words, but very carefully. They can be used to show a product exactly as it is or they can be used to conjure up an image which is completely false. Do you remember what Estate Agents used to get away with? "Bijou old world cottage, idyllically situated away from noisy traffic – some improvements needed for which grants may be available." This really meant – "a very small, un-modernised;

tumble-down shack; damp; needing re-wiring; no mains water or drainage; reached down a mile long pot-holed track."

Similar are the lies that are told about God! "He is far away; he's not concerned about you; there are many ways to him; he's not really bothered about sin; you may do as you please for he doesn't notice and he's soft."

John says, "You want to know the truth; then listen to the WORD. Listen to JESUS. He will not only tell you about God – He is God!"

Jesus Christ the True Light

The true light that gives light to every man was coming into the world.

Have you ever been out for a long country walk on a spring evening? When you set out the sun is shining. There are wonderful colours lighting the hedgerows. You take in all the details and colours of the blossoms and the leaves; you wonder at the beauty of it all. But as the light fades, the detail and colour slowly disappear. Shapes, silhouettes are still sharp and fascinating, but the colour has gone. Gradually as the light fades still further the shapes become shadowy, unreal, frightening. Your mind plays tricks and you imagine all manner of weird objects. Finally the sun has set. Clouds obscure the sky. Tonight there is no moon; no stars; just total blackness. Looking round you realise you are lost. It is hopeless. You cannot see the way. Your sense of direction leaves you, and panic follows.

Why do I paint that picture? Have you ever watched the tragedy of light draining out of a life, perhaps even out of the life of someone near and dear, one of your loved ones? I remember Nick in Brighton in the early days of the drug culture. He had come to Brighton to go to Sussex University. His parents were proud of him. Much promise lay ahead, but he got in with the wrong group. I knew him through the outreach of Youth for Christ. He had arrived at the bottom of the pile. He'd given up his student flat – he couldn't pay his rent as well as buy his drugs. He slept with some others, sometimes under the pier, sometimes further along the front under the arches of the Marine Parade. He was pleased with the shelter of the Youth for Christ Saturday night outreach; the free coffee, buns and biscuits. He would come too on a Sunday night to the meeting in the basement of the Park Royal Hotel. Sadly for Nick, the light went out completely. When he didn't come either on Saturday or Sunday a group went looking for him. They found his body in a disused beach hut. He had taken his own life. For Nick the drugs had brought darkness. The light had gone.

But it doesn't have to be dramatic like that for light to go out in life. The writer of Ecclesiastes declares:

"Vanity of vanities, all is vanity." (Ecclesiastes 1.2)

When you think seriously about life he is right, unless you have the light of God in your life.

In him was life, and that life was the light of men.

Do you see what John is saying? He says, "If you want real life, satisfying life, you will only find that in Jesus, for he is the light of God." He also says, "When Jesus comes into your life, he brings what is best described as the Light of Life." The Life and Light of Christ are inseparable. The man or woman who rejects the light of Christ rejects real life. Later in his gospel John records the words of Jesus:

"And this is the condemnation, that light is come into the world, and men loved darkness rather than light, because their deeds were evil." (John 3.19)

To reject Jesus is to bring condemnation on yourself.

Do you know the Old Testament verse about walking in darkness?

The wise man has eyes in his head, while the fool walks in darkness. (Ecclesiastes 2.14)

Do you know what else the Bible says about fools?

Fools mock at making amends for sin. (Proverbs 14.9)

The fool says in his heart, 'There is no God.' (Psalm 53.1)

So what is the Good News, the gospel, in our passage? Many people live in darkness today. The good news is that life doesn't have to be dark. We don't have to live outside the light. Look again at two verses from our passage as we close.

The true light that gives light to every man was coming into the world.

Jesus the Word, Jesus the Light (John 1.1-14)

Every man includes you. God's intention is that you have the opportunity to respond; to see the light; to come to the light – to have LIFE.

The tragedy is to remain in darkness, to love darkness because of your sins and your evil deeds. Wonderful victory over darkness and new life is possible for you. It is made clear in verse 12:

Yet to all who received him, to those who believed in his name, he gave the right to become children of God.

You may say, "I've rejected him so often; life is dark; so much of life seems depressing – hopeless." You need to see that Jesus is so great, so strong is his light in the darkness of this world, that all the evil, all the darkness that this world puts up, cannot overcome, cannot put out the light of Jesus. At Concarneau in Brittany there is a lighthouse close by a Mission to Seamen Chapel at one end of the harbour. On it are the words – La Croix, The Cross. The cross of Jesus shines out as an everlasting light to the entire world. He is our guiding light. His light still shines like a great harbour light, a beacon, radiating, calling – "Here is safety - here is forgiveness - here is peace."

Remember these words of Jesus:

Then Jesus spoke again to the people. He said, "I am the light of the world. Whoever follows me will never walk in darkness, but will have the light of life." (John 8.12)

9. I am the Good Shepherd
John 10.1-15

"I am the good shepherd: I know my sheep and my sheep know me – just as the Father knows me and I know the Father – and I lay down my life for the sheep." (John 10.14-15)

One of the facts that we have learned recently in Home Groups is that parables, though they may sometimes seem simple on the surface, are not easy to understand unless someone, preferably God's Holy Spirit, interprets them to us. Each of the parables of Jesus has a sting in the tail; a sting that affects us because it challenges our mode of life, and our relationship with Jesus Christ.

Tonight's scripture passage is built around a parable. It recognises that we count ourselves as religious, but it asks: Do we really follow the call of Jesus, or are we enchanted by some other siren god?

Listen to the parable that Jesus told in John 10:

Jesus said, "I tell you the truth, a man who does not enter the sheep pen by the gate, but climbs in some other way, is a thief and a robber. The man who enters by the gate is the shepherd of his sheep. The watchman opens the gate for him, and the sheep listen to his voice. He calls his own sheep by name and leads them out. When he has brought out all his own, he goes on ahead of them, and his sheep follow him because they know his voice. But they will never follow a stranger; in fact they will run away from him because they do not recognise a stranger's voice." Jesus used this figure of speech, but they did not understand what he was telling them.

Likening people to sheep is an age old picture. We may not like to be identified with sheep but since it is a God given image we would do well to stop and give the comparison due consideration. Let me pull out a few Bible verses. In 2 Chronicles, Israel is going through a bad time. Jehoshaphat is proving a distinctly bad king. He offers no real leadership and is forming an alliance with the pagan King Ahab of Samaria. However, he calls in the prophet of the Lord for counsel:

Then Micaiah answered, "I saw all Israel scattered on the hills like sheep without a shepherd." (2 Chronicles 18.16)

The psalmist writes:

You gave us up to be devoured like sheep and have scattered us among the nations. (Psalm 44.11)

Know that the Lord is God. It is he who made us, and we are his; we are his people, the sheep of his pasture. (Psalm 100.3)

You will remember when Jesus fed the five thousand:

When Jesus landed and saw a large crowd, he had compassion on them, because they were like sheep without a shepherd. So he began teaching them many things. (Mark 6.34)

Following the resurrection, Peter was recommissioned by Jesus with the words:

"Feed my sheep." (John 21.17)

So having taken on board the biblical nature of this image; let me draw a few parallels between people and sheep. The first is that sheep without a shepherd get lost.

Sheep have a herd instinct; like us they like to be part of a crowd. They go about in flocks, but it is also common for an individual sheep, or a small group of sheep, to become parted from the flock, to wander off on their own, and to get completely lost. Sheep, I am told, have a very poor homing instinct. Once they are out of sight of other members of their flock, they will go on straying farther and farther away.

Sheep need a shepherd to lead them; to keep them together; to protect them; to care for their day to day needs; to chase off their enemies; to find them food and to provide them with shelter. Another sheep cannot fulfil that role! They need someone other than themselves; someone who is not a super-sheep but a shepherd.

People need a shepherd too. Even leaders need a leader. Show me a lost person. They are lost because they have no leader. Actually we need hierarchies of leadership. We have pastoral carers and deacons and a pastor, and we need a supreme leader who is not just a super-person. We need a leader other than ourselves. We need God.

Think of situations that you know. A wife biblically follows her husband who sadly dies. Whether she is lost and bereft, or whether she copes really well, so often revolves around the issue of the couple having had God as their supreme leader. Where this is the case, the wife draws on God and finds fresh resources which renew her strength, and she goes on in her own right to be a blessing and example to many.

Think of the church which is too closely attached and too dependent on its pastor rather than on God. The pastor leaves and for whatever reason the people get scattered. The work breaks down. The work for the kingdom falls away because the leadership has not been really under girded with dependence on God.

Jesus said, "I tell you the truth, the man who does not enter the sheep pen by the gate, but climbs in some other way, is a thief and a robber."

In Jesus' day sheep were a very valuable commodity. There were no banks, no stock exchanges, and no building societies. The ordinary man invested in sheep. A rich man might employ a shepherd all of his own, but in many a small village one shepherd would look after the sheep of several families. Sheep rustling was very common, especially among nomadic groups. To snatch a few sheep and move on with them could prove very profitable.

Now we need to be clear concerning the parable. The image which Jesus has in mind is not the summer sheepfold out in the hills, but the winter quarters. These were large permanent constructions with strong walls and a door with a watchman or gatekeeper on duty. All the sheep from a village, hundreds of them, would be overwintered in such a sheepfold. Despite the watchman thieves would still climb over the wall and steal sheep. The door or gate and the gatekeeper were supposed to keep the sheep safe. Legitimate owners could have access to their sheep via the gate and the gatekeeper. Jesus says in his picture that the wall climbers had evil intentions.

"The thief comes only to steal and kill and destroy; I have come that they may have life, and have it to the full." (John 10.10)

Life is full of people who call us to follow their way. Usually the only real interest they have at heart is their own. The most unscrupulous seek to profit from us, to exercise influence over us. Some in ignorance call us to follow the way they have found, in order to bolster up their own uncertainty. They believe they have found a way, but really they are lost. The problem with illustrating the gurus who would lead us astray is not where to start but where to stop. So let me first lay down a firm and trustworthy guide. Every system, every leader who does not call people to adopt God's biblical standards; who does not expect people to make Jesus their Lord, is ultimately opposed to Christianity. He or she leads people away from God, and ultimately leads to the disaster of a godless eternity.

Ideas which may distract us are -

Humanism

Humanism calls people to cast off the shackles of God, but it is without hope. It makes no offer of eternity. It believes that death is the end.

Communism

This suggests that everyone can be equal. All things are owned in common. Sounds good but in fact it leads to a total loss of personal freedom. The ordinary individual is exploited and oppressed. Despite the experiments of history, we find that power-conscious dictators continue to emerge.

New Ageism

New Ageism suggests that mother earth is god, and that we are gods too. It wanders off, leading people into paths full of mystery. These paths get nowhere except away from the saving grace of Jesus Christ.

The Occult

Whatever its guise the Occult recognises the spiritual, but gives it over to the control of Satan and all his evil ways. It ensnares little by little. It devalues and debases those who get caught in its trap. It counterfeits God's gifts, claiming to offer healing and enlightenment but its experiences are all temporal. Instead of receiving the gift of salvation a convert sells his own soul.

The Sects claiming to be Christian

These will tell you they have special insights that have not been revealed to the orthodox churches, yet all - every single one - ultimately denies the divinity and authority of the Lord Jesus Christ. They call us to work for our salvation; a gospel by which we know we cannot be saved.

Listen again to the words of Jesus:

Jesus said, "I tell you the truth, the man who does not enter the sheep pen by the gate but climbs in some other way, is a thief and a robber. The thief comes only to steal and kill and destroy.... I have come that they may have life, and have it to the full."

Listen to the wise words of the Old Testament prophet Jeremiah:

"My people have been lost sheep; their shepherds have led them astray and caused them to roam on the mountains. They wandered over mountain and hill and forgot their own resting place." (Jeremiah 50.6)

The only shepherd to follow is Jesus:

Salvation is found in no one else, for there is no other name under heaven given to men by which we must be saved. (Acts 4.12)

Who really is your shepherd?

I am the Good Shepherd – John 10.1-15

"The man who enters by the gate is the shepherd of his sheep. The watchman opens the gate for him, and the sheep hear his voice. He calls his own sheep by name and leads them out."

If you mix up several hundred sheep belonging to different flocks; how do you sort them out? My friend John keeps a few Jacob's sheep in his field near Hassocks in Sussex. Once while visiting when we went down to the gate of the field he asked me, "Can you can call the sheep over for their treats?"

I tried, "Come on, over here, over here, come and get it!" Nothing happened. The sheep went on munching the grass placidly as if they hadn't heard at all.

"I'll show you how it's done," said John. He called out just as I had done, "Come on, come on!" At once the sheep came running towards him, eager for their treats. "You see," he said to me with some pride, "They know the master's voice. I am their shepherd. They don't know you."

This was a perfect illustration to me that sheep really do know the shepherd's voice. Somehow, despite the claimed simplicity of their sheep's brains, they have learned that this is no stranger's voice. This is the voice of one who really cares for them. This is the one who keeps them safe; the one who finds them food; the one who tends their wounds. At the end of their winter in the Bible sheepfold, his voice is like music to their ears. His call to follow is one they have been longing for, and they are quick to respond.

The influence of voice is tremendous. We all respond. The advertiser exploits this knowledge ruthlessly. You need to listen very carefully to what the advertiser says. He is not actually allowed to lie, so he snappily presents all the images that you will perceive as positive concerning his product. He leaves unsaid all the drawbacks that might cause you to stop and think a second time about buying it.

You need to be even more careful when listening to voices which would call you to follow their way, their faith, their system of belief. If you need to be careful with the currency of day to day purchases, how much more careful you should be concerning the eternal destiny of your very self, your life, your soul!

There is only one voice which can be really trusted – only one voice to follow, and that is the voice of Jesus. Have you listened for his voice, for his call? When he calls there is no mistaking his voice. Perhaps he is calling today?

Listen to the voice of Jesus:

"I am the good shepherd. The good shepherd lays down his life for the sheep. The hired man is not the shepherd who owns the sheep. So when he sees a wolf coming, he abandons the sheep and runs away. The wolf attacks the flock and scatters it."

The role of the shepherd was total commitment to his sheep. He must be prepared to take on the thief or the robber, the lion, the wolf or the bear. He must be prepared even to lay down his life for the sheep, to keep them safe, so that they might be brought home to their rightful owner.

Remember that Jesus is in Jerusalem as he gives this account. Here we begin to see the full significance of it all. The lambs in the fields around Jerusalem, particularly in Bethlehem's fields, were being bred especially for sacrifice.

The old way of dealing with sin was by the sacrifice of lambs. Lambs were costly. I am told that for the ordinary family, their life savings might well be represented by just two or three sheep. We have seen in our studies of sacrifice in Leviticus just how serious sin is in God's eyes, and how costly it was to pay the price of sin. We tend to trivialise sin and can be guilty of offering cheap forgiveness. We need to be aware that our sin is an offence and an affront to Almighty God, who says that the wages of sin is death, and that for forgiveness the price must be paid.

The men and women listening to Jesus knew all about sacrifice, and about sheep. Suddenly we realise that what Jesus is saying is that he will stand in our place. He will be our sacrifice. The Good Shepherd will be our sacrificial lamb. He will allow them to nail him to the cross that he might die in our place, in order that we might go free.

The prophet Isaiah puts it so much better than I can:

I am the Good Shepherd – John 10.1-15

We all, like sheep, have gone astray, each of us has turned to his own way; and the Lord has laid on him the iniquity of us all. (Isaiah 53.6)

But he was pierced for our transgressions, he was crushed for our iniquities; the punishment that brought us peace was upon him, and by his wounds we are healed. (Isaiah 53.5)

This is why we must listen to the voice of Jesus. This is why we must follow Jesus. This is why Jesus is Lord. This is why Jesus must be your Lord.

10. I am the Way - Snakes and Ladders
John 14.1-21

"Whoever has my commands and obeys them, he is the one who loves me. He who loves me will be loved by my Father, and I too will love him and show myself to him."(John 14.21)
Do you love the Lord? Are you obedient to the Lord's commands? Are you sure that you enjoy the Father's love? Do you know God – Father, Son and Holy Spirit?

I am amazed how many folk in our churches today find it hard to face up to questions like these. The truth of their lives is that they see and hear others who talk about having a relationship with God in Jesus, but whilst they know about God and know about Jesus, there is no real relationship. They are not sure that they are really loved by the Father, nor are they sure they really love the Lord. Perhaps I have already touched on something at the heart of your Christian life. God willing, it may be that this morning you can take a great step forward.

There is a golden rule which you must always remember when studying scripture. Set it in its context. Look what comes before, and look what comes after, for these will be sure to illuminate the passage. Today's passage is set on that dreadful evening when Jesus shared a final meal with his disciples before going out to

Gethsemane where he would be arrested, tried and the next day put to death on a cross. Jesus has washed his disciples' feet, setting them that amazing example of humble service one for another. He has predicted his betrayal and shared bread with Judas. He has warned Peter that before the cock crows he will deny his Lord three times. There can be little doubt in anyone's mind that the end is very near – tomorrow Jesus will die!

You need to get your mind around that in coming to this passage. If possible you need in your imagination to put yourself among the disciples in the upper room, for if you don't you may treat the passage lightly. This final teaching of Jesus is very important.

The disciples are confused and upset. Their world is in turmoil. All sense of security has gone. If self-confident Peter is about to fail utterly, what hope is there for the rest? They too surely must fail, for like you and me they are frail and weak. If this were a game of snakes and ladders: this is the snake. Everything will go wrong. If the disciples are not about to be gobbled up by the snake, they are at least to go plunging downwards.

Jesus begins his teaching with amazing words:

"Do not let your hearts be troubled. Trust in God; trust also in me."

This passage explains why all true followers of Jesus have no need to worry or to be upset. There is no reason to be afraid. I will outline his discourse briefly.

Jesus firstly reassures them concerning eternity. He is going ahead to his Father's house. This is a place where the Father has a gracious welcome and plenty of rooms. No one need be excluded. Jesus promises to prepare a place especially and individually for each believer. Jesus promises to come again and accompany each believer through the gates of death to the new life. We will not be alone, for the Saviour will take us to be with him. There is nothing the believer need fear.

Assured of eternity, we can begin to enjoy eternal life: that is life with the same quality which Jesus himself enjoys; right here and now. From the moment when we believe in Jesus a new destiny is ours.

Secondly, Jesus tells them about the way. Thomas, true to form, bravely asks the question which is on all their hearts:

"Lord, we don't know where you are going, so how can we know the way?"

This prompts the magnificent response of Jesus:

"I am the way, the truth and the life. No one comes to The Father except through me."

This claim that Jesus is the Way, and the only Way, is a stumbling block to many. It is not a claim that Christians have invented in order to make the faith exclusive. It is what Jesus said. Those who argue against it will say that this way is too narrow. In reality it is wide enough for every single person who has ever been born if only they choose to accept it. Instead of worrying about it, each one of us should be on our knees saying, "Thank you God for providing a sure and certain way for me to come to you." Hence our title – unless Jesus died, unless Jesus opened the door – there would be no way to the Father. Jesus provides the ladder by which I may come to him.

This brings us to today's verses. I want to draw out four affirmations from the passage. These will enable us to climb the ladder, to become nearer to and more confident in God. Jesus wants and enables you to really know God.

Philip said, "Lord, show us the Father and that will be enough for us." Jesus answered: "Don't you know me Philip, even after I have been among you such a long time? Anyone who has seen me has seen the Father. How can you say, 'Show us the Father'?"

Jesus has already told his disciples to trust him. He has reassured them concerning eternal life. He has told them that he is the way, the truth and the life. They only have to believe in him. But Philip, and probably some of the others, are still not sure. If only they could see the Father in some way, like Moses had, or as Aaron, or as Isaiah. If they could have a divine revelation, then they could be sure.

Philip is no different to many of us. We find it easier to go on asking questions about God and about Jesus, than we do to step out and believe on the basis of what has already been shown to us. We too say, "If God would only perform our own personal private miracle – if he would reveal himself in some splendid and dramatic way – if God would satisfy all the conditions that I lay down – then I would believe in him." Put another way we have a desire for assurance; we want bomb-proof evidence before we will believe. We have a desire for feelings; "Lord, if I can feel you so close that it is like an embrace, if I can have a radiant glow inside, then I will believe." We have a desire for knowledge; "Lord, let me first learn everything about you, then I will believe."

If we want to really know God, then we have to give up setting conditions. We have to submit to God in Jesus. We have to recognise that he is in charge, not us! We have to step out in faith and believe. Then, and only then, it may well be that God in his grace will give us all these other things.

Did you by any chance watch that programme on ITV where someone is challenged to overcome a long held fear? Yesterday it was a young man terribly afraid of heights. They took him to New Zealand to the Sky Tower in Auckland; the highest tower in the Southern Hemisphere. At the top there is an observation platform on the outside. Running from this is a strut, three feet wide with no hand rails, which goes out some twenty feet further to support the flood lights which are situated away from and around the tower one thousand feet above the ground. His task was to walk across the strut to the ledge which held the lights and walk on right round the tower. If the young man had remained on the ground, debating if he could possibly walk right round the tower on the ledge, he would still be afraid of heights. But because of his girl friend's encouragement and because of his desire to overcome his fear, he stepped out, and found he could complete the challenge. He has overcome his fear because he trusted. It is just the same with God. The only way to really know God is to take him at his word – to trust him – to step out with him. Then you will prove that all he says is completely trustworthy and true. Have you taken that step of faith?

Jesus is quite disappointed in Philip. He has been with Jesus for the best part of three and a half years, and still has doubts concerning Jesus as the Son of God.

"Don't you believe that I am in the Father, and that the Father is in me?"

It was Philip who had said that two hundred denarii would not buy enough bread to feed the five thousand, and then had witnessed what the Lord had done with the little lad's five barley loaves and two fishes. Philip had listened to Jesus' teaching, had heard his discourses with the religious leaders; Philip had seen so many signs and wonders. Tomorrow Jesus will die, so it is important that Philip believes. Jesus puts it to him straight:

"The words I say to you are not just my own. Rather, it is the Father, living in me, who is doing his work. Believe me when I say that I am in the Father and the Father is in me; or at least believe on the evidence of the miracles themselves."

Is Jesus disappointed in you today? You may not have had the privilege of being with Jesus, but you know about his teaching; you know about his miracles; you have seen men and women whose lives have been transformed. He has been gracious to you. You can really know God if you will take Jesus at his word and trust in him.

Jesus wants to revolutionise your witness and your prayer life:

"I tell you the truth, anyone who has faith in me will do what I have been doing. He will do even greater things than these, because I am going to the Father. And I will do whatever you ask in my name, so that the Son may bring glory to the Father. You may ask me for anything in my name, and I will do it."

Wow! Can you think of anything more mind-blowing than what Jesus says here? "Because I am going to the Father – you will do even greater works than I have done. Because I am going to the Father, and in order to bring glory to the Father, whatever you ask in my name, that I will do!"

I know these verses present a real problem to some of us. Let's think first about doing even greater things than Jesus did. I have picked four passages out of Acts which would appear to confirm Jesus' promise. These are wonders which Jesus didn't perform.

1. In the streets of Jerusalem the very shadow of Peter healed the diseased. (Acts 5.15)

2. At Ephesus diseases were cured and demons cast out simply by applying to the affected person handkerchiefs and aprons which had been touched by Paul. (Acts 19.12)
3. By the word of Peter, Ananias and Sapphira died. (Acts 5.9-10)
4. At Paphos Elymas the sorcerer was struck blind by the word of Paul. (Acts 13.11)

All this was done in the name and through the power of Christ. If we wish, we can take these examples and others which are similar, and we can build quite a strong case that Jesus is talking about an on-going signs and wonders ministry. It is only when you go through the gospels and Acts and count the signs and wonders performed that you realise that there are actually not a huge number. And though there were clearly many which were not recorded we will be talking about hundreds, not thousands, of miracles.

This is important, because while I think we should have much more faith and be much more expectant of God to continue to do the miraculous today; there are too many spurious claims of miracles which cannot be tested, and people can easily be disappointed when God does not perform a miracle for them.

What was the real work of Jesus? The great work of Jesus was to found a kingdom. The great work of Jesus was to be a Saviour. The good news is that because of Jesus we can be forgiven; we can live; we can know purpose and direction and joy. The final command of Jesus to his disciples was to do his work.

"Therefore go and make disciples of all nations, baptising them in the name of the Father and of the Son and of the Holy Spirit, and teaching them to obey everything I have commanded you. And surely I am with you always, to the very end of the age." (Matthew 28.19-20)

Christ preached only in Judea, and only in the language of that country; but the apostles preached through most of the then known world, and in all languages of all countries. Following the resurrection there were only one hundred and twenty believers. Through the witness and ministry of believers down through the years, countless millions have come to believe.

What a difference Jesus will make if you take him at his word! Your life and testimony will become credible. People will notice the change in your life since you really believed. They will want to learn about your Saviour. Your word will carry with it the authority of the living Lord Jesus. Through your witness others will come to believe. You will become a builder of the kingdom of God.

Consider these words of Jesus:

"Whatever you ask in my name, I will do it."

When Jesus says we can ask for anything, we must remember that our asking must be in his name. Asking in Jesus' name is not tacking the phrase, "for the sake of Jesus Christ our Lord," on to the end of a selfish prayer. Asking in Jesus' name is seeking to do his will. Asking in Jesus' name is asking in line with what he wants. Asking in Jesus' name is having the glory of Jesus at the forefront of our minds. If we pray for things which will glorify God; if we pray for others to be brought into the kingdom; if our prayers are genuinely founded on love and concern for our brothers and sisters, then God will hear and answer. Prayer will become an exciting and fulfilling activity. You will have answers to your prayers that amaze you, for God is good and the word of Jesus is faithful and true.

"And I will ask the Father, and he will give you another Counsellor to be with you for ever – the Spirit of truth. The world cannot accept him, because it neither sees him nor knows him. But you know him, for he lives with you and will be in you."

Jesus wants you to have the power to keep going. It must have been terrible for the disciples to experience Jesus being arrested and dying on a cross, his body savaged by the beatings, the crown of thorns, the nails and the mid-day sun. But as so often happens when a loved one dies, a measure of the pain is for ourselves. However will we cope without the one who was so precious to us?

What would the disciples do? How could they go on? How could they possibly manage without Jesus? But Jesus explains: when he returns to the Father, he will ask the Father to send the Holy Spirit, the very Spirit of God who will come into the heart of every believer.

I am the Way – Snakes and Ladders – John 14.1-21

Everyone and anyone had been able to listen to Jesus, but the gift of the Holy Spirit would be very special indeed, for he would come and actually be in – live in – the heart and life of every individual believer. As the Spirit took up residence each believer would experience an awareness of God's love; a sense of guidance and purpose in life; the power to persevere and obey and bring glory to Jesus; an assurance of salvation and being one with God; an awareness of what is right and true and good, and a deep desire to live a life pleasing to God.

The Holy Spirit is God's special gift to everyone who believes: to everyone who will put their trust in Jesus. Jesus explains:

If you then, though you are evil, know how to give good gifts to your children, how much more will your Father in heaven give the Holy Spirit to those who ask him!" (Luke 11.13)

There are some simple conditions which go with this promise. Listen to them:

"If you love me, you will obey what I command. Whoever has my commands and obeys them, he is the one who loves me. He who loves me will be loved by my Father, and I too will love him and show myself to him."

Do you say? "If only God would reveal himself to me. If only God would show me what to do. If only God would give me assurance concerning salvation. If only God would assure me that my sins are forgiven. If only God would really use me. If only God would answer my prayers. If only God would give me the gift of the Holy Spirit.

God wants to do all that. God is able to do all that because Jesus died. The missing link is faith – trust – obedience on our part. We need to take Jesus at his word and come to him. Then our Christian experience will no longer be one of plunging down snakes. We will find ourselves climbing ladders, nearer and nearer to God each day.

11. I am the Vine
John 15 1-17

"I am the vine; you are the branches. If a man remains in me and I in him, he will bear much fruit; apart from me you can do nothing."

This is our final message in the series on the "I am" sayings of Jesus. We've studied The Bread of Life, The Light of the World, The Good Shepherd, The Way, and now The Vine. You will remember from the earlier messages that these are far from gentle sayings of Jesus. We often get the wrong picture of Jesus. We think of him as a very gentle person who told wonderful stories. If this were the case, then why did the people hate him? Why did they cry out for him to be crucified? Today Jesus' claim to be "The True Vine," perhaps helps us to understand the opposition, for this is one of the most dramatic, outrageous, inflammatory claims of his whole ministry.

In Israel the Jews were clear that as a nation they were the vine or the vineyard of God. There are many Old Testament references:

You brought a vine out of Egypt; you drove out the nations and planted it. You cleared the ground for it, and it took root and filled the land. (Psalm 80.8-9)

I am the Vine – John 15.1-17

The vineyard of the Lord Almighty is the house of Israel, and the men of Judah are the garden of his delight. (Isaiah 5.7)

Isaiah goes on to challenge the people, saying they are producing sour grapes. Jeremiah warned his listeners:

I had planted you like a choice vine of sound and reliable stock. How then did you turn against me into a corrupt, wild vine? (Jeremiah 2.21)

Israel saw itself as the Vine of God – the vine had become their national symbol.

In Jesus' day, the Roman coinage had to be changed for use in the temple. The people would be given coinage from the Maccabean era. Stamped on the coins was a picture of a vine.

In the very centre of the temple was, of course, the Holy Place, where the High Priest alone was allowed to go at Yom Kippur. The Holy Place was decorated with a huge golden vine which was the glory of the temple. It was a great honour for any citizen to be allowed to subscribe for a bunch or even a single gold grape to be added to a bunch on the glowing vine.

Just a few days before this event Jesus has been in the temple courtyard overturning the tables of the money changers with his stern condemnation:

"My house will be called a house of prayer, but you are making it a den of robbers." (Matthew 21.13)

Now standing among the people he says:

"I am the true vine, and my Father is the gardener."

Can you see that with this background his words are dynamite!

I believe this passage remains dynamite today. It is a key passage for our Christian discipleship. Jesus is the vine and the Father is the gardener. The passage is all about us, as the branches of the vine bearing fruit. God's intention is that we should bear much fruit.

"This is to my Father's Glory, that you bear much fruit, showing yourselves to be my disciples." John 15.8)

What is this fruit? Whilst it is true that in Romans 1.13 Paul refers to converts as fruit, I am confident that what Jesus is talking about here is the Fruit of the Spirit.

But the fruit of the Spirit is love, joy, peace, patience, kindness, goodness, faithfulness, gentleness and self-control. Against such things there is no law. (Galatians 5.22-23)

Paul speaks of:

Lives filled with the fruit of righteousness that comes through Jesus Christ – to the glory and praise of God. (Philippians 1.11) or as The Good News Bible puts it: *Your lives will be filled with the truly good qualities which only Jesus Christ can produce, for the glory and praise of God.*

Think of a luscious bunch of black grapes, kissed by the sun, with a velvet coating of bloom, absolutely lovely, desired by everyone. Have you watched people picking over the grapes in the supermarket? The poor and squashy ones are ignored.

God wants our lives to be like good grapes, for then the difference will show. People will know that we have been transformed by the power of God. People will see the beauty of Jesus reflected in us. God will be glorified, and men and women will be drawn to him. This is God's purpose for our lives.

Notice in the passage that four states of fruiting are mentioned. Firstly in verse 2 is the branch which bears no fruit. What happens?

He cuts off every branch in me that bears no fruit,

The branch is cut out completely, bundled up and burned, unless mildew should get in and spread to the rest of the vine.

We need to recognise that there is a Christian responsibility, not a Christian option, to bear fruit. There is much in the scriptures about disciples who in effect do not bear fruit. Just for a moment remember the person who put his hand to the plough and then looked back. Jesus' judgment was that this person was not fit for the kingdom of God. Remember the person who hid his talent? Jesus said:

"Throw that worthless servant outside, into the darkness, where there will be weeping and gnashing of teeth." (Matthew 25.30)

If you claim to be a Christian, yet bear no fruit, the matter is serious indeed. It needs urgent action, even today!

Secondly, there is the branch that fruits:

Every branch that does bear fruit he prunes so that it will be even more fruitful.

It bears some fruit. What happens to this branch? It gets pruned, cut back so that the goodness being drawn from the vine goes into producing grapes and not into luxuriant rambling growth. Left on its own a branch of a vine can run for up to one hundred feet. Various translators use different words concerning the pruning. The NIV 'trims clean,' the AV 'purgeth,' whilst the Good News Bible 'prunes so that it will be clean.'

I used to think it was just in Jesus' day that they talked about cleaning vines, until a dear friend of mine, David Stone, head gardener at Mottisfont Abbey, spoke about this passage in his testimony. He talked about how as a lad one of his tasks was to clean the vines, getting rid of anything that might hinder fruiting. That rang bells with me. How important for me and for you, as Christians, to allow God to cut out everything unprofitable. What is the secret in your life which needs to be purged? Have you locked the greenhouse door, preventing God, who is the gardener, from coming in?

Thirdly, and still in verse 2, there is a reference to bearing more fruit. I did some reading about growing grapes and learned that in the first year the vine should not be allowed to bear fruit. In its second year there can be one bunch to each branch. By the time the vine is five years old; it can be expected to bear a heavy crop. A vine properly pruned, grown against a sunny wall, can be expected after five years to bear up to two hundred pounds of fruit!

More fruit? Yes! God expects us to grow. Suppose I challenge you about the fruit of the Spirit in your life? You say to me, "I'm not very good at loving." Are you more loving than last year? "I don't have much joy." Is there more joy than last year?

"I'm not very gentle, my self-control is poor." Maybe, but how do you compare with last year?

If things are not better, if you have to admit, honestly, that things are in decline, do you see the cause? Is it because you are not letting the Father, the head gardener, cleanse you? If this is the case, you need to do something about that now, today.

The final state of fruiting is found in verses 5 and 8:

If a man remains in me and I in him, he will bear much fruit.
This is to my Father's glory, that you bear much fruit.

The aim is to bear much fruit because this glorifies God. What do your neighbours say about you? Do they say – "What love that person shows to all around her, to what lengths she goes to help others!" "I don't know how she came through that difficult time!" "Have you noticed her peace and serenity? It must be her faith!"

Remember the words of Jesus:

"In the same way, let your light shine before men, so that they may see your good deeds and praise your Father in heaven." (Matthew 5.16)

"Pastor," you say, "you are putting pressure on me. You make me feel guilty." My dear friends, that is not what I want to do in the least. I want you to bear much fruit, because I want your joy to be full. Let me, in closing; point out from our passage the secrets of fruiting.

Jesus says in verse 4:

"No branch can bear fruit by itself."

That seems obvious, but it is a difficult lesson to learn. A branch cut out of the vine will very soon wither and die. Unless it is in living contact with the main vine the branch gets no sap, no goodness, no strength. The branches must be joined, must be united with the main stem of the vine so that they are one plant.

If you are bearing no fruit, do you have a living relationship with God? There is a world of difference between knowing about God and knowing God. I know about the Queen, I know about Michael Atherton. I know about John Major. I know my wife and my children. I can hug, hold, share, trust and share my time with them. I miss them when we are apart.

All of a sudden I have the secret of what it means to abide. Abiding in Jesus is trusting him, listening to him, loving him, giving time to him, living in his company, sharing an intimate relationship with him. If it hurts to miss a day with Jesus, you abide.

I believe there are people in church this morning who have no real joy, who bear no real fruit. The honest comment would have to be – they are not abiding.

What stops you from abiding? Are you so busy trying to bear fruit that in fact you have no time to listen to God? You have no time to talk to God. You don't really have time to spend with his Word. You are so anxious to get on with life that you don't have time to trust him. You have never really learned to develop that relationship. To you God says, "STOP – start abiding now!"

Many a husband has been so busy providing for his wife and children that he ends up estranged from them, and divorced. Are you divorced from God?

You may be resisting pruning. There is that area which needs to be cut out. God may have put his finger on it before now. You think of it as your secret sin, the hidden room in your life – but there are no secrets from God, and it spoils your relationship with him. God says it has got to go, but you won't let him cut it out.

TODAY Jesus wants you to abide in his love.

TODAY Jesus wants your joy to be full.

TODAY Jesus wants to you as his intimate friend.

TODAY Jesus loves to forgive and redeem your misspent years.

Did you notice verse 13 in our reading today?

"Greater love has no one than this, that he lay down his life for his friends."

That is exactly what Jesus has done for you.

TESTIMONY

OF

REVEREND

GODFREY W. BUTLER

From the Pit

Spoken
in a common tongue
the words,
closer than his eyes;
though softened with rags,
and wrapped in tears,
rose up
like a child's cry
to his father.

This is part of a sermon which was given on 9th January 1997 at
Ferndown United Church

12. Goff's Testimony

*"He is in your hands," King Zedekiah answered. "The king can do
nothing to oppose you." So they took Jeremiah and put him into the
cistern of Malkijah, the king's son, which was in the courtyard of the
guard. They lowered Jeremiah by ropes into the cistern; it had no
water in it, only mud, and Jeremiah sank down into the mud.
(Jeremiah 38.5-6 NIV)*
     Nearly forty-eight years ago, I was sitting on a backless
bench, in a marquee, in a field at Whitecliff Bay on the Isle of Wight.
I was listening to this story being told, when God spoke to me. It was
as if I could see Jeremiah in the bottom of the pit – and I could sense
his predicament. It must have been bad enough to have been in the
prison, but thrown into this mud – at the bottom of the pit – how long
could he possibly survive? Then I became aware of the damp and cold
of the mud and of how dirty Jeremiah must have been; he couldn't
even touch himself without spreading mud!
     Now all that is a reasonable response of a young lad's
imagination, but the bit I can't explain came next. From nowhere I

saw in my mind a vivid picture of a bride dressed in white. She was radiant – pure – clean. And a voice said to me, "You are as dirty as the man in the pit – and I want you to be as clean as the bride."

Jeremiah had no means of helping himself. Survival in the pit would have been a matter of days at the most. There was no way he could climb out. But, thank God, there was a righteous man among King Zedekiah's officials, Ebed-Melech the Cushite. Ebed-Melech went to the king and pleaded for Jeremiah. Let the Bible tell the story.

Then the king commanded Ebed-Melech the Cushite, "Take thirty men from here with you and lift Jeremiah the prophet out of the cistern before he dies." So Ebed-Melech took the men with him and went to a room under the treasury in the palace. He took some old rags and worn-out clothes from there and let them down with ropes to Jeremiah in the cistern. Ebed-Melech the Cushite said to Jeremiah, "Put these old rags and worn-out clothes under your arms to pad the ropes." Jeremiah did so, and they pulled him up with the ropes and lifted him out of the cistern. And Jeremiah remained in the courtyard of the guard. (Jeremiah 38.10-13)

There on that bench God said to me, "Can't you see, can't you see that is what Jesus has done for you? You are the one in the pit. You are the one in the mud. You are the one who cannot help yourself. You cannot be clean however much you try – but Jesus died to rescue you – to make you clean – to make you safe."

You may not have rated me as a bad youngster – but I sat on that bench sobbing – because I knew that in God's eyes my sin made me dirty. Until I came to Jesus I would be unforgiven. And I knew that Jesus had died on the cross – because he loved me.

What could I do? What could I say? "Jesus – forgive me – come into my heart."

PART 4

THE

HEALING MIRACLES

OF JESUS

The Woman who touched His Hem

Women's problems, the doctors called it,
dismissing me, time after time
with a potion or pill
which did nothing to stop
the blood running continually.

I should have been married, with children,
instead of seeking physicians,
year after year; destitute, weary
and shunned because of the smell
of the blood running continually.

I hurried when I heard that Jesus was here,
but Jairus was taking him home to his
daughter.
What chance of him speaking to me
a pauper
with blood running continually?

Frantic I pushed through the crowd.
Go away, said one, *you're not the right sort,*
but I prayed and hoped
as I grasped his cloak
and at once - the blood flow stopped.

He turned his kind eyes to me,
so trembling, I started to tell
of my searching in vain, the long years of pain,
My daughter, he smiled, *Go in peace,*
Your faith has made you well.

13. Jesus heals a Paralysed Man
Mark 2.1-12

I began last week with a warning about healing – that we are on dangerous ground. We are in the realm of the mystery of God who is Sovereign and whose concern for us is always greater even than our own. We have a God who longs for all of us to be whole; but for us, while we are part of this earth's fallen creation, that wholeness may be found in physical or mental healing, or it may be in spiritual wholeness that we find Jesus.

Now of course in our better moments we realise that spiritual wholeness is much more important than physical or mental wholeness. We know in our better moments that in the new creation, that is heaven, there will be no more suffering or crying or pain. We will be completely whole; but until then we struggle because we are human. We are in danger of finding miraculous physical healing far more impressive than a man's sins being forgiven. We would talk far more about a woman freed from her paralysis than we would about a woman delivered from terrible guilt.

We are challenged in this passage to stop and think again about these issues; to try to get our perceptions right, and to move into the wholeness that God intends for each one of us.

What does our passage actually show us about this healing issue? We must examine the text.

Finding the Real Jesus

A few days later, when Jesus again entered Capernaum, the people heard that he had come home.

If you go on a visit to the Holy Land today you will certainly be taken to see the ruins of Capernaum at the northern end of the Sea, or Lake, of Galilee. You will doubtless be impressed by the ruins of the ancient synagogue and by the houses; not much more than cottages by our standards; but which may well be the remains of the homes of Andrew and Peter, James and John and others in the fishing community who earned their living from the lake. If your overall impression is that it was just a small place you need to stop and realise that it was the largest of all the towns and cities built around the shores of the lake. It was the principal city of Galilee. So while we have no idea when Jesus left Nazareth and settled in Capernaum, nor whether Mary and Joseph had acquired a home there or if Jesus relied on the hospitality of his friends, we do see that it was a strategic place for him to begin and to conduct much of his ministry.

We can understand that what happened in the synagogue in Capernaum would soon be talked about throughout the region. What Jesus taught and the miracles he did would soon be known all around the lake.

From Chapter One of Mark's gospel we learn that fishermen had given up their livelihood to follow Jesus, and that Jesus taught in the synagogue with authority and not like the established teachers of the law. We know that Jesus had cast out evil spirits, had healed Peter's mother-in-law from a dreadful fever and had healed many others from various diseases. When he taught, it was hardly a surprise that many came to hear him:

So many gathered that there was no room left, not even outside the door, and he preached the word to them.

What I want you to notice this morning is not the crowd; that speaks for itself, but what Jesus is doing. He is preaching the Word. He is teaching them about his Father and about the Kingdom of God. He is doubtless expounding the Old Testament scriptures and their relevance in the daily lives of the people. He is showing them what God would have them to be. He is endeavouring to ensure that they have a good and true picture of God and what God requires.

Jesus heals a Paralysed Man – Mark 2.1-12

At times in his ministry we will find Jesus being extraordinarily scathing concerning those who have only come because of the signs and wonders. Being a Christian, then and now, is always first and foremost discovering and doing what God requires.

Some men came, bringing to him a paralytic, carried by four of them.

Now here is a vital marker regarding healing, the marker of faith. I am always very critical of people who suggest that a person is not healed because of a lack of faith. I am sure you have come across the situation where onlookers say, "If only they had more faith." What we must understand is that faith is an important element in healing.

I cannot answer the question "Why?" so won't waste time pontificating, but I do observe in virtually every healing miracle of Jesus that faith is a significant factor. What is faith? Gethin Russell-Jones offers an interesting suggestion. He writes, "Faith is the powerful understanding that human solutions alone will not alter the situation facing us, but the belief that God can, or must, do something."

If I put it into simple terms, I would say, "Faith is recognising that while I am helpless to do anything about it, God can and will." Or how about this from Oliver Wendell Holmes, "Faith is when a man decides he is not God."

But there is something else which is important, especially in this account. Whose faith is it? Whilst faith may be later engendered in the paralytic, at the outset it is certainly not his faith. It is the faith of the four friends. Doubtless they have heard about the wonderful healings that have been ministered by Jesus in Capernaum. Importantly they have a deep love and a real concern for their paralysed friend. Believing that Jesus can do something about his infirmity, they bring him to Jesus.

We sometime forget just how often in the gospels healing comes not as result of the prayer of the faith of a sick person, but because of the prayer and actions, the faith of a friend or relative. Consider the occasion when Jairus came to plead with Jesus on behalf of his daughter, or when friends brought the deaf mute to

Jesus. Think of when the Syro-Phoenecian woman begged Jesus to heal her daughter, or when at Bethsaida, his friends brought a blind man to Jesus.

We exhort others to have faith. The scriptures show us and today's passage shows us that it is when we have faith; when we pray and bring our friends and relatives to Jesus, that we open the door to forgiveness and healing and wholeness.

Will you notice too that there is a time to pray and a time to act? I am sure these four men had prayed often in the synagogue and in their homes for their paralysed friend. They may even have pinned up a prayer card on the synagogue notice board. But their friend would never have been healed unless they were prepared to act and bring him to Jesus. I dare to suggest that we are good at the praying, but that our confidence evaporates when it comes to the doing. We chicken out when it comes to the point of telling our friend that we are going to bring them to church and introduce them to Jesus. But these friends not only have faith, they have persistent faith: faith which takes whatever action is necessary.

Since they could not get him to Jesus because of the crowd, they made an opening in the roof above Jesus and, after digging through it, lowered the mat the paralysed man was lying on.

When they saw the crowd filling the house, and many people all around the door straining to hear the Master, no one would have been surprised if they had given up. They would have assessed the situation as hopeless. They could not get their friend to Jesus that day. Perhaps they would try again on another occasion.

Would it be wicked to suggest that if it were some of us, we might even be glad to see the crowd, for it would give us a good excuse not to press on with bringing our friend? But these men know that their friend is beyond human help. It is a mark of their faith, and it is also a mark of their true love for their friend that they devise the strategy of digging through the roof.

Assuming this to be a traditional Middle Eastern roof on a fairly substantial house of the time, the construction would have been that beams ran one way across the roof. These would have been covered with a layer of twigs and then a second row of lighter beams to the first set would be laid. The space between these would be filled with a mixture of mud and straw, and when it had baked in the sun it would be tiled with small paving slabs. So the paralysed man's friends have quite a demolition job on their hands: to prise the tiles away; to dig down through the baked mud and straw; to remove joints and twigs, and all before they can lower their friend to Jesus.

This is what I call faith! Sometimes when I have told this story I have commented on what might be the reaction of the crowd as they find these men breaking through the ceiling. The four friends believe that with Jesus anything is possible. For us they pose the challenging question – what do we really believe Jesus can and will do?

Let me add another observation regarding the digging through the roof. You see, it was hard work. It needed perseverance. It involved taking a risk. They could have been chased off before they broke through. They are inevitably going to have to pay the cost of putting things right afterwards, whether or not their friend is healed.

The point I want to make is that it is often difficult to get to Jesus, either for yourself or for a friend. There are times when it is as if Jesus himself has prepared the way. You feel you could walk right into his presence and make your request; but I observe that more often that not, as if God were testing our earnestness, the way is hard and we need roof digging perseverance. All kinds of issues challenge our minds. We perceive problems in every direction. We are called to persevere how ever long it may take, either for our own sake or for the sake of our friend.

In a sense it was really good that there were four of them together. What a good idea it is to take our friends into our confidence when we need healing or when we have a friend who needs a touch from the Master. Their prayers and their faith and their determination will be effective in reinforcing ours.

It is at this point in the story that the dynamite explodes:

When Jesus saw their faith, he said to the paralytic, "Son, your sins are forgiven."

How often, when someone is ill, do we treat the symptoms of their disease, rather than treating the cause of the disease? Very often we treat symptoms because we do not have the means of treating the cause of the disease, because we are unable to give the time, or do not have the insight to discover the root cause of the problem.

So we treat the depressed person with antidepressants, hoping his or her circumstances will change so that the cause of the depression will pass and that when the tablets are withdrawn he or she will be able to cope. All too often that is not the case. We treat back pain with anti-inflammatory drugs and pain killers without diagnosing the real cause for the tension which puts those muscles into spasm, or what traps the nerves. We treat high blood pressure with medication which will dilate the vessels. We deal with asthma with drugs which dilate the tracheoles. When we withdraw the medication the original problem still remains.

Jesus saw the cause of this man's paralysis. It was because he was gripped by sin. We have no idea what his sin was, but the guilt of that sin had so gripped this man, spiritually, emotionally and physically, that he was unable to walk. Jesus knew that what this man needed was forgiveness and assurance that his sins were forgiven completely.

Listen carefully. I am not suggesting that sin is at the root of all diseases. Many diseases are because we have encountered a bacteria or a virus. Many diseases are because of some genetic imperfection. Many disabilities are because of accidents, and so on. But I am clear that we seriously underestimate the effect of sin and guilt in gripping us and making us ill.

We now come to the crucial point in the story:

Now some teachers of the law were sitting there, thinking to themselves, "Why does this fellow talk like that? He's blaspheming! Who can forgive sins but God alone?"

They are right of course. Only God can forgive sins. In telling this man that his sins are forgiven Jesus is putting himself on an equal footing with God – he is claiming to be God. I come back to what I touched on earlier. The Jewish teachers of the law would have been far more impressed to see a paralytic healed than to see him forgiven. But it is in fact far, far more important that he should be forgiven than that he should be able to walk again. The wonderful thing in our passage today is that both occur – the man's sins are forgiven and his body is made whole.

Immediately Jesus knew in his spirit that this was what they were thinking in their hearts, and he said to them, "Why are you thinking these things? Which is easier: to say to the paralytic, 'Your sins are forgiven,' or to say, 'Get up, take your mat and walk?' But that you may know that the Son of Man has authority on earth to forgive sins…" He said to the paralytic, "I tell you, get up, take up your mat and go home." He got up, took his mat and walked out in full view of them all. This amazed everyone and they praised God saying, "We have never seen anything like this!"

It was George Bernard Shaw who said, "We have not lost faith, but we have transferred it from God to the medical professionals." If you agree with him I hope you will agree with me that this was an extraordinarily foolish thing to do. We bless God for the medical professions, but they are not God and would be the first to acknowledge that they hold only a few of the answers. Today there is a fresh realisation about the spiritual dimension in healing, health and wholeness. More and more we hear about "holistic treatment." This reaction against science holding all the answers is good, but what is sad is that at present so much attention is directed towards alternative medical practices which mostly have their spiritual roots in Eastern mysticism rather than in an Almighty God.

Remarkable advances are achieved through some of these alternative treatments, but we still do not see people being made really whole, because these treatments cannot put people back in relationship with Almighty God. Although they can be helpful physically, some of them may trap people into beliefs that ultimately remove them even further from God. At last there is a growing co-operation between the medical profession and the Christian faith. More and more surgeries are finding the value of specifically Christian counselling. Gradually more and more patients are pleased to be referred for Christian counsel. What is more, remarkable improvement is reported in the rate of recovery and the degree of recovery, both in physical and mental health among patients who receive this dual treatment.

Finally, can I put to you a 'supposing'? Suppose the paralytic man had had his sins forgiven, but had not been able to walk again. You see, his friends' concern was that he should be physically healed. They had that one straightforward aim, but Jesus saw that it was far more important that his sins should be forgiven. His physical disabilities were life-long but the spiritual damage of his sin was eternal.

This morning you may feel fit as a fiddle, as strong as an ox. The matter of physical healing may seem totally irrelevant and inapplicable to your life today, but if you have never had your sins forgiven you are spiritually terminally ill. You are desperately in need of forgiveness, before sin pays its wages – death.

There is not one of us, nor is there anyone in the whole wide world who does not need to be brought to Jesus. We all need to find his love and forgiveness, and for some of us, his release from the bonds of guilt may well be the key to us being made completely whole.

14. Jesus heals a man with demons
Luke 8.26-39 GNB

Jesus and his disciples sailed on over to the territory of Gerasa, which is across the lake from Galilee.
The Good News Bible rendering, "the territory of Gerasa," is a good one for it is difficult to say exactly where this miracle took place. Three names appear in the ancient texts; Gerasa, but the town of Gerasa is nearly 30 miles south east of the Sea of Galilee; Gergese, which is on the shore of Galilee to the south eastern end of the lake, and Gadara, which is situated five miles south east of the Sea of Galilee but which does have territory stretching to the shore of the lake.

The other name we will have heard of in connection with this miracle is the Decapolis, or "the ten towns." There was a region to the south east of Galilee, Gentile land, where there were ten towns, including the ones we have mentioned. They had originally been settled by the Greeks, and in Jesus' day had not been conquered by the Romans, nor were they under the control of any other power block. They had been left alone and were simply known as the Decapolis.

We know the region. We can't be sure of the exact location, though I came across one lovely comment regarding the town of Gerasa, "If the miracle took place in Gerasa the stampede of pigs from Gerasa to the lake would have made them the most energetic herd in history!"

Try to picture the scene typical of that south eastern end of the lake; very steep, almost sheer limestone cliffs coming down to the lakeside with just a few yards of beach. In the cliff there were many tombs, some in natural limestone caves, and many more were carved into the hillside and large enough to serve as family mausoleums. Some were sealed for they were in use; some opened were prepared in advance by families to receive their dead when the sad occasion arose. Such graveyards were often some distance from a town for many believed that the spirits of the dead haunted such places.

As Jesus stepped ashore, he was met by a man from the town who had demons in him. For a long time this man had gone without clothes and would not stay at home, but spent his time in the burial caves.

Try to imagine the sight of this poor man. How he had come to be possessed we can only speculate, but scripture tells us that this had been his condition for a long time. The evil spirits are under Satan's control and they torment him. He is not his own. His body and soul are possessed by the demons whose only interest is his ultimate destruction. He has long since given up caring for himself. He is naked, unwashed, and unkempt, and Mark tells us that he cut himself with stones. That he would not stay at home is an understatement. His family could not control or contain him. He was an outcast, shunned, unclean, living among the tombs.

Perhaps he served one useful purpose, that of keeping other people away. It is William Barclay who speculates concerning the herd of pigs. He suggests that whilst Jews were forbidden to keep pigs; many Jews, despite pig meat being declared unclean because of the parasites the flesh often contained, in fact liked pork and a black market in pork went on with Jews making trips to the Decapolis to purchase supplies.

Make what you will of that – I do not agree with the commentators who say that the demoniac came down to the shore to scare Jesus and the disciples away. This was no chance meeting, Jesus had planned it. It was in the purposes of God for this man and

102

that we might be sure that Jesus is far greater than Satan and all his demons.

When he saw Jesus, he gave a loud cry, threw himself down at his feet, and shouted, "Jesus, Son of the Most High God! What do you want with me? I beg you, don't punish me!"

Is it the demoniac who speaks or is it the demons within him who speak? It doesn't really matter – all at once the power and authority of Jesus is recognised and the man throws himself down at Jesus' feet. At the name of Jesus every knee must bow. The title he uses is interesting – 'Jesus, Son of the Most High God.' The Most High God was a term used by the Gentiles for Jehovah God. They used it when they recognised that Jehovah was superior to any of their idols. The demoniac has no doubt concerning Jesus – he is the incarnate son of this one true God.

"I beg you, don't punish me," or in Mark's words, *"Swear to God that you won't torture me." (Mark 5.7 NIV)*

What does the poor fellow believe is about to happen? Luke immediately seeks to help us:

He said this because Jesus had ordered the evil spirit to go out of him.

The man knew what had happened when others had tried to restrain him – of the pain and double torment it had caused.

Many times it had seized him, and even though he was kept a prisoner, his hands and feet tied with chains, he would break the chains and be driven by the demon out into the desert.

Those were the very worst times for the demoniac, but Jesus is not like that. Jesus deals with us with the utmost care and compassion. Just watch Jesus in ministry!

Jesus asked him, "What is your name?"

This is a gentle but masterful ploy. To know someone's name is to gain a real measure of control and authority over them. The first task of the successful teacher is to get to know the names of all the children in their class. If he calls, "The boy in the third row, two seats from the back," his call will have no effect. But when he calls, "Neil!" or, "Alan!" it is amazing what just the sharp mention of a name will do to pull that pupil back into line.

"My name is Mob," he answered, because many demons had

103

gone into him.

Most translators use the name Legion. A legion was the largest unit in the Roman army. Some have suggested that this man had been abused by the Roman legions and the demons had entered as a result of this abuse.

I quite like this Good News rendering - *"My name is Mob."* It is not just one demon; this man is possessed by many demons, and they are just like an unruly mob seeking to destroy him.

There must have been a time when the demons entered this man. The Life Application commentary retells an old fable about a scorpion and a frog. The scorpion asked the frog to carry him on his back across a creek. The frog said 'No,' fearing the scorpion would sting him. The scorpion swore he would not, so the frog warily allowed the scorpion to hop on and started out across the stream. Sure enough, when they were half-way across the scorpion stung the frog. 'Why did you do that?' yelled the frog. 'Now I will die and you will drown!' 'I know.' replied the scorpion, 'but it is in my nature to sting.'

Time and again Satan tempts us – to risk sinful activity – to get involved in the occult and other dodgy practices. "You won't get harmed, it won't affect you, you are strong enough to stand," he coaxes.

But Satan and his minions have only one goal, to take control of your life, to separate you from the love of God, to little by little destroy you. It is the nature of Satan, the nature of sin is to sting.

The message is clear, so be careful what you get involved in, in case you allow Satan entrance into controlling your life.

The demons begged Jesus not to send them into the abyss.

If you study Revelation the Abyss is the final place of imprisonment of Satan and all his angels. The demons know by now that Jesus is going to cast them out of the man who is possessed. To be sent away into the Abyss would mean that they would no longer be able to torment anyone or anything. It was the place demons feared most.

Why didn't Jesus destroy the demons, or send them into the Abyss? There is a clue in Matthew's account of this miracle:

"What do you want with us, you Son of God? Have you come

to punish us before the right time?" (Matthew 8.29)

This suggests that the demons knew their ultimate fate, but the time for that had not yet come.

We find it hard to understand. We ask, "Why does God allow evil? Why doesn't Jesus stop all the evil in the world?" The only answer we can give is that God's time for that has not yet come. It most certainly will come. The final victory over Satan, his demons and all evil is sure, but it is God's time and purpose. His plan and timing has not been fully revealed.

There was a large herd of pigs nearby, feeding on a hillside. So the demons begged Jesus to let them go into the pigs, and he let them. They went out of the man and into the pigs. The whole herd rushed down the side of the cliff into the lake and was drowned.

Mark tries to number the pigs and says there were about two thousand. The Jews would have considered pigs to be an appropriate place for demons to end up – unclean spirits in unclean animals. But to us it shows the value Jesus puts on a soul – it is much more valuable than a whole herd of pigs.

What a sight it must have been, a stampede of pigs charging headlong down the exceedingly steep hillside and into the lake. I imagine the noise! I imagine the amazement of the disciples!

But I cannot imagine the release and the relief of the demoniac; free after years of torment; restored and in his right mind.

The destruction of a herd of pigs raises all manner of issues I know. Animal lovers will protest on behalf of the pigs. Is the farmer entitled to claim compensation from Jesus?

Luke tells us a fair deal about the response. We suddenly learn that there were other people about; the swineherds.

The men who had been taking care of the pigs saw what happened, so they ran off and spread the news in the town and among the farms.

They are astounded. Perhaps they are afraid they will be blamed for the loss of the pigs. They run everywhere telling about the deliverance of the deranged man, and about Jesus and his authority. Can it possibly be true?

People went out to see what had happened, and when they came to Jesus, they found the man from whom the demons had gone out sitting at the feet of Jesus, clothed and in his right mind; and they were all afraid. Those who had seen it told the people how the man had been cured.

What will be the reaction of the people?

Then all the people from that territory asked Jesus to go away, because they were terribly afraid.

What an incredible reaction – a wonderful miracle – a man they had been unable to restrain is healed and in his right mind, and they ask Jesus to go away!

What are they afraid of? Someone once suggested that there were others who were possessed and they were afraid of losing more of their livestock! But that is frivolous.

This is serious – people are always sending Jesus away. They are not demon possessed, but their lives are spoiled by sin. When confronted by Jesus people have to make a decision. Will I let Jesus deal with the sin in my life? Will I let him deal with my unclean areas, my unpleasant habits, my materialism, my little addictions? Will I let him have his way and change my life? So many people send Jesus away. They would rather maintain the status quo with all its pain, with all its troubles, than let Jesus come and make them whole.

Have you been sending Jesus away, rather than facing up to him dealing with the sin and shame in your life?

If you have – first let me give you a warning from our passage tonight – note these very next words:

So Jesus got into the boat and left.

As far as we know, Jesus never went back to the Decapolis again. They had their chance and they turned Jesus away. It may be that you have often been challenged to allow Jesus to be Lord in your life. There will come a time when he will go away. The opportunity will have passed and you will not be able to say you were not warned. If the story of Jesus has challenged you tonight – you should respond to him.

What about the man who has been healed?

The man from whom the demons had gone out begged Jesus "Let me go with you."

That seems perfectly reasonable. Jesus has done wonderful

things for this man.

But Jesus sent him away saying, "Go back home and tell what God has done for you."

"Jesus, why didn't you let this man come with you? He could have testified at all your meetings regarding his wonderful deliverance. He would have been a great witness." But Jesus is realistic. This man will be a far more effective witness in the Decapolis, witnessing to those who knew his previous condition and could attest that he really had been miraculously healed. Jesus could use his witness to give, even to those who had sent him away, another chance to respond to the gospel.

What we need to learn is that when God touches a life, the most effective witness is not in telling strangers. It is in living a new life and sharing what God has done among family and friends.

The man went through the town, telling what Jesus had done for him.

15. They knew Jesus would not fail them
Luke 8.40-56

Jesus did many other miraculous signs in the presence of his disciples, which are not recorded in this book. But these are written that you may believe that Jesus is the Christ, the Son of God, and that by believing you may have life in his name. (John 20.30-31)

Jesus' miracles were not only to bring relief to people in dire need in his time, they were not only to wow the crowds and cause them to ask, "Who is this man?" They were in order that you and I might believe, and through believing we might have eternal life – life with a God-like quality, because of what Jesus has done.

That wonderful news is what took me into the preaching ministry. It is what I have sought to share, and what I want to share with you tonight as we look at two of the healing, restoring, life-giving miracles of Jesus.

I want you to know that Jesus will not fail you, that Jesus is sufficient for your every need, that no one and nothing else can satisfy the deepest longings of your heart. I want you to see just how personally Jesus will treat you when you turn to him in your need. Let us turn to our scripture passage:

Now when Jesus returned, a crowd welcomed him, for they were all expecting him.

They knew Jesus would not fail them – Luke 8.40-56

Luke writes this in order to set the scene for us. Thirty-six hours earlier Jesus had set out with his disciples in one of their fishing boats for the Decapolis. What a time it had been: that dreadful storm on the lake, when all the disciples had thought that they must drown, but Jesus had calmed the storm with his word of command, *"Peace, be still."* Then across the lake, Jesus had delivered the Gadarene demoniac; the poor man who for years had been tormented by evil spirits. Now Jesus is back in Capernaum, his base in Galilee. Here the crowds, who love his stories, who love his jibes at the self-righteous religious leaders, who are stunned by his miracles, meet and throng around him, wondering what will happen today.

Jairus

Then a man named Jairus, a ruler of the synagogue, came and fell at Jesus' feet, pleading for him to come to his house.

In order for us to appreciate the full wonder of what will happen we need to understand a little about Jairus. He's the synagogue ruler, a real big-wig in the community. He is respected, prosperous, and he has significant authority. He is not a cleric but a layman appointed by the community to see that everything at the synagogue is done properly. Besides his administrative duties he acts as a community magistrate. He is the one to approach for advice over family and community problems. It was the highest honour a local community could confer to make a man ruler of the synagogue!

For Jairus to come to Jesus is quite remarkable. Already the teachings of the carpenter turned rabbi, from Nazareth have offended and threatened the authority of the Jewish leaders. By now the chief council in Jerusalem has issued warnings against the teachings of Jesus, so why does Jairus come?

His only daughter, a girl of about twelve, was dying.

Desperate times dictate desperate measures! Despite all his money and despite all the knowledge of the best doctors in the land, his one and only daughter lies dying! Where else can he turn? What is important to him at that moment is not what people think of him, or his position as ruler of the synagogue, but the precious life of his daughter. Desperation drives him to Jesus.

Are you one of those respectable people, looked up to at your place of work, in the community, at the Rotary or Probus club? Are you perhaps a leading lady in your social circles? That's fine – but what is the greatest need in your life? Do you want to do something about it? Are you willing to come to Jesus; to tell him about the troubles in your life? Until you do, you may succeed in finding a palliative, but you will not succeed in finding a cure for your heart's greatest need.

Jesus, who never turns away anyone who comes to him humbly, sets out at once. The crowd is such that it is difficult to make headway through the narrow streets of Capernaum.

The Woman

As Jesus was on his way, the crowds almost crushed him. And a woman was there who had been subject to bleeding for twelve years, but no one could heal her.

Have you heard of Eusabius? Eusabius was a Bishop of Caesarea in Palestine from 313 to 339 A.D. He was an avid writer and a good historian. He tells us about this woman. "She was a God-fearer who dwelt at Paneas, near the source of the river Jordan." He writes that, in his day her house was still standing, and at its entrance two brass statues had been erected on stone pedestals. One represented a woman on her knees with her hand outstretched, and the other, a man, with his cloak thrown over his shoulder, and with his hand reaching out towards the woman. Clearly, her home had become something of a shrine, and doubtless there were those who made money out of it, but I am pleased that this early record is preserved for it adds to the picture we can draw concerning her.

This poor soul had suffered bleeding for twelve years. As long as Jairus' daughter had been alive her bleeding had made her ritually unclean. She was not allowed in the synagogue, and certainly not in the temple. Anything or anyone she touched was also to be considered ritually unclean and had to be washed and remained unclean until the evening, the beginning of a new day. She would not be allowed at the well when other women were there drawing water, nor was she allowed in the market place. No one would want to associate with her. She was required keep away from other people and if she didn't they would insult her.

They knew Jesus would not fail them – Luke 8.40-56

She had been treated by many doctors. Mark tells us that she had spent all her money, but instead of getting better she got worse all the time. Does that sound familiar? Do you know people like that? Is that perhaps you?

I'm sure that now you have a picture in your mind: a small, anaemic woman; despised, rejected, downcast. This woman is no leading figure in the community, but a person who felt she was of little value; who was unloved and desolate, having spent all she had trying to find relief.

I am beginning to think that like Jairus she is coming to Jesus out of desperation. However when I look back to Mark's gospel I find that she had heard about Jesus and that determination made her come all the way from Paneas to Capernaum! She walked more than thirty miles, down the Hula valley and over the hills. She came to the place where she knew she could meet with Jesus.

I am so pleased that we know that, for I might wonder if she too is coming to Jesus as a last resort. "I've tried everything else – I might as well try Jesus." But it wasn't like that. When she heard about Jesus her faith was immediately kindled. If he could do wonderful things for other people, he could do wonderful things for her too.

Her only worry was that she was not good enough to come to Jesus. As an unclean woman she dare not approach the Master face to face. She was strictly forbidden to touch him, but she thinks, "if only I might be able to touch the edge of his cloak, the hem of his garment."

As a rabbi, Jesus would almost certainly have worn the shawl-like garment of a strict Jew, draped so that two corners hung down his back. On those corners were tassels, tassels that were there to remind everyone of the commandments of God. Such is the woman's faith and trust in Jesus that she determines, "I will not touch the Master. I will only touch the holy tassels on his robe, but it will be sufficient." So tentatively, and yet determinedly, she creeps up behind Jesus, reaches out and touches him!

She came up behind him and touched the edge of his cloak, and immediately her bleeding stopped.

Wonderful!

Do you need to reach out and touch Jesus? Are you downcast, at your wit's end? Perhaps your problem is a physical illness, perhaps it is something totally different, but you are anxious, worried, depressed. Let me remind you; as soon as this woman heard about Jesus, she came. The sad thing is that so many hear about Jesus and fail to come. It is also sad that many carry burdens for years and years and only come to Jesus as a last resort.

The wonderful thing about Jesus is that he still says, "Come!" However long you have delayed, however unworthy you feel, "Come!" He still longs to help you in your difficult situation.

There is one last point about this story before we go back to see what happens regarding Jairus' daughter.

"Who touched me?" Jesus asked. When they all denied it, Peter said, "Master, the people are crowding and pressing against you."

Jesus, you are crazy. There are crowds all around you. All sorts of people are jostling you.

But Jesus said, "Someone touched me; I know that power has gone out from me."

What I want you to see is that Jesus makes this woman stand out in front of the entire crowd.

Then the woman, seeing that she could not go unnoticed, came trembling and fell at his feet. In the presence of all the people, she told why she had touched him and how she had been instantly healed.

Jesus, why are you making a spectacle of this woman? She didn't want any fuss. She was more than content just to touch the hem of your garment and believe she would be healed.

It is because it is vital that the crowd know that she has been healed. This is why Jesus makes her come forward. No more is she to be an outcast. She is to be allowed to go to the priest and make the sacrifice of two doves. Then she will be fully integrated back into the community.

Then he said to her, "Daughter, your faith has healed you. Go in peace."

Jesus deals with the woman from Paneas in exactly the way she needs, just as he will with you when you come to him. The words, "Go in peace," are, more literally, "Go into peace." The woman has not only received her physical healing, Jesus gave her back fullness of life. Her cure was permanent and her cure was complete. Jesus gave her renewed health for her body and eternal salvation for her soul.

Now what about Jairus?

While Jesus was still speaking, someone came from the house of Jairus, the synagogue ruler. "Your daughter is dead," he said. "Don't bother the teacher any more."

What worse news could there possibly be? Whilst Jesus has spent time with this unclean woman his dearly beloved daughter has died. We don't know if the ruler had heard how Jesus had restored a son back to the widow from Nain. Her joy will be his joy, but reading the text it would seem he had not. The synagogue ruler and his servants are ready to return home, totally dejected.

Hearing this, Jesus said to Jairus, "Don't be afraid; just believe, and she will be healed."

Jairus had heard Jesus commend the woman from Paneas for her faith and now Jesus tells him not to be afraid but to exercise faith. He had come to Jesus hoping beyond hope that Jesus would heal his daughter. Could he now believe that Jesus could bring her back to life?

There must have been at least a flicker of hope in Jairus' heart, for impossible as the situation now seems, and though his heart is breaking with grief, he allows Jesus to continue the journey to his home, and he clings on to that glimmer of hope.

What a wonderful lesson! When you experience intense grief, be it over the loss of a loved one, the break-up of a marriage, the loss of a job, rejection by a close friend; whatever it is, don't abandon hope. Don't turn away from the one person who can help you. Do what Jairus did and cling to the hope that is always there in Jesus.

When he arrived at the house of Jairus, he did not let anyone go in with him except Peter, John and James, and the child's father and mother.

The scene which met Jesus is one we have all seen on our television screens. The crowds of neighbours, in fact most of the town folk who were not with Jesus, have assembled at the dead girl's home. The women have put on their black mourning clothes and are shouting and wailing; maybe even the professional mourners have arrived too. Some of the wailing will have come from real grief, but custom demanded that there was much wailing, for the louder the wailing the more people would know how much the lost one was loved. Luke puts it clearly:

All the people were wailing and mourning for her. "Stop wailing," Jesus said. "She is not dead but asleep." They laughed at him, knowing that she was dead.

The reaction of the crowd would probably have been our reaction too.

Watch now the sheer loveliness of what happens next. Remember this is a rich house, with a number of rooms. The little girl's body will have been laid in the coolest room in the house. Jesus takes Jairus, the girl's mother, and Peter, John and James into that cool bedroom. I perceive Jesus putting his arm around the shoulders of the distraught mother. I see him look reassuringly straight into the eyes of Jairus. There they stand. In front of them is the ashen corpse of the little girl who has been so ill and who now has died. She was the pride and joy of their lives. So many hopes had centred on her. What could the Master do now?

But he took her by the hand and said, "My child, get up!"
I love those old words of the Authorised Version: *"Damsel, I say unto thee, arise!"(Mark 5.41)*

Her spirit returned, and at once she stood up. Then Jesus told them to give her something to eat. Her parents were astonished, but he ordered them not to tell anyone what had happened.

What an understatement, 'Her parents were astonished!' What tears of relief and joy must have rolled down the cheeks of Jairus and his wife that day! What a lovely ending! Jesus brought everything back to normality. "Give the little girl something to eat, and by the way, don't go around telling people about this. We don't want her to be a spectacle all her days. We don't want her to become a curiosity. We want her to be able to get on and enjoy life, life in all its fullness."

These stories have been recorded in order that you and I might believe, in order that you and I might have life, life in all its fullness. The story of the woman with a haemorrhage reminds us that whatever problem we have, Jesus is sufficient to meet our need; and the story of Jairus' daughter has an even greater relevance.

It is likely that there are dead persons here tonight. They may be suffering, distressed or depressed. They are not physically dead of course. No, it is much worse than that – they are spiritually dead. The Bible describes such folk; describes you if you have not come to Jesus, as dead in trespasses and sins, with no hope of eternal life with God. Listen to the words of Jesus.

"I am the way, the truth, and the life; no one comes to the Father except by me." (John 14.6)

"I have come that you might have life, life in all its fullness."(John 10.10)

To come to Jesus was the most important decision in the whole of Jairus' life. It involved humbling himself. It involved admitting that he had no other hope except in Jesus. The woman possibly came full of expectation, trusting that Jesus could heal her, that Jesus could save. Whatever sparked their coming, both came recognising their need of a Saviour.

It always involves that. You too must admit your need of a Saviour, and the Saviour will not turn you away. Jesus invites you to come, and he will supply the deepest need of your heart.

Romsey Baptist Church 18th February 1996,
Ferndown United Church 7th July 2002 and 25th January 2004

16. The Man Born Blind
John 9.1-41

Do you believe in Jesus? Of course you know about him. You believe he was a really good man who did wonderful things and died on a cross: but do you believe in him? Do you believe in him more than you believe in your doctor, your husband, your wife? Do you believe him more than you believe in your parents?

The account of "The Man born Blind" in John is one of the longest single accounts in the gospels. Tonight we only read a small part of it. I want you to especially remember two short sentences. The first one was said by Jesus:

"While I am in the world, I am the light of the world."

And the dramatic statement of the man born blind in verse 38:

The man said, "Lord, I believe," and he worshipped him.

The question I want to put to you is – Have you really met Jesus, the Light of the World? Do you really believe?

Let me set something of the scene for this miracle. In Chapter Seven Jesus has been up to Jerusalem for the Feast of Tabernacles. There he gave some amazing teaching in the temple courts. If not actually claiming to be the Messiah, he has certainly been claiming a very close relationship to God the Father. The outstanding claim that he made was:

The Man Born Blind — John 9.1-41

"I am the light of the world."

The very climax of the feast was the lighting of the great temple candelabra or Menorah. Its light was said to shine throughout the courts of the temple and could be seen from anywhere in the whole city. It stood for the light of God shining in the world. Jesus has dared to say:

"I am the light of the world. Whoever follows me will never walk in darkness, but will have the light of life." (John 8.12)

The general public are amazed that the authorities have allowed him to get away with it and have not put him on trial for blasphemy there and then. The conversation in Jerusalem is, "Is Jesus the Messiah?" To some it seems that the authorities must have concluded that he is. Opinions vary. Many are saying, "Surely this man is at least the prophet Elijah." Others are saying, "No, He is the Christ!"

The Chief Priests and the Pharisees are in a corner. Their immediate response is to attempt to totally discredit Jesus. They know of a woman having an affair. They decide to catch her in the act of adultery, drag her before Jesus and demand a verdict according to the Law of Moses. If Jesus affirms the ancient punishment and says, "Stone her!" his reputation as a man of compassion, as a man of the people, will be destroyed. If he simply lets her go, they will have him for refusing to recognise the authority of the Law of Moses. The answer Jesus gives utterly confounds them, and as Chapter Eight closes he goes on the offensive against the Scribes and Pharisees.

He tells them they are so worldly they will die in their sins. (John 8.23-24)

He accuses them of belonging to their father the devil, and of carrying out his desires. (John 8.44)

Jesus makes the astonishing claim that he is receiving praise and glory from his Father who they claim to be their God. (John 8.54)

The Scribes and Pharisees, who wanted to stone the adulterous woman, pick up stones to stone Jesus. (John 8.59) Jesus is forced to hide and to slip away from the temple grounds.

117

With that background we begin to see the real significance and the purpose of the miracle which follows. Healing a man who was born blind not only demonstrates the power of Jesus to bring light and physical sight to a man, which was wonderful for him; it also illustrates how Jesus can bring spiritual light to our lives, where before there has been impenetrable darkness. He really is the Light of the World.

As he went along, he saw a man blind from birth. His disciples asked him, "Rabbi, who sinned, this man or his parents, that he was born blind?"

It was not unusual to meet blind people, for eye disease was common in Palestine and even today is much more common in the Middle East than it is here.

There are various accounts of Jesus healing blind men, but what makes this especially significant is that this man has been born blind. It is assumed that he suffers from his dreadful handicap because of sin: either the sin of his parents or of a member of a previous generation; or even possibly because of a sin committed in the womb or in some pre-existent state. This is not the place to discuss this strange theology.

The Jews would point you to verses in Exodus:

"I the Lord your God, am a jealous God, punishing the children for the sin of the fathers to the third and fourth generation of those who hate me." (Exodus 20.5)

He does not leave the guilty unpunished; he punishes the children and their children for the sin of the fathers to the third and fourth generation. (Exodus 34.7)

But Jesus is quite clear. He asserts:

"Neither this man nor his parents sinned," said Jesus, "but this happened so that the work of God might be displayed in his life."

Let me remind you again that John is clear that all the miracles recorded in his gospel are signs which bring glory to God and which point to Jesus as the Messiah; the one who was to come. Let us look at that working out in this miracle. Firstly I want us to consider the effect of blindness on this man, and then to see how it parallels the effect of spiritual blindness on any person who does not know God.

The Man Born Blind – John 9.1-41

The Blind Man's Problem

His problem is obvious to a degree. Since he cannot see he cannot work. There are no social services, no welfare state in his day, so the only way he can survive is by begging. These are the obvious problems, but what are his real deprivations?

Born blind, he can know so little of the beauty of the earth. He has never seen the countryside, the sky at night, the beauty of a rose, the face of a baby. He learns something through his other senses and through what people tell him, but it is much less than he ought to perceive. It is the same with communication. He can hear the spoken word, but he can never read for himself. He has never seen a smile and never looked into eyes that say, "I love you." He knows what it is to lose direction, to bump into people and things, to fall over on the pot-holed roads.

One could go on, but let me make my point by recalling a conversation I had with a blind lady who played the organ in a Methodist chapel in Buckinghamshire. She had not been blind from birth but had become blind as a result of diabetes. In conversation I asked her about becoming blind and how she coped with it. She told me, "It was awful at first, but I've got used to it and some days I scarcely notice." I recognised this lady's wonderful spirit, but what struck me was the tragic spiritual parallel her blindness held.

Very few today are physically blind, but the vast majority are spiritually blind, unaware of the things of God. They have never known his beauty, his holiness, his presence, his peace, his forgiveness. They have never really communicated with him through prayer; through his holy word in the Bible; through the indwelling presence of his Spirit. They cannot sing, "For he walks with me and he talks with me and he tells me I am his own." Nor do they know God's direction in life: his purpose; his assurance both for this life and in the life to come – and the dreadful result is they get used to it. They have little or no awareness of what they are missing. Am I talking about you?

Jesus says:

"I am the Light of the world." "I am the way, the truth and the life." (John 14.6)

So many don't understand. When I am wrestling with this, and asking myself, "Why should this be?" I remember:

The god of this age has blinded the minds of unbelievers, so that they cannot see the light of the gospel of the glory of Christ, who is the image of God. (2 Corinthians 4.4)

God wants his light to shine, but unless men and women will come to Jesus, they are trapped by the blindness of a fallen world. Instead of beauty theirs is ugliness: the ugliness of violence; dishonesty; pornography; Spiritism; hatred. Instead of communication theirs is loneliness: the loneliness of broken relationships; families torn apart; loss of true friends. Instead of direction, their lives have very little real purpose, and there is no assurance for tomorrow, just darkness.

It is then that we look back to our scripture:

"As long as it is day, we must do the work of him who sent me. Night is coming, when no one can work. While I am in the world, I am the light of the world."

We see something of the urgency of involving ourselves with spreading the gospel message. Jesus knew of the growing hostility towards him. He knew that his time was short and that all too soon he would be put to death, but I believe there is a wider prophetic element too. For now we have the opportunity to share the Good News, yet increasingly we will find it challenged. It is hard to believe that this country which has been open to the gospel for so long could soon find, having given up its Christian heritage; having sold out to multi-faith and multi-culturalism, that seeking to make converts in any way will become an illegal activity. Yet remember, Jesus has passed the torch to us. He has told us:

"You are the light of the world – let your light shine before men." (Matthew 5.14)

At the Pool of Siloam Jesus meets a man born blind. What is he to do?

He spat on the ground, made some mud with the saliva and put it on the man's eyes. "Go," he told him. "Wash in the Pool of Siloam." (this word means Sent). So the man went and washed, and came home seeing.

The Man Born Blind – John 9.1-41

Let me first tell you a little about the Pool of Siloam. Visitors to Jerusalem are rarely taken to see the site because it is in a poor Arab quarter of the city. For generations it was lost and people even debated its very existence. Then one day, now over a hundred years ago, two Arab boys, playing in a derelict pool of water, discovered a tunnel. They had discovered one end of Hezekiah's tunnel. In Old Testament times most of Jerusalem obtained its water from a spring known either as the Fountain of Gihon or the Virgin's Fountain. It was actually a well fed by a spring in the Kidron valley to the east of the city. The women folk would go out to collect water and carry it into the city.

When Hezekiah became king (2 Kings 16-20), the first good strong king for many years, he realised that battle against the Assyrians was imminent and inevitable. He also knew, if Jerusalem was to be able to withstand a long siege, that water would be the secret to survival. So he extended the city walls, built a large pool as a reservoir and then in a wonderful piece of civil engineering for his day, had a five hundred and eighty yard long tunnel dug to the spring which fed the Fountain of Gihon. It was dug from both ends, and bends were built into the tunnel so that it avoided the sacred burial tombs of David and Solomon. Where the two ends met an inscription was placed on the wall. Then the well was filled in and water from the spring fed through the tunnel to the Pool of Siloam.

To the Jews this pool was a special and revered site. It had been a life-line. It stood as a symbol of life. In Jesus' day it was the main place where people went to collect water. As they entered the concourse the faithful were taught to stop to pray and give thanks to God for water, for life, for deliverance. The road to the Pool of Siloam was a good place for a blind beggar. He could expect to receive alms there.

With that context we begin to see the significance and the purpose of the miracle which follows. Healing a man who was born blind not only demonstrates the power of Jesus to bring light and physical sight to a man – it illustrates too how Jesus can bring spiritual light where before there has been impenetrable darkness. He really is the Light of the World.

Finding the Real Jesus

Meeting Jesus is fundamental to finding real life. Most of us who have met Jesus associate that meeting with a special place. We would describe it as the place where for the first time we really saw. Here for the first time our spiritual blindness was taken away. Here we realised how much Jesus loves us. Here we came to him and received new life – real life.

There was the woman at the well in Samaria who met Jesus. She was completely changed that day.

Jesus answered, "Everybody who drinks this water will be thirsty again, but whoever drinks the water I give him will never thirst. Indeed, the water I give him will become in him a spring of water welling up to eternal life." (John 4.41-43)

I met Jesus in a marquee in a field near Whitecliff Bay on the Isle of Wight. Many have met Jesus in this chapel here in Ferndown. You could meet Jesus right here today. He could turn your darkness to light – you could find real life in him.

I wonder what we think about the prospect of meeting Jesus? Are we afraid of his awesome purity, his utter holiness? Do we ask ourselves, "How will he deal with me? If he knows all about me he will be aware of my total unworthiness. Will he condemn me because of my sin?"

How then did Jesus deal with the blind man? He didn't turn away in disgust at yet another beggar. He didn't say he'd already helped enough people for one day. I believe he looked at the man with compassion. Then he spat on the ground, made clay or mud and he anointed the eyes of the blind man.

Do you find this treatment repulsive or unhygienic? To us it might be; in Jesus' day things were different.

Pliny, the prolific Roman writer, put together a collection of so called scientific information. In it he devoted a whole chapter to the curative properties of saliva. It is, according to him, effective against the poison of snakes; against epilepsy; against leprous spots; against carcinomas; against stiff necks and against eye disease. Before you laugh him to scorn, what do you do today when you burn yourself, have an itch etc?

In Jesus' day they firmly believed in the curative properties of saliva, and here is the interesting point. They also believed that the more famous the person, the more effective would be their saliva in healing disease. Jesus the Rabbi is well known for his wonderful cures. The treatment which Jesus offers to the man born blind is exactly what will inspire his faith.

That is how Jesus treats everyone – lovingly; with compassion; in a way which inspires faith. We could rehearse a whole catalogue of Bible incidents, and every time we would find Jesus deals with the person exactly according to his or her need. Do you need to come to Jesus? Have you been holding back because of what Jesus may think of you? Jesus will deal with you with compassion, with love, according to your need.

Jesus' anointing of the eyes of the blind man made it possible for him to be healed, possible for him to receive his sight, but of itself the anointing did not heal him.

There was a command from Jesus to be obeyed:

"Go," he told him, "wash in the Pool of Siloam."

Just like the crippled man at the Pool of Bethesda, this man is confronted with a choice – to obey, or to decide that the suggestion is nonsense. How could he possibly see, having been blind from birth, simply by going and washing mud from his eyes in the Pool of Siloam?

Perhaps the most important sentence in this account comes next:

So the man went and washed, and came home seeing.

I think that is wonderful. He took Jesus at his word. He obeyed, and so he recovered his sight.

When Jesus died on the cross he made it possible for me, for you, to receive forgiveness of all our sins. He made it possible for me to receive spiritual sight, but this act didn't forgive my sins automatically, nor did it give me spiritual sight automatically, nor did it make me a son of the living God automatically.

The scriptures tell us that there is our part to play. We must repent and believe. We must turn away from our present life and turn to Jesus. We must actively put our trust in him. It is only when we do that, that what is possible becomes a reality. We have to trust and obey.

One of the things I like when using this story as a vehicle for sharing the gospel, is the seeming nonsense of it all – that a man born blind should have saliva mixed with mud applied to his eyes – and when he washed he could see! I like it because the gospel is like that. A man nailed to a Roman gibbet two thousand years ago could be the means whereby I can receive eternal life? It sounds like nonsense!

But because he met Jesus, the blind man was convinced. Perhaps tonight you have met Jesus. You are aware of his presence. He is speaking into your life. He invites you to come, to see the truth of what he offers – to live!

Jesus said, "I am the light of the world. Whoever follows me will never walk in darkness, but will have the light of life."

"Go," Jesus told him, "wash in the Pool of Siloam." So the man went and washed and came home seeing.

Will you tonight say, "Lord I believe" and worship him?

PART 5

THE

PARABLES

OF JESUS

Good Samaritan

I didn't stop
for the man knocked down
in the London Road;
the hit and run.
I went on past.
If anyone asked -
I hadn't seen.
It was none of my business,
I'm not a Samaritan.

but -
if I was the one
mugged by the Sailor's Inn,
lying there bleeding;
if I was the one
crouched in the stairwell
with a plastic cup
held up,

then -
if you came,
black, Christian, or Muslim,
you would be my knight in armour.
You would be my friend,
my neighbour.

.

17. Are Parables Allegories?

The great German preacher Helmut Thielicke described the parables as, "God's Picture Book." A popular definition of a parable is "an earthly story with a heavenly meaning."

These statements are attractive, but if we look no further we avoid one of the difficult statements of scripture. Jesus said:

"The knowledge of the secrets of the kingdom of God has been given to you, but to others I speak in parables, so that, though seeing, they may not see; though hearing, they may not understand." (Luke 10.8)

Our problem when confronted with a verse like this is that many of us know the parables well. We have heard them often. They have been explained to us time and again and have become as familiar as nursery rhymes. We forget that Jesus told his parables without explanation. On a number of occasions, concerned lest his disciples had missed the point; he took them aside perhaps later on in the day to explain the parable. The hearers heard the parable once and once only, unless they became followers of Jesus, when I expect it is likely they heard the stories on more than one occasion.

Now, if only you could stand back from your familiarity with the stories you would perhaps realise that unless you see, hear and understand the parable from a Christian standpoint, from Jesus' point of view, then the word pictures which Jesus paints are merely that. They may be lovely stories, but you may not realise what they are really all about.

Let me try and illustrate what I mean with two of Jesus' shorter parables.

"Look at the birds of the air; they do not sow or reap or store away in barns, and yet your heavenly Father feeds them. Are you not much more valuable than they? Who of you by worrying can add a single hour to his life?" (Matthew 6.26-27)

"And why do you worry about clothes? See how the lilies of the field grow. They do not labour or spin. Yet I tell you that not even Solomon in all his splendour was dressed like one of these." (Matthew 6.28-29)

Seen through Christian eyes, Jesus shows us what his Father is like. His love is such that he cares for birds and plants. He ensures that birds are fed and lilies of the field are clothed with flowers. Then the heart of the matter dawns on us – we are more important than the birds and plants. So why does worry, worry in general, form such a major part of our thinking? It will shorten our lives rather than lengthen them. Why do we not trust our Father?

We realise that these parables are telling us what God is like. If we don't know that, the parables don't make sense, and we end up confused as we try to sort them out.

Now you may have been surprised that I recounted those two short extracts from the Sermon on the Mount as parables. Yet if you think in terms of a parable being an illustration from this world to show us what God is like and what the Kingdom of God, or the Kingdom of Heaven (for they are the same thing) is like, then it is amazing how much of Jesus' teaching is in parables.

Matthew tells us that there was a phase in Jesus' ministry when he only used parables:

Jesus spoke all these things to the crowd in parables; he did not say anything to them without using a parable. (Matthew 13.34)

Various Ph.D.'s have been earned researching the parables and many books have been written about them. A.M. Hunter in 'Interpreting the Parables,' says that parables account for almost a third of all Jesus' recorded words. I find there is tremendous variation between writers in calculating the number of parables.

Are Parables Allegories?

Hunter identifies 60 parables: Archbishop Trench said there were only 30: A.B. Bruce, a New Testament scholar at the end of the last century (not to be confused with F.F.Bruce) reckoned 41: Julicher counted 53. The record number is held by B.T.D. Smith, who claims 62.

It boils down to the breadth of your definition as to what you accept as a parable. The Hebrew word for parable is 'Mashal'. There is a similar Aramaic word, 'Mathla'. They are inclusive terms. So you could include sayings, proverbs, fables, riddles, jokes, apocalyptic predictions, as well as the stories and allegories which make up the best known parables in the New Testament.

But are parables allegories? You just may have noticed that I slipped in the comment that; 'stories and allegories,' make up the bulk of well known parables. What I am really asking is, do parables simply make one main point, or are they full of hidden meanings? Should we seek to tease out every phrase to discover the mystery within?

The length to which this dispute rages in the various academic books is enough to drive one up the wall. It becomes pretty obvious that some parables have just one main point to make, while in others there is a great deal of spiritual truth. It is all too easy to be trapped into trying to read far too much into a parable. You can try to make it fit all situations, when it is supposed to be an illustration. Remember the words which so often introduce a parable – "The Kingdom of Heaven is like…"

It is interesting to look at some of the early church allegorisation of parables. I have dug out some examples based on the parable of The Good Samaritan. The parable of The Good Samaritan, (Luke 10.30-37) is in fact a devastating attack on racial prejudice. It says, 'a neighbour is in need of help: no human being is to be beyond the range of our compassion.' The parable is in fact timeless, and if we could only really learn that one simple central principle, we would revolutionise human relationships.

Listen to what Origen did to it. Origen who lived from 185 to 254 A.D. was one of the great Bible scholars of the early church and undoubtedly we owe a significant debt to him for preserving and drawing attention to the importance of scripture. In his interpretation the man who fell among thieves became Adam; Jerusalem was heaven; Jericho was the world; the robbers were the devil and his dominions. The priest represented the law; the Levite the prophets whilst the Samaritan was Jesus himself. The ass was Christ's body, whilst the inn was the church. Two pence represented the Father and the Son, while the promise to come again and pay the further debt was Christ's second coming!

Do you really think that Jesus' listeners were supposed to take all that in, or even think all that out, as a result of a single hearing to a story told in response to a Pharisee or Sadducee who hoped to trip Jesus up with the question, *"And who is my neighbour?"*

St. Augustine (354-430 A.D.) was also well known for his elaborate interpretations. In his account of this parable the traveller represents fallen man. The fact that he was half alive (actually half dead) indicated that he had some knowledge of God, but was only half alive because of his slavery to sin. The binding up of his wounds was Jesus restraining his sin; the pouring in of oil and wine stood for the comfort of good hope and the exhortation to spiritual work. The innkeeper was the apostle Paul, and the two pence were the two commandments to love God and your neighbour.

Let me bamboozle you with one more. There remains a copy of a sermon preached on the parable of The Good Samaritan by an English friar. Most of it is totally incomprehensible, so being as fair as I can be; I have tried to pull out the salient points. The friar read the text accurately, then went on to say, "It was the man who went down from Jerusalem when Adam sinned and the thieves he fell among are the demons. The priest passed down the same way, when the order of patriarchs followed the paths of mortality. The priest left him wounded, having no power to aid the human race while he himself was wounded with sins. The Levite went that way inasmuch as the order of prophets also had to tread the path of death. The Lord was the Good Samaritan. He went down this way when he came from heaven into this world. Two pence are given to the innkeeper when the doctors are raised on high by scriptural knowledge and temporal honour."

Are Parables Allegories?

The point I am making is this. The parables can all too easily be destroyed when we try to get clever with them. Many parables are simply similes; statements which capture our attention by speaking about something with which we are totally familiar, and then saying, "Now think about it – God is like that - the Kingdom of Heaven is like that – the way God wants you to respond and behave is like that."

Let me give you an example:

"Again, the Kingdom of Heaven is like a merchant looking for fine pearls. When he found one of great value, he went away and sold everything he had and bought it." (Matthew 13.45-46)

And here is another example:

"Once again the Kingdom of Heaven is like a net that was let down into the lake and caught all kinds of fish. When it was full, the fishermen pulled it up on the shore. Then they sat down and collected the good fish in baskets, but threw the bad away." (Matthew 13.47-48)

These followed in the teaching of Jesus, one after the other. Each is a bit like a cryptic crossword clue. Until you understand the meaning, you struggle to make sense of it. Once you see the answer, you wonder how anyone can possibly not see it. When you understand them, you find each of these parables makes one point. The point challenges you to the core, and that is what is supposed to happen.

There are longer parables, like the parable of The Prodigal Son, or the parable of The Sower, that go much further. Heaven forbid that we should do an Origen or Augustine with them, but they deserve careful and deep examination, because we may find our own lives being described, and they may well demand that we change our ways in order to conform to the Kingdom.

I like Roy Clement's description of these story parables. He writes: "In these parable tales Jesus is not merely seeking to tantalise or educate his hearers, he wants to challenge them at a fundamental level. On the surface the stories seem innocuous, charming little narratives, full of familiar images that easily capture your attention. In reality they are a kind of stealth bomber, especially designed to evade our psychological defences, insinuating themselves inside our minds in spite of every barricade we may seek to erect, and then dropping a highly explosive charge targeted at the most vulnerable point in our spiritual complacency."

You can apply that very clearly to the parable of The Good Samaritan. Jesus has not directly answered the question, "Who is my neighbour?" but the expert in the law has no doubts. Jesus dropped a bombshell of a practical example. Jesus has challenged the lawyer to put together Samaritan and neighbour, and to think of them as one and the same person. In his culture this is unthinkable! In fact when Jesus presses the point, he asks the lawyer:

"In your opinion, which of these three was like a neighbour to the man who was attacked by the robbers?"

The lawyer cannot bring himself to say, "The Samaritan." He has to say:

"The one who was kind to him."

but the point has been made. The lawyer has seen for a moment through the eyes of Christ and has no doubts.

I have come full circle. Parables are difficult to retell today, because they have become so familiar. I guess Jesus would come to Ferndown with a whole range of new ones, probably making the same points. For us too they would have a sting in the tail, a punch line which would creep up on us and then kick us in the gut just when we were not expecting it. He would challenge our complacency and our failure to live like sons and daughters of the living God.

18. A Widow and a Lost Sheep
Luke 15.1-7, 18.1-8 GNB

There is a joke doing the rounds at the moment and I'd like to share it with you this morning. The bishop was visiting a particular parish to assess how a new curate and his wife were settling in. Part of his assessment was to hear the curate preach. The curate stood up and began his sermon. "The best times in my life were spent in the arms of another man's wife." Understandably the congregation gasped, and the bishop felt himself distinctly colouring up. The curate continued, "that woman was my mother!" There was a great roar of laughter from the congregation, all except the bishop, who somehow managed to miss the point of it all and spent the rest of the service trying to work out what the joke had been. Over lunch he asked the curate to tell him why everybody had laughed, and the curate carefully explained. With his anxiety gone, the bishop and curate talked about what good teaching tools stories could be. In fact the bishop decided to add this story to his repertoire. So the very next Sunday, he stood up in the Cathedral and began his sermon, "The best times in my life were spent in the arms of another man's wife." The congregation gasped, as if to order, but then the bishop faltered, "I can't for the life of me remember who she was... but we all had a good laugh about it last week!"

Today we consider two of the parables told by Jesus. A parable is a bit like a joke, in that if you have to explain it, the danger is that the impact will be lost.

If you make a catalogue of Jesus' parables you will find that they all were stories about everyday subjects – farming, wedding banquets – tax collectors and the like. The attractive thing about them was that they all had a punch line, an unexpected twist, something that would come across as a bit of a shock to the people to whom they were directed. It was the shock value that made people sit up and think.

Today as I look at the two parables we have read together, I must take care not to destroy the message which God would get across to us today.

The Persistent Widow

In a certain town there was a judge who neither feared God or respected man. And there was a widow in that same town who kept coming to him and pleading for her rights, saying, 'Help me against my opponent!' For a long time the judge refused to act, but at last he said to himself, 'Even though I don't fear God or respect man, yet because of all the trouble this widow is giving me, I will see to it that she gets her rights. If I don't, she will keep on coming and finally wear me out!' (Luke 18.2-8)

Now, if we try to pick that story to pieces, we will get into the most awful muddle. You can't make the judge God, for he is described as a godless man. You can't identify the woman, in fact from the way Jesus tells the story she comes across as something of a nag. So why did he tell the story? What does he say?

Listen to what the corrupt judge said. Now, will God not judge in favour of his own people who cry to him day and night for help? I tell you, he will judge in their favour and do it quickly.

In effect what Jesus is saying is, "Father God is nothing like this judge, who answers the woman's pleas for all the wrong motives, because he is fed up with her." Jesus says, "Think what wonderful answers to prayer God will give, if you appeal to his loving and just heart from all the right motives."

Let us ask ourselves again: Why did Jesus tell this story?

A Widow and a Lost Sheep – Luke 15.1-7, 18.1-8

Then Jesus told his disciples a parable to teach them that they should always pray and never become discouraged. (Luke 18.1).

It is a single, and simple, yet immensely important point that Jesus is out to make. Notice first that it is directed to his disciples, so it is directed to us. Notice secondly that Jesus says they should pray, that they ought to pray, that they needed to pray. It is not an invitation – you may pray if you wish. It is an obligation – you need to pray.

How is that reflected in our lives? I'm talking more about prayer tonight, but let me commend to you the prayer meeting, as well as a personal prayer time. The prayer meeting is the barometer of the health of the church.

Thirdly, Jesus says that they should not give up. They should persist in prayer. C.H. Spurgeon gave valuable advice. "If it is anything for my own personal advantage then I should ask God three times, and be content if there seems to be the answer – No." He based this on Paul's example:

'Three times I prayed to the Lord about this and asked him to take it away. But his answer was : "My grace is all you need, for my power is strongest when you are weak." I am most happy, then, to be proud of my weaknesses, in order to feel the protection of Christ's power over me.'(2 Corinthians 12.8-9).

Spurgeon continued, "If our prayers are for someone's material good, we should pray between seven and seventy times seven times. At some point the Holy Spirit will tell us that our prayer will be answered or that we should ask no more.

But if our prayers are for someone's spiritual good, for their salvation, I quote, 'Here if we would prevail, we must persist, we must continue incessantly and constantly, and know no pause to our prayer till we win the mercy to the fullest possible extent.'"

Friends, what is on your heart? Who is on your heart? Men ought always to pray, and not give up. All too often we hardly begin.

The Lost Sheep Luke 15.1-7

Suppose one of you has a hundred sheep and loses one of them - what does he do? He leaves the other ninety-nine sheep in the

pasture and goes looking for the one that got lost until he finds it.
When he finds it, he is so happy that he puts it on his shoulders
and carries it back home. Then he calls his friends and neighbours
and says to them, 'I am so happy I found my lost sheep. Let us
celebrate!'

We have heard talks about shepherds, and the love of God who goes after the lost sheep; but today, for a change, let us look at the context and the direction of the parable.

Jesus has built up a following of tax collectors, assumed to be rogues, and other so called notorious sinners. This is not surprising when you realise he has called the tax collector Matthew to be one of his close disciples, and when Zaccheus, a chief tax collector, has had his life transformed. When Mary Magdalene, reputedly a high class prostitute, follows Jesus, and the woman taken in the very act of adultery has seemingly been forgiven, many eyebrows must have been raised. It's not surprising then that:

The Pharisees and the teachers of the law started grumbling,
"This man welcomes outcasts and even eats with them." (Luke 15.2)

The scribes and Pharisees saw sinners and tax collectors as a totally unacceptable strand of society. They called these people, "The People of the Land." There were regulations and sayings concerning them. One saying was, "It is better to expose your daughter bound and helpless before a raging lion than to allow her to marry one of the People of the Land." Another said, "When a man is one of the People of the Land, entrust no money to him, take no testimony from him, trust him with no secret, do not appoint him guardian of an orphan, do not make him custodian of charitable funds, do not accompany him on a journey." A Pharisee was forbidden to be the guest of any such man or to have him as his guest.

And here is Jesus welcoming them and eating with them! The strictest among the Pharisees had a saying, "There will be joy in heaven over one sinner who is obliterated before God."

It is to these people that Jesus speaks:

"There will be more joy in heaven over one sinner who repents
than over ninety-nine respectable people who do not need to repent!"

A Widow and a Lost Sheep – Luke 15.1-7, 18.1-8

My word, Jesus! You twisted the knife as you told them that story. No wonder they hated you. No wonder they wanted you out of the way.

But should we not identify with the story too? God, the Good Shepherd, goes after the lost sheep until he finds him and carries him home rejoicing.

Do we not feel a certain security in church? If we are totally honest, are there not people in society who we would rather did not join our fellowship? If this is so then we must be warned, for Jesus tells the story to us. He calls us to have a burden, a love, as he did, for the outcasts and sinners. He calls for us to stir ourselves into action and look for the sheep that are lost.

But do you feel like one of the lost sheep? No one seems to hear your cries for help. You feel left behind. You dare not reveal your true self, for fear of the rejection. You feel you are one of the outcasts, one of the tax collectors, one of the sinners.'

I want you this morning to see that there were two groups who Jesus addressed with this story. The scribes and Pharisees were cut to the heart. But if they were one part of the throng, the rest were people like you and me. The same story Jesus tells them isn't cutting at all. It is wonderfully good news. You are more important than the ninety and nine who need no repentance. Jesus the good shepherd is out looking for you. Not that you should limp back into some sort of respectability, but that he might carry you home on his shoulders rejoicing! His only requirement is that you turn around, stop running and let the shepherd enfold you in his arms. Will you let him?

In conclusion let me go back to the first parable. To be prayerless is just as sinful in God's eyes as being lost. Jesus longs that you should come back into full fellowship. He longs for you to turn around so that once again you may play your full part in the family of God.

I tell you there will be more joy in heaven over one sinner who repents than over ninety-nine respectable people who do not need to repent.

If you will turn around today, there will be rejoicing in heaven!

19. The Waiting Father
Luke 15.11-24

The story of The Prodigal Son, or to turn it round, The Waiting Father, is possibly one of the best known stories in the Bible. Every one of Jesus' parables is powerful. There is something in each which speaks to us. Tonight try to put yourself in the position of the son, and remember this parable was told to tax collectors and outcasts.

The younger son had problems. From where he stood his big brother always seemed to get the best deal. There was no situation in which he was the boss. If it wasn't his brother on at him, then it was his mother, or his dad. In fact the old man really got on his nerves. "You're not to do that; do what I tell you; you mustn't go there; behave yourself!" He wanted to cry out, "If only I could do my own thing!"

His father was not really trying to lord it over him. He was recognising his responsibility towards his son: his son's need of guidance; his need of boundaries. He wanted the very best for his son. He probably said, "You should count your blessings my boy!"

Can you imagine his son's reactions: the rows; the slammed doors? I think the boy's problem was really fear, prompted by Satan, that he would not get everything life had to offer. I don't think he had any intention of being wicked. He just wanted a good time while he was young. So one day at breakfast he came out with it:

"Father, give me my share of the estate."

Imagine the shock and distress for his father and mother. Imagine the pleading, the anguish they must have gone through. Then, when all are exhausted; see the father going sadly to the safe; getting out the deeds and money, and letting him go.

God forces no one. It always hurts to let go of someone you love, even in good circumstances. All parents know this. How ready have we been to assert ourselves, and to hurt others? How often have those who claim to belong to the Father, hurt him by not doing what he wants, but going their own way?

The younger son leaves and gets as far away from home as possible. In his new country he lives in grand style. He has many friends of both sexes. He has a wardrobe of the latest fashion. He has good taste, good food, lavish parties; but the money is running through his fingers.

He has failed to recognise that everything came from his father. Now that he is out of relationship, there is no more money coming. He thought life would be great, but it's flat. Each new excitement lasts such a short time. He needs more and more stimulation. He cannot face himself so constantly seeks entertainment. He has things in abundance; but purpose, peace and joy; he doesn't know what they are any longer, though he remembers good times at home.

The more unhappy and lost he feels, the more wildly he celebrates, trying to divert himself from the fact that his life is really poverty-stricken. What has he done that's wrong? How has he gone wrong?

We can see that he has given up the ties of home for a greater bondage. He misses home more than he admits. He's finding that seeking friends and amusement doesn't calm the emptiness inside. Riotous living doesn't satisfy the deep urges within him.

In fact, he is not free, he is a slave. He needs the grace that

Charles Wesley wrote about when he was converted: "My chains fell off, my soul was free."

When finally his money runs out things go from bad to worse. He has to seek employment. It's bad enough having to work for a farmer; the only work he knows; but to end up with the pigs! Pigs were unclean animals. His father would not have kept pigs. To touch one was to become unclean; now he had to live among them. After his rich life, he has fallen to the depths of degradation. He lives the life of a slave.

We can see he has exchanged one master for another. We are always subject to a master. Our lives are not really our own. We were made to glorify God. Either we are his, or we belong to Satan, the prince of this world. Luther said, "Human life is a battlefield between two masters." I imagine the younger son, sitting with the pigs, thinking, "I wanted to be free, now look at me!"

Helmut Thielicke writes, "You could hear the Devil's bitter laugh from the pigsty."

To have left home seems now the most ridiculous thing he has ever done, but how can he go home? He has forfeited his rights. He has no cash, no sonship any more. Perhaps he now remembers the sadness and love in his father's face.

"I'll turn around. I'll face in the other direction. I will leave all this behind. I'll go back."

All this time the father has been waiting, looking for him down that dusty road. Day after day after day he watches; he hopes.

One day in the mist a long way off, he sees his son struggling along, tired and dishevelled. Straight away his heart is filled with compassion. He runs to him, throws his arms around him, kisses the grime on his face. And his son didn't say, "Dad, I've changed. I've learned my lesson. I've grown up. I'll do better now." He couldn't. His words were:

"Father, I have sinned."

Notice he was not accepted back on any merit of his own, for he had no merit left. He had no claim on his father for he had rejected his life at home. It was the father's great love which re-instated him as his son.

"Bring the best robe and put it on him, - for this my son of mine was dead, and is alive again."

Can you hear the father's joy, his delight that his son is home once more?

This is my heavenly father rejoicing when a sinner turns round for home. When I see myself as I am, I turn around, I begin a journey. I am no longer full of self, but have a deep desire to know and serve God. Because he is God, I can trust him.

Do you need to go home tonight?

As a postscript to this address I include The Lost Daughter, compiled by the Youth Alpha Group at Ferndown United Church on January 8th 1999.

The Lost Daughter
based on Luke 15.11-32

There was once a woman who had two daughters. Jenny, the younger daughter was fed up with life at home: the rules, the work, and no one approving of her boyfriend. So Jenny nicked her father's credit card, the best things from Mum's wardrobe, and her sister's car and went off to Ibiza to live with her boyfriend.

Jenny spent her money on groovy raves, pub crawls, sun cream, CD's, and generally keeping her boy friend happy. When she tried to use dad's credit card she found he had put a stop on it. When the money ran out, her boy friend left her. So she went to work for a pimp who offered her a sordid flat in the red light district of Ibiza.

As Christmas approached, Jenny became terribly depressed. She longed to be back with her loving family. She thought, "Even the loo cleaner at my mum's home is much better off than me! I will go home and say, "Mum, I'm grovelling. I'm very, very sorry. Please can I come back and do all the chores at home."

She had only just reached West Moors when her Mum, peering longingly from her bedroom window, saw her a long way off. Zooming out of the house, she raced down the street and embraced the dirty, spotty frame that was once her attractive daughter. "Mum, forgive me!" Jenny cried, "Make me your unpaid family loo lady." "Come inside," Mum replied. Find new undies, book a room at the Tap and Railway. Everyone will have "Hungry Man" meals. For my daughter who was lost is home safe and sound and is not pregnant!"

Meanwhile, Lindsey, coming home from the January sales, laden with presents bought at bargain prices for next Christmas, seeing her sister dressed in her favourite sequinned dress, fumed, "What's she doing in my clothes! Why is everyone getting ready to go out and party?"

"My dear daughter," Mum said. "Jenny has come home. My daughter is alive and well; we must rejoice and be glad!"

Lindsey really blew her nut! Stamping her feet she ranted, "You never as much as took me to MacDonald's, but this Jenny stole the credit card, stripped the wardrobe, stole my car and frittered the lot on dirty old men in Ibiza.!" She stormed out, never to be seen again.

20. The Wise and Foolish Virgins
Matthew 24.36-25.13

Chapter 25 of Matthew is all about a grand sorting out at the end of time when Jesus brings about the culmination of history. Wise virgins are separated from foolish virgins; those who have used their gifts are separated from those who have hidden them away; sheep are separated from goats.

Firstly we learn there will be separation. In each parable one group rejoice with their master, the other group is cast into outer darkness, where there is wailing and gnashing of teeth. Secondly we are to learn there will be reward and punishment.

In the stories this happens when the bridegroom comes; when the owner returns; when the shepherd sorts out his flocks, and in each parable it is made clear that this happens when the Son of Man comes in Glory.

Do we know if Jesus is really coming again? He consistently taught that he would.

And if I go and prepare a place for you, I will come back and take you to be with me that you also may be where I am. (John 14.3)

The angels said Jesus would come again:

"Men of Galilee," they said, "Why do you stand here looking into the sky? This same Jesus, who has been taken from you

into heaven, will come back in the same way you have seen him go into heaven." (Acts 1.11)

The apostle John taught that he would come again:

"Look, he is coming with the clouds, and every eye will see him, even those who pierced him; and all the peoples of the earth will mourn because of him. So shall it be! Amen." (Revelation 1.7)

Through the ages people have found the delay in Jesus' return to be a problem. It is clear in the epistles that Paul expected the return of Christ to be imminent. He lived and exhorted others to live in the light of this expectation. The disciples also wanted to know when it would be:

As Jesus was sitting on the Mount of Olives opposite the temple, Peter, James, John and Andrew asked him privately, "Tell us, when will these things happen? And what will be the sign that they are all about to be fulfilled?" Jesus said to them: "Watch out that no one deceives you. Many will come in my name, claiming, 'I am he,' and will deceive many." (Mark 13.3-6)

We are not meant to know:

He said to them, "It is not for you to know the times or dates the Father has set by his own authority." (Acts 1.7)

There is only one person who knows when it will be:

"No one knows about that day or hour, not even the angels in heaven, nor the Son, but only the Father."(Matthew 24.36)

It will happen at a time when life is going on as it always does:

"As it was in the days of Noah, so it will be at the coming of the Son of Man. For in the days before the flood, people were eating and drinking, marrying and giving in marriage, up to the day Noah entered the ark; and they knew nothing about what would happen until the flood came and took them all away. That is how it will be at the coming of the Son of Man.

Two men will be in the field; one will be taken and the other left. Two women will be grinding with a hand mill; one will be taken and the other left.

Therefore keep watch, because you do not know on what day your Lord will come. But understand this: if the owner of the house had known at what time of night the thief was coming, he would have

kept watch and would not have let his house be broken into."
(Matthew 24.37)

Jesus will come when we least expect him:

"So you also must be ready, because the Son of Man will come at an hour when you do not expect him."

His coming may well be sudden:

For you know very well that the day of the Lord will come like a thief in the night. (I Thessalonians 5.2)

Despite all these scriptures, and because there has been a delay of two thousand years between his first coming and his second coming; a majority, (dare I say it?), even within the churches, are sceptical concerning this really happening. That is not new; they were sceptical less than fifty years after his ascension into heaven. Peter had to address the issue:

They will say, "Where is this coming he promised? Ever since our fathers died, everything goes on as it has since the beginning of creation." (1 Peter 3.4)

The waiting time for us really demonstrates the mercy of God:

But do not forget this one thing, dear friends; with the Lord a day is like a thousand years, and a thousand years are like a day. The Lord is not slow in keeping his promise, as some understand slowness. He is patient with you, not wanting anyone to perish, but everyone to come to repentance. (2 Peter 3.8-9)

So, having taken some time to make clear that we are to expect the Lord's second coming, let me add one final point before commenting on the parable itself. Paul, as I have said, believed that the Lord would come again while he was alive. Countless Christians have believed that the Lord would come while they were alive. Without detracting one iota from my firm belief that in God the Father's good time there will be this apocalyptic return of Christ on clouds of glory; I want to say there is a sense in which every person who has ever lived will experience the return of Christ – when he returns for them in death. The issue will be: were they prepared? Were they ready? When the call comes it is too late to make preparations. Our standing before God at that time is our standing before God for eternity. When Jesus returns he will find both true and false Christians in the church.

At that time the kingdom of heaven will be like ten virgins who took their lamps and went out to meet the bridegroom. Five of them were foolish and five were wise.

The idea of the coming of Christ as the bridegroom and the church as his bride is deeply rooted in scripture, in the Old Testament in passages such as Ezekiel 16, Hosea 2 and Isaiah we read:

As a young man marries a maiden, so will your sons marry you; as a bridegroom rejoices over his bride, so will your God rejoice over you. (Isaiah 62.5)

This theme is represented in the New Testament, especially in the book of Revelation. So I think it is fair to see the ten virgins as representing the church. We must not push the image too far, for traditionally we see the virgins as the bridesmaids, though you might wish to think about them as representing the bride.

What I do notice is that they all had lamps, though only five of them had reserves of oil to refill the lamps. They all believed they were going to take part in the bridal celebrations. Commentators like William Barclay provide plenty of detail about the culture of the day. Weddings often took place in the evening. Normally the bridegroom with some close friends left his home to go to the bride's home, where various ceremonies would take place. Afterwards there would be a torch-lit procession round the village back to the groom's home where the ceremonies would be completed and the marriage consummated. Everyone in the procession was expected to provide and carry his or her own torch. Most commonly the torches would be made from rags on a stick, and the rags would need periodic dowsing with oil to keep them burning. Prudent members of the procession would bring along a flask with an additional supply of oil. Anyone in the procession without a burning torch would be assumed to be a party crasher or even a brigand and they would be forcibly ejected.

So in his parable Jesus says:

The foolish ones took their lamps but did not take any oil with them. The wise, however, took oil in jars along with their lamps.

The Wise and Foolish Virgins - Matthew 24.36-25.13

Wise are perhaps better thought of as prudent or prepared: foolish as careless and unprepared.

Now if you accept that the virgins represent the whole of the church I think you see a powerful picture of how things really are. The church is made of a mixture of people. All those who are members have been baptised, either as infants, or scripturally as believers. All call themselves Christians, all profess to have faith, and they all have lamps. But though all profess to be Christians, not all really listen for his voice. Not all follow him. Not all have really repented. Not all have really sought the filling of the Holy Spirit in their hearts. Not all are what they profess to be.

It is not for me to judge concerning any individual's standing before the Lord, but I do have to tell you that I believe in every church there are those who have been truly converted, and those who have not yielded their wills to Christ. There are real Christians and spurious believers; wise and foolish virgins, sheep and goats, wheat and chaff.

Whilst I must never judge, it is my responsibility to challenge, to make sure those questions are asked, that you are duly warned. Which class will Jesus find that you belong to; wise or foolish; alive, forgiven, prepared and fulfilled; or dead in trespasses and sins, unprepared?

Incredible as it may seem, the Middle Eastern bridegroom would not always announce his wedding day. The expectation was that, once betrothed, the bride and her bridesmaids should hold themselves in readiness for whenever the bridegroom chose to come for his bride. But even in the ordinary family, when the day had been firmly fixed; and it was normally on a Wednesday to allow time for a full period of feasting before the Sabbath; part of the fun of the day was to endeavour to catch the bride's party unawares. So a watch would be set for the bridegroom. Here is a story with which Jesus' listeners would become fully engaged.

The bridegroom was a long time in coming, and they all became drowsy and fell asleep.

Has that ever struck you as a curious feature of the parable? We would expect it to say that the wise remained alert and awake watching for the bridegroom while the foolish fell asleep; but they all fall asleep, and Jesus recounts this without any criticism whatsoever.

This insight belongs to Helmut Thielicke, and I am grateful for it. He writes, "We must not think of the waiting of the wise maidens as if they never had another thought in their heads except waiting, praying and hymn singing. In his goodness, Jesus knows that his people need rest. The disciples were invited to 'rest a while.' Nor can we pray all day long or do nothing but think of how soon the Lord may be coming again."

This is right, but there is a vast difference in the sleep of the wise and the sleep of the foolish. The wise sleep in confidence and at peace because their trust is in the Lord. They are ready. The foolish slumber in their unpreparedness, for they simply don't expect the bridegroom to come.

At midnight the cry rang out: "Here's the bridegroom! Come out to meet him!"

I think we can all identify with this little bit of the story. We will all have had the experience of waiting and waiting for something to happen, and of being in various states of consciousness as we have waited. Then suddenly we are totally awake when the cry goes out, "He's here, its happening!"

But will we be prepared? Will we be ready? Bishop J.C. Ryle said that he feared, "The Lord would find the vast majority of mankind utterly unbelieving and unprepared." He is right. It will be just as in the days of Noah when the flood came. Men will be going about their business, buying, selling, pleasure seeking, feasting, grumbling, involved in controversy, engaged in politics, on holiday, just as they are today. Preachers will still be calling men and women to repent and come back to the Lord. Men and women will still be putting off the day of decision: when suddenly, like a thief in the night, the Lord will return.

The vitally important point is this: when that occurs, and it could be at any time, then we are summoned to stop what we are doing and appear before the judgment seat of Christ. The challenge is: Will we be ready or caught utterly unprepared?

Many people will discover the truth about Jesus too late.

The Wise and Foolish Virgins - Matthew 24.36-25.13

Then all the virgins woke up and trimmed their lamps. The foolish ones said to the wise, "Give us some of your oil; our lamps are going out." "No," they replied, "there may not be enough for both us and you. Instead, go to those who sell oil and buy some for yourselves." But while they were on their way to buy the oil, the bridegroom arrived.

When the cry goes up, "Here's the bridegroom. Come out and meet him," all unbelief disappears. All the virgins want their torches to be ready for the procession. They all set about trimming their lamps. They have no doubt now about the reality of the bridegroom coming, for the shout has gone up. It is then that the foolish virgins realise their predicament. The bridegroom has come but they have no reserves of oil for their lamps. They beg their companions "Give us some of yours." But oil is like grace. It is individually acquired and it is only sufficient for our need. We have to get grace for ourselves from the Saviour.

So the wise counsel the foolish, "Go and buy oil for yourselves." The foolish had been told many times about the need for oil, but had not believed that the groom would come and catch them unawares.

So it is with repentance and forgiveness, exercising faith, finding grace, working at holiness. We know the need, but for too many, we are sadly careless, negligent, unprepared. The prayer of the preacher is that you will be convicted concerning your need of a Saviour, before that day when you hear the clarion call, "The bridegroom is coming!" For on that day it will be too late.

Do you sometimes get mocked because of your faithfulness to Jesus? Do people sometimes call you a fool for being so committed to the cause of the Christian Church? Listen, for we are told that when the bridegroom came:

the virgins who were ready went in with him to the wedding banquet. And the door was shut.

Every Jew knew that picture, and we find it easy too. Heaven was likened to the happiest of celebrations - the wedding feast. No expense spared – the very greatest rejoicing – eternal bliss.

Finding the Real Jesus

When the Lord comes again he takes those who love him to be with him and he shuts them in. He closes the door. No longer are they open to pain or sorrow. They are free from all the wickedness of the world, immune from temptation to sin. There is no longer any doubt or fear. Everything is perfect peace. It is a wonderful prospect. It is that prospect that we must hold on to when the going seems hard or the Lord seems to tarry. When Jesus comes - all will be well.

But the parable has a solemn ending. *"Open the door for us!" But he replied, "I tell you the truth, I don't know you."*

They had been invited. They could have come, but they never prepared themselves. Oil was not in short supply. It was available for the asking, but they never stocked up. They always believed there was tomorrow. Now it was too late. They were shut out for all time. What about you?

Therefore keep watch, because you do not know the day or the hour.

21. The Great Banquet
Luke 14.1-24

Banqueting and feasting were a major part of the social and religious life in Biblical times, and as you know it was an image widely used when talking about the heavenly kingdom of God. Take, for example, the picture in Isaiah. The prophet foresees a day when the reign of the Lord is finally established. He writes:

On this mountain the Lord Almighty will prepare a feast of rich food for all peoples, a banquet of aged wine, the best of meats and the finest of wines. On this mountain he will destroy the shroud that enfolds all peoples, the sheet that covers all nations; he will swallow up death forever. The Sovereign Lord will wipe away the tears from all faces; he will remove the disgrace of his people from all the earth. The Lord has spoken. In that day they will say, "Surely this is our God; we trusted in him, and he saved us. This is the Lord; we trusted in him; let us rejoice and be glad in his salvation." (Isaiah 25.6-9)

It is a tremendous picture, for Isaiah perceives a banquet, not just for the Jews, but for all the peoples of the earth – all people everywhere are invited to the banquet.

Celebration meals often followed sacrifices, and were held in the belief that one day the Lord would hold a great feast, where there would no longer be tears or death or reproach for the people of God.

The greatest banquets were wedding celebrations. That is almost certainly the reason why in Revelation the final banquet in the kingdom of God is specifically and powerfully described as a wedding feast:

Let us rejoice and be glad and give him glory! For the wedding of the Lamb has come, and his bride has made herself ready. Fine linen, bright and clean, was given her to wear. (Fine linen stands for the righteous acts of the saints.) Then the angel said to me, "Write: "Blessed are those who are invited to the wedding supper of the Lamb!" And he added, "These are the true words of God." (Revelation 19.7-9)

In the parable which we are examining this morning Jesus is teaching that those excluded from the banquet have only themselves to blame. Whatever else you hear this morning this is the vital central point. It is essential that you take hold of it. **Those who fail to get to heaven have only themselves to blame**. The invitation is available to all and it is we who accept or refuse the Lord's gracious invitation.

Let us set the scene of the parable. It is a Sabbath day. Jesus is guest at the house of a prominent Pharisee who doubtless felt sure that his piety would earn him a place in the kingdom. Luke tells us about Jesus that he was being carefully watched by the Pharisee and others there, (verse 1). To their way of thinking Jesus has acted and spoken provocatively, and the other guests will be feeling uneasy. Try to imagine being there yourself. Would you be cheering Jesus on, or feeling distinctly on edge knowing how the Pharisee felt about such matters? Jesus has healed a man suffering from dropsy on the Sabbath. The healing has been received with the stony silence of disapproval, and Jesus has remarked how they would surely have rescued a son or an ox that had fallen into a well even on a Sabbath day.

When they sat down Jesus remarked on the scramble that took place for the best seats at the table, and has rubbed in his comment with a parable about taking a humble position, so that you might be invited to come up higher, rather than being so full of your own importance that you sat too near your host and had the shame of being demoted.

The Great Banquet – Luke 14.1-24

Finally, Jesus has, it seems, been directly critical of his host: *Then Jesus said to his host, "When you give a luncheon or dinner, do not invite your friends, your brothers or relatives, or your rich neighbours; if you do, they may invite you back and so you will be repaid. But when you give a banquet, invite the poor, the crippled, the lame, the blind and you will be blessed. Although they cannot repay you, you will be repaid at the resurrection of the righteous."*

If you have been picturing all this in your mind, you will be well aware of the tension in the air. One man at the meal seems anxious to calm things down, and seizes his chance. Jesus has been speaking about giving banquets, and about the last days, the time of the resurrection of the righteous. It is time for a pious interjection:

When one of those at the table with him heard this, he said to Jesus, "Blessed is the man who will eat at the feast in the kingdom of God."

No doubt the person who speaks up thinks that all at the table will agree with this blessing, but it only prompts Jesus to tell another parable:

Jesus replied, "A certain man was preparing a great banquet and invited many guests."

There are two facts which Jesus' listeners would notice in this opening sentence of the story. Firstly, this was to be a really grand occasion, for Jesus describes it as a *great* banquet. Though their thoughts may not immediately have jumped to the conclusion; as they considered it they would certainly realise that Jesus was talking about *the great banquet,* which was heaven.

Secondly what would have registered with them was the matter of invitations. Banquets were costly affairs. They took a long time to prepare. You needed to know who was going to accept the invitations to come, so custom was that many months before the banquet, formal invitations would be sent out; invitations which required a reply. Eastern rules of hospitality meant that once you had accepted a banquet invitation you were committed, even if the precise date had not been given. Nothing else must go in your diary. There is a banquet to attend, and you have said you are going.

Normally there would be some time between the invitations going out and the replies being expected. On some occasions your reply would be expected via the messenger who brought the invitation.

I am always impressed by the way that Jesus' stories "hit the nail on the head." Many are invited. They have time to decide whether to accept or refuse their invitation, but they must make up their minds.

How long have you had the invitation to follow Jesus, to be really committed to him, to make yourself a guest at the "Marriage feast of the Lamb?" Is the invitation still on the mantelpiece? Are you still humming and haa-ing as to whether you want to be counted in? Jesus invites you to come. He doesn't force you to come, but he expects you to reply to the invitation. You must make that response. Perhaps for you, today is the closing date to return your reply. Perhaps for you the invitation will close, never to be sent again!

At the time of the banquet he sent his servant to tell those who had been invited, "Come, for everything is now ready."

This may seem strange to us, but is exactly what happened at a Middle Eastern banquet. Sometimes this courtesy was simply a reminder; the original invitation having been sent a long time ago. Sometimes the original date had been a bit vague: 'My daughter is getting married in June' – 'One day in the autumn we are going to celebrate.' Whatever the reason for the feast, a few days before the event, servants would go round to make sure the invited guests were coming. Now the commitment to the host is being called in. They had said they were committed. Now they have to show their commitment by coming.

What happens is astonishing! The refusals pour in, and they are pretty pathetic:

But they all began to make excuses. The first said, "I have just bought a field, and I must go and see it. Please excuse me."

Surely he had seen the field before he agreed to buy it. Of course he had, but this was one of the stock excuses of the day. Some ancient purchases did require a post-purchase inspection before the monies were finally handed over, to ensure that the goods delivered were the goods you had originally inspected. Such dates though, were invariably flexible. This is an excuse on a par with – "Oh I'd love to come but we are having the car, the boiler, the washing machine, serviced."

I think this excuse highlights the matter of priorities. I'll fit things in for the church, for the kingdom, for Jesus, if it is convenient, but Jesus doesn't have first call on my life.

Does Jesus have first call on your life? Is he more important than friends, or family, or work, or hobby, or yourself?

Another said, "I have just bought five yoke of oxen, and I'm on my way to try them out. Please excuse me."

It is easy to miss the cutting edge of this excuse. We miss it if we simply say, "Well surely anyone buying oxen would have examined them before buying them." Would you buy a Rover, a Ford, a Porsche, a BMW, a Daewoo, without first insisting on a test drive? But that is not really the point. This man is buying five yoke, five pairs of oxen. To need five yoke indicated that his man had a huge estate and was very rich. Have no doubts, in this excuse Jesus is alluding to the pursuit of wealth and its hindrance to really becoming a member of the kingdom. Materialism is the very devil to our society today. How true is Jesus' comment – "You cannot serve God and Mammon!"

What I have noticed is that money seems to be the biggest hindrance, not to the really rich, or to the really poor, but to the vast majority of people in between. These people actually, if they are not always striving to keep up with the Joneses, have perfectly adequate resources to live happily, but because they want their success to show, they are always striving to get more.

Still another said, "I have just got married, so I can't come."

Once again there is more to this refusal than immediately meets the eye. It is true that only men were invited to banquets. You were not permitted to bring the wife along, unless, as was the case with Queen Vashti (Esther 1.9), while King Xerxes held a banquet for the men, she held one for the women. A newly married man may well not want to leave his bride, but he had accepted the invitation. Marriage was not a snap decision so was hardly likely to have been a real factor intervening between the first and second invitations. No, the point is much sharper than that. He is saying, "My spouse prevents me from coming!"

What an enormous problem this is today! How my heart goes out to those of you who have non-Christian partners, especially those of you who have come to faith since forming that partnership. But I think I have to point out to you that whilst God understands, and whilst I believe that God does hear your prayers for your non-Christian partner; still God says that is not an excuse for you to draw back. The fact that you are here shows that your heart is with my heart. You are determined to press on with the invitation to be a devoted follower of Jesus despite all the problems it presents. Yet we know of many who have lapsed, or given up on the faith because of the relationship with a non-Christian partner.

Will you allow me a word this morning, directly to non-Christian partners? I want to tell you from the bottom of my heart, that I believe if you really loved your partner, you too would make a real commitment to Jesus Christ. How can you spurn the faith which means so much to your loved one? You say you can't believe, but you know in your heart that you need forgiveness. You see the difference that faith makes in your loved one's life. Are you so proud as to believe that it cannot make a difference to you? If your loved one was to die today, you would be utterly devastated by the separation, yet blithely, because of your refusal to believe, you choose of your own free will to be separated for eternity. My friend, what is the sense? Who has blinded your eyes? Are you going to go on rejecting the invitation? Today may be the last time that God will invite you to come!

The servant came back and reported to his master. Then the owner of the house became angry and ordered his servant, "Go out quickly into the streets and alleys of the town and bring in the poor, the crippled, the blind and the lame."

The master had every right to be angry. Preparing the feast had been exceedingly costly, just as the preparations for heaven have cost the Father dearly. The rejections are a personal insult to the Jesus who hung on the cross that we might be forgiven. How solemn to realise that we incur the anger of a Holy God when we continue to reject his invitation.

If the first invited guests will not come, then others must be invited, and verses 21-23 indicate the breadth of God's invitation. No one is to be excluded.

"Go out quickly into the streets and alleys of the town and bring in the poor, the crippled, the blind and the lame."

These words have very specific meanings. The streets were the main thoroughfare of the towns, where the ordinary people would be going about their business. The alleys were the little narrow sideways, where the very poorest lived and to an extent hid themselves away. Here you would find the out-of-work, the uneducated, the outcasts of society.

"Sir," the servant said, "What you ordered has been done, but there is still room." Then the master told his servant, "Go out to the roads and country lanes and make them come in, so that my house will be full."

This is going outside the town. The roads were the highways between towns and the country lanes were just what they say, the little roads where the humble folk lived. "Go to them all," says the master, "I am determined that my house shall be full."

People say that in this parable Jesus was showing how the gospel would be offered to the Gentiles. I'm far from sure about that. Jesus' parables invariably made one point and made it very clearly. This parable is about people who say one thing but in fact do another. It is about people who are sitting on an invitation and who finally turn it down.

The real punch line comes with the closing verse:

"I tell you, not one of those men who were invited will get a taste of my banquet."

Not a taste. The door will be firmly barred. They will be sent away. There is no further chance. They have missed the invitation. It is just like that with the kingdom. Jesus extends the invitation today, but if we do not respond we will miss the blessing. What about you?

22. The Talents
Matthew 25.14-30

His master replied, "Well done, good and faithful servant!"
I hope that one day Jesus will greet me with words like that, but I have a deep awareness that I do not deserve such praise. There is so much I have left undone. There have been opportunities missed, challenges rejected. I have made many mistakes. If I had the energy, I could do so much more.

I could easily become terribly afraid for my destiny, if it were not for my assurance concerning God's love, and God's promise that those who have repented and come to Jesus for forgiveness, who have been baptised and who have sought to serve him, will be saved. If it were not for that knowledge I could worry endlessly that I might still be among the lost.

This is a difficult parable because for some, it could serve to accentuate the fear that, "I too, will be judged as unprofitable." It is true that the parable is given as a warning. It is an exhortation to be found working profitably for the master, but it is not meant to stir up dread among those who love Jesus and who seek to do their best for him. The Master's praise is won for faithfulness and not for the quality of one's achievement.

"Well done, good and faithful servant!"
Let us begin to tackle the text.

The Talents – Matthew 25.14-30

Again, it will be like a man going on a journey, who called his servants and entrusted his property to them.

You will remember, in my introductory talk on the parables, that I said we must be careful to concentrate on the one main point that Jesus is making as he tells his story, rather than seeking to allegorise every tiny detail. Hang on to that, but at the same time be amazed at the richness of the story Jesus tells.

This is one of the three parables in Matthew concerning the grand sorting out that will take place when Jesus returns in glory. Wise virgins are sorted from foolish virgins, sheep are sorted from goats and profitable servants are sorted from unprofitable servants. In each case there are those who think they belong, or who pretend that they belong, who end up excluded from the kingdom of God. The phrase, "It will be like," begins a story for his listeners in which they can draw a parallel between a situation they know well and what will happen when Jesus returns.

I was interested, looking at some of the old allegorical interpretations of this parable that the man going on a journey was said to represent Christ ascending into heaven following his resurrection, and the entrusting of the talents was said to represent the bestowal of gifts of the Spirit. Now that is clever, but I think it reads too much into the text. These details are probably simply setting the scene.

To one he gave five talents of money, to another two talents, and to another one talent, each according to his ability. Then he went on his journey.

Let me hurry to dispel the suggestion that this text teaches that God sees some as better than others. It is recounted for effect in the story. If you are concerned about God's love and care for you, how he rates you, whether you matter in his eyes, you must look outside this parable and at the whole counsel of scripture. Scripture is realistic. It acknowledges how things are. Some are leaders, some are led. Some are rich, some are poor. Some are more capable, some are less capable. But God comes out on the side of the poor, the under-valued, the widow, the fatherless, the sick, and the powerless. Jesus dies for "whosoever" will respond in repentance. All are accountable. The responsibility of those who have much is greater than that of those who have little; but we are all loved. All are precious in the sight of a Lord who is not willing that any one should perish.

We can be led astray by the word, "talent." In our English language today we use it to describe skills and mental powers, but in New Testament times a talent was an amount of money.

If we compare the notes in our Bibles and concordances, we find tremendous variation in the estimate of the value of a talent. There are a variety of reasons for this. Very often Bibles go on being printed and footnotes never get updated. Think what a thousand pounds would have bought fifty years ago, and what its value is today! A talent was a measure of weight, about thirty kilograms; between sixty and seventy pounds. You could have talents of gold or silver or even copper. They would vary greatly in value.

If you do want to put value on a talent it is probably best to think of it in terms of earning power. In New Testament days, according to the most reliable sources, a talent was worth six thousand denarii. I think we all know that a working man's daily wage was one denarius, so a talent was a huge sum. It would take a working man some twenty years to earn that amount of money.

So significantly none of the servants gets a miserly amount. They all have plenty if they are willing to show enterprise. The master has entrusted his money, as he is entitled to do, according to how he rates his servants' abilities to steward it well.

Duncan Derrett, who is one of the acknowledged experts on life in Palestine at the time of Jesus, points out that this was a common way for a master to treat his servants, a way that would be well understood by Jesus' listeners. A wealthy entrepreneur would look for trustworthy individuals and give them considerable responsibility and authority. The law saw people put in this position of trust, more or less as business partners. They were entitled to a share in the profits they made. They were accountable at all times. They had an obligation, entrusted with the master's resources, to use them profitably.

The man who had received the five talents went at once and put his money to work and gained five more. So also, the one with the two talents gained two more.

The good servants recognised they had a responsibility. They had been entrusted with money to use. There was an expectation that they would work diligently, so at once they set to work. Both of these servants carried on some kind of business and worked with the capital to make it grow. This inevitably involved venture, daring, taking risks, exercising faith. Their enterprise was rewarded. Both of them doubled their capital.

But the man who had received the one talent went off, dug a hole in the ground and hid his master's money.

The important point to see is that this servant is unwilling to work or to take risks for his master. He will preserve the capital against the day of accounting, but by digging a hole and burying the money, there is no way in which he can make a profit.

You can attempt a defence for this servant. You can properly argue that the money was safer buried than entrusted to the money lenders for they were notorious both for robbing people who borrowed from them and people who entrusted capital to them. The Old Testament forbade Israelites from charging interest if they lent money to a fellow Jew, and who would risk lending money to a Gentile? When money lending did take place, according to Roman law the interest rate must not exceed twelve per cent. The whole point about this third servant is simply that given a charge from his master, he did nothing about it.

After a long time the master of those servants returned and settled accounts with them. The man who had received the five talents brought the other five. "Master," he said, "you entrusted me with five talents. See, I have gained five more."

His master is delighted.

His master replied, "Well done, good and faithful servant! You have been faithful with a few things; I will put you in charge of many things, come and share your master's happiness!"

Once again, it is important to see that this is simply part of building the story. It is not meant to be applied allegorically. In the story the servant is promoted, given greater responsibility. What we are meant to take on board is not the extra responsibility but the master's delight, and the fact that the servant is going to be richly rewarded. He will celebrate with the master and share in the master's joy. But, as I said at the beginning, be careful to note that he is praised, not for the quantity of money he has earned, but for being faithful and doing what the master expected of him.

The second servant has also been faithful, and the praise he receives from the master is exactly the same.

The man with the two talents also came, "Master," he said, "you have entrusted me with two talents; see, I have gained two more." His master replied, "Well done, good and faithful servant! You have been faithful with a few things; I will put you in charge of many things. Come and share your master's happiness!

The third servant is different.

Then the man who had received the one talent came. "Master," he said, "I knew that you are a hard man, harvesting where you have not sown and gathering where you have not scattered seed. So I was afraid and went out and hid your talent in the ground. See, here is what belongs to you."

It is quite an accusation he lays against the master. "You are a hard man. You are grasping, you exploit the labour of others. I was not prepared to take the risk of incurring your wrath, so I've kept your money in a safe place. Here is what is yours, no more and no less."

O the blindness of this third servant! He has completely overlooked his responsibility as a chosen servant. There would have been hundreds if not thousands of men who would have given their right arm for the opportunity that had been given to him; to have a whole talent with which to trade and make more. He has been afforded a tremendous privilege. Yet he has seen it as an impossible, onerous burden. So he blames the master and seeks to exonerate himself. He has no real love for the master who has chosen him and trusted him. He has not even considered the inflation that has probably occurred during the long period the master has been away. Perhaps he is even angry that he had been trusted with much less than the other two, so he has done nothing, and has nothing to show as the fruit of his endeavour over those many years.

The master condemns the third servant on the basis of his own words. He reckons the master to be a hard man, yet he has dared to do nothing.

The Talents – Matthew 25.14-30

His master replied, "You wicked, lazy servant! So you knew that I harvest where I have not sown and gather where I have not scattered seed? Well then, you should have put my money on deposit with the bankers, so that when I returned I would have received it back with interest. Take the talent from him and give it to the one who has the ten talents. For everyone who has will be given more, and he will have an abundance. Whoever does not have, even what he has will be taken from him. And throw that worthless servant outside, into the darkness, where there will be weeping and gnashing of teeth."

What are we to learn from this parable tonight? First, it is a privilege and not a punishment to be called to be a servant of God. Just as the master in the story is tremendously generous towards his servants, God is tremendously generous to us. His gifts are bountiful. His gifts are given to be used, not to be hidden away.

To be called to be a follower of Jesus should be a delight, not a sentence to hard labour. To serve Jesus should be our greatest pleasure, not an awesome obligation. To work for the Master should fill our hearts with joy and not with dread. In following Jesus, in being a pilgrim for him we should find fulfilment and not discontent. If we cannot understand our calling, if we see it as anything less than that, then we have missed just how much God loves us. We have missed the cost of our salvation. We have missed the fact that God has chosen us and called us to be his servants and his disciples.

Secondly, it is in our response to this parable that we check our own standing before God. Inactivity is inexcusable. Christians have a responsibility, not to work for their salvation, but to work because of their salvation. There are a few folk in our churches who are inactive. These folk have completely the wrong picture of God. They have not experienced his compassion; they have never really seen the love which is radiating from him. They have never understood the implications of the cross. They really believe God to be a hard master and his service to be drudgery. So from fear, or hurt, they bury their talent and do nothing.

In our endeavour to be gentle, we would say they are to be pitied, but I fear that God would say they are unprofitable and therefore wicked, for they have not responded to his amazing love which has been freely offered.

The majority of people in our churches who are inactive have a quite different, but also completely wrong picture of God. They believe that God is so kind, so loving, so forgiving, and so weak, that he expects nothing. He will always forgive and never condemn. They become lazy and indifferent to the demands of God. They bury their talent in the ground and spend their lives pleasing themselves with hardly a thought as to whether or not they are pleasing God.

There is a third small group who are in immense danger. They are those who are smugly satisfied. They are sure that their good works have put them in a position of deserving heaven's rewards. They are a cut above other men and women. They are Pharisaic, and their reward will be that of the Pharisees.

So we check our standing by checking the path we walk. Is ours a devotion to the Lord born out of love? Is ours a humble recognition of our failure to fulfil all that God requires? Is his service our joy and delight? Do we find pleasure as we bring him praise and worship and offer him service loyal and true? Are we mindful of God's grace? Are we aware of the privileges of being chosen?

If we find ourselves in this final category we have little to fear. We will be judged as faithful. Our good works will serve as evidence of God's grace at work in us. They will be a sign of our loving spirit towards the Master. They will be our assurance that the Lord will welcome us as good and faithful servants.

In closing, let me remind you that the man who was given two talents received exactly the same praise and reward as his fellow servant with five. It was Spurgeon addressing trainees for the ministry who said, "It is better to be faithful in the infant school than to be unfaithful in a class of noble men. Better to be faithful in a hamlet of two or three score people than to be unfaithful in a great city parish, with thousands perishing in consequence. Better to be faithful in a cottage meeting, speaking of Christ crucified to half a hundred villagers than to be unfaithful in a great building where thousands congregate. I pray you, be faithful in laying out all that you are and have for God."

The final word and illustration is in case there is anyone here tonight who is inactive in the service of the Master. The teacher looked up from her desk and spotted John. "What are you doing John?" she called out. "Nothing Miss," John replied, quite indignantly. "That's exactly it." said the teacher. "You've got work! You ought to be doing the work I set you just a few minutes ago."

Suppose that the return of Jesus should be today and he should call, "What are you doing?" It will be no excuse – it will be condemnation if you answer, "Nothing sir." Your idle inactivity will show that you have not really responded to his love. Heaven forbid, that you or I should also be called, "a wicked and slothful servant." Heaven forbid that we should be candidates for outer darkness.

23. The Rich Man and Lazarus
Luke 16.19-31

The first thing to note is the context of the parable. Except for verses 16-18 the whole of Chapter 16 of Luke's gospel deals with managing money. It repeatedly asks, "Does money control you, or do you use money wisely and generously for the sake of the kingdom of heaven?"

The closer context of the parable is that while Jesus is teaching his followers about money, the Pharisees; who Luke tells us loved money, had overheard and were sneering at Jesus and his teaching. This parable is told in their hearing, if not specifically directed at them. So, the parable asks: Do you love money or God? Where do you stand in an unequal and unfair world?

There was a rich man who was dressed in purple and fine linen and lived in luxury every day. At his gate was laid a beggar named Lazarus.

It is Roy Clements, pastor of Eden Baptist Church in Cambridge, who points out a similarity between the American Constitution and the Communist Manifesto. The Americans talk about every person having, "equality of opportunity in a competitive society," - a fair chance for all. The Communist Manifesto calls for, "equality of distribution in a co-operative society," - fair shares for all. But as experience teaches us, equality in this world just does not happen, however positive an ideal it may be, however right it may be to strive for some sort of equality. Even Jesus himself says:

"The poor you will always have with you."(Matthew 26.11)

There could hardly be a greater contrast than between the two characters in Jesus' story. The word used to indicate the wealth of the rich man might well be translated – there was a phenomenally wealthy man. I don't know about the fashion world of Jesus' day, whether there was a Vogue magazine or Harpers Bazaar, but this man was dressed expensively. He had the very best that money could buy. True purple was fabulously expensive. It was the very finest woollen cloth, dyed with a dye which could only be obtained from the Purpurea shellfish which were only found in the shallow water off Tyre and Sidon. It had always been a symbol of royalty. It said you had arrived. You could afford the best. His fine linen likewise, was not from Marks and Spencer or even Harrods or Liberty. It was cloth personally made up by his very own skilled and expensive tailor.

He lived in luxury every day.

He ate the finest foods. He probably entertained his fellow rich men lavishly. If he wanted it - he could afford it - and he had it! The other point we pick up from Jesus' opening remarks is that the rich man's house had a gate or portico. It was the custom, if you were really rich, to build a huge ornamental gate-house, such as might adorn a palace or a temple. It was a symbol to the whole world that you had made your pile and could afford whatever you wanted.

Lest you begin to covet his riches and his life style, notice we are told remarkably little about him. We don't know how he earned his money, what friends he had, and most significantly, we don't even know his name.

At his gate was laid a beggar named Lazarus, covered with sores and longing to eat what fell from the rich man's table. Even the dogs came and licked his sores.

Let me comment first on the matter of names. In Home Group someone asked me about the name Lazarus and I needed to go home and look it up. Lazarus was a common name and is the Greek form of the Hebrew name Eleazar. It means, "Whom God has helped."

Finding the Real Jesus

In our prosperous society, it strikes me hard, especially when I look at his lot in life, that his name should say that God has helped him. I struggle to understand. He was *"laid,"* literally, sprawled, dumped in a heap, at the gate of the rich man. Virtually everyone who passed by would look down on him. Just a few might offer him alms, but the vast majority would sneer. In their minds, if not in their words, they would assess that he was some sort of useless, sinning, dreg of society. His belly was empty. He longed to be fed the left-overs from the rich man's banqueting table, but they almost certainly went to the dogs. His body was covered with sores, maybe not leprous, probably the result of severe malnutrition. And the ultimate humiliation; the dogs, perhaps the very ones who ate the rich man's left-overs, came and licked his oozing wounds. Yet in this state, his name declared God was his helper.

We must not get carried away, for Lazarus may not have existed. This Lazarus is a character in a story. What we are intended to see is Lazarus as a type of millions across the globe, both in Jesus' day and now, whose lot is very hard indeed – but still they look to God. They see no other source of help. They could curse God and blame their misfortune on God. They could be full of resentment or wallow in self-pity, but they do not. They simply struggle faithfully on. By giving him a name, (interestingly the only person in all of Jesus' parables to be given a name), Jesus says, "Though he was at the very bottom of society, he was known to God. In God's eyes he was more important that the rich man."

A name meant much in Jewish society. To be known by name was to have standing; to be important. A name gives a person significance. Not to have a name is the very opposite; not to matter; to be someone who can be passed over. Jesus, tellingly, omits any name for the rich man, (Dives is merely an invention of tradition). As far as God is concerned he is a nobody. He is unknown to God. He has no relationship with the Lord Almighty.

Now don't misunderstand me. There is nothing intrinsically wrong with being rich. It may be that God has blessed you with material prosperity and trusts you to handle it. The hard question is; in the final analysis, who would you rather be - the rich man, with everything that this world has to offer but unknown to God - or

Lazarus, abjectly poor, his life desperately tough, sick and suffering, but known to God and glory bound?

Jesus has painted the extremes, and somewhere in between we find ourselves. Jesus said:

"Indeed, it is easier for a camel to go through the eye of a needle than for a rich man to enter the kingdom of God." (Luke 18.25)

"What good is it for a man to gain the whole world, and yet lose or forfeit his very self?" (Luke 9.25)

"Blessed are the poor in spirit, for theirs is the kingdom of heaven." (Matthew 5.3)

The psalmist confidently declares:

Better is one day in your courts than a thousand elsewhere; I would rather be a doorkeeper in the house of my God than dwell in the tents of the wicked.(Psalm 84.10)

But who do you stand with: Lazarus or the rich man? What have you decided concerning your final destiny? I want to remind you that in a parable Jesus is seeking to make one main point and maybe a few ancillary challenges. We are not intended to allegorise every detail of the story. I say this because some people have tended to read too much fine detail concerning life after death into this story. Overall the scriptures do not teach that the redeemed end up nestled in Abraham's bosom (AV) or alongside him (NIV), neither do they teach instant translation to hell, but that hell follows the final judgment. What we need to realise is that Jesus is homing in on the classic understanding of the rabbis in his day. Equally we need to realise that Jesus would not have taught anything which was a falsehood. So the key point, that decisions and actions in this life will irrevocably determine our eternal destiny, stands firm.

The time came when the beggar died and the angels carried him to Abraham's side. The rich man also died and was buried. In hell, where he was in torment, he looked up and saw Abraham far away, with Lazarus by his side.

What a dramatic reversal of roles, and how hopping mad the Pharisees will be by now as they listen to Jesus' story!

The beggar may not even have been be afforded the dignity of a burial. Lazarus' body would have been thrown, like the body of an executed criminal, on the city refuse tip, where it would be incinerated along with all the city rubbish. The stench from Gehenna was notorious; it was a synonym for hell.

How outrageous can you get! This beggar does not simply die and be buried – he is borne away by angels to Abraham's side! One rabbinic understanding of heaven was to liken it to a great banquet at which Abraham, as father of the Jewish race, is at the head of the table. Lazarus, who longed for the scraps from the rich man's table, is not merely in heaven. He is at Abraham's side, a place of the very highest honour.

The rich man too, had died and been buried, but his lot is worse than the life of the beggar at his gate. He is in hell. Hell is like a fire, and the searing pain of hell is far worse than the weeping sores which afflicted Lazarus.

So he called to him, "Father Abraham, have pity on me and send Lazarus to dip the tip of his finger in water and cool my tongue, because I am in agony in this fire." But Abraham replied, "Son, remember that in your lifetime you received your good things, while Lazarus received bad things, but now he is comforted here and you are in agony."

As the story progresses the screws turn even tighter as far as the Pharisees are concerned. It was unthinkable that a religious Jew, who saw himself as a "son of Abraham," should be condemned to hell. Jews were surely God's Covenant people by birth. Heaven was theirs by right. Yet losing heaven was not the only part of his agony to come. Abraham acknowledges the rich man as a son, but as a son who has been lost; not as a son with any claim on heaven's rewards.

Anyone who thinks that parables are gentle stories had better think again. Jesus makes it clear that once this life is done there is no second chance. There is no redemption earned in Paradise. There is no all forgiving God who asks you again at the gates of heaven if you repent. No! These questions must be answered on earth. The questions at that time will relate to your relationship with Jesus and how you served him with the gifts entrusted to your stewardship.

"And besides all this, between us and you a great chasm has been fixed, so that those who want to go from here to you cannot, nor can anyone cross over from there to us."

The Rich Man and Lazarus – Luke 16.19-31

A garden path stood between the rich man at his table and the poor man at his gate. But a gulf that cannot be crossed stands between heaven and hell.

There is another saying of Jesus which sums up the rich man's condemnation.

No servant can serve two masters. Either he will hate the one and love the other, or he will be devoted to the one and despise the other. You cannot serve both God and Money. (Luke 16.13)

Remember what I said at the beginning – we must look at this parable in its context. This chapter in Luke is all about a follower of God and his or her money.

Was it being rich that condemned the rich man? Clearly not or the parable would be a mockery. Abraham, by whose side Lazarus rested, was fabulously wealthy at the end of his life. He had enormous amounts of property and vast power. So whilst God is on the side of the poor, he does not discriminate against the rich.

Was it how he obtained his riches that condemned the rich man? No! The story makes no suggestion that his riches were dishonestly obtained. He may have inherited riches. He may have been a merchant trader. He may have been a land owner and farmer. The parable is not a diatribe against capitalism, however evil some may see that as being.

So why was the rich man condemned? The clue, of course, is in the parable and in the context of the chapter. It is how he used his riches; how his riches controlled him. Who could really claim to serve and follow God and allow Lazarus to languish at his gate? Notice the relevance of the teaching about judgment in Matthew's gospel:

"For I was hungry and you gave me nothing to eat. I was thirsty and you gave me nothing to drink. I was a stranger and you did not invite me in. I needed clothes and you did not clothe me, I was sick and in prison and you did not look after me." They also will answer, 'Lord, when did we see you hungry or thirsty or a stranger or needing clothes or sick or in prison, and did not help you?' He will reply, "I tell you the truth, whatever you did not do for one of the least of these, you did not do for me." (Matthew 25.42-45)

It was not the bad things that he had done that condemned the rich man. It was the good things he had left undone. He had many good things in life, but the beggar at his gate had never benefited one iota. He had every opportunity to help but he consistently refused. Money mattered more to him than people and so he stood condemned.

Do you recall that much less well known story at the beginning of the chapter? It is an odd story. A manager had been slack concerning his master's affairs and is about to get the sack. He is distraught for he doesn't know what will happen to him. So he goes to all the folk who owe the company money and tells them that he will settle their bills if they pay half of what they owe. In so doing he wins lots of friends who he can go to when he is out of work. His master has the good grace to commend him for his shrewd action; for he will need those friends once he is sacked. Jesus makes the comment:

"I tell you, use worldly wealth to gain friends for yourselves, so that when it is gone, you will be welcomed into eternal dwellings." (Luke 16.9)

What Jesus seems to be saying is, "You can't take earthly wealth with you, so use your treasures on earth to make sure that you build up treasure in heaven." The rich man in our parable may in his mind have gained the whole world, but he had not used it for the benefit of others, and his soul was forfeit.

What will convince men and women of their need to change? The rich man has learned his lesson too late, and realises he has five brothers heading in the same direction. The five brothers are of course, representatives of people still alive. They represent you and me. The rich man becomes concerned lest they should share his dreadful fate.

He answered, "Then I beg you, father, send Lazarus to my father's house, for I have five brothers. Let him warn them, so that they will not also come to this place of torment."

It seems an admirable request, surely one that a God whose name is love will be unable to refuse. If Lazarus is sent back to earth, surely they will listen to him and repent. So what is the reply?

The Rich Man and Lazarus – Luke 16.19-31

Abraham replied, "They have Moses and the Prophets; let them listen to them."

If we translate that into words which we plainly understand it says, "They have the scriptures. They have all that they need. The Bible more than adequately shows them all they need to know to find eternal life."

The rich man protests:

"No, father Abraham," he said, "but if someone from the dead goes to them, they will repent."

I note his request and smile. It is still around in our culture today. Show them a few signs and wonders and they will believe. Let a few folk fall over, slain in the Spirit; that will surely bring them in in droves. I understand that the very latest idea is; "let their hands be covered with gold dust or all their tooth fillings turn to gold." Let me again quote from Roy Clements who says, "Signs and wonders may establish the faith of the faithful, and may confirm the spiritual blindness of the unbelieving, but it is the word of God which awakens spiritual life."

In the closing verse of the parable Jesus presses the point home.

He said to him, "If they do not listen to Moses and the Prophets, they would not be convinced even if someone rises from the dead."

Jesus knew of his coming death and resurrection. It would do wonders for those who already believed; but the masses, the unbelievers would simply do all they could to discredit it.

"No," says Jesus. "God has given you a tremendous gift – his Word. If you will not take it seriously and listen to what it says, then you will not listen to anyone or anything. If you are not changed by God's word, you will not be changed at all."

God's word tonight challenges us concerning our treasure:

"Store up for yourselves treasure in heaven, where moth and rust do not destroy, and where thieves do not break in and steal, for where your treasure is, there your heart will be also." (Matthew 6.20)

173

PART 6

THE

GLORIOUS

TRANSFIGURATION

Vision on a Mountain

It seemed I climbed a hill
through rocks and heather; there were others too,
hurrying after him.

Among the summit trees;
a deep glade like a room, where primroses
were lights in gloom.

He was transfigured there,
in shining robes of gold and white; a king
breathing his power.

And as we watched in awe,
bathed in the cloud of Presence; thunder spoke:
This is my Son!

In hazy after-glow,
he led us down by way of thorns and pine;
our senses tingling.

24. The Glorious Transfiguration
Mark 9.2-9

Tonight we come to one of those mysterious passages of scripture –
The Transfiguration. Last week I said that the retreat at Caesarea
Philippi marked a turning point in Jesus' ministry. It was there that
Jesus asked his disciples who they thought he was. To his great joy
Peter answered:

*"You are the Christ, the Son of the living God." (Matthew
16.16)*

From that point on the path of Jesus turns towards the cross.
He begins to make his way to Jerusalem for the last time, and the
focus of his teaching is on the cross and what it will mean. It seems
therefore, that the transfiguration was an experience that would
sustain and encourage the disciples, especially in the dark days
between the cross and the resurrection and at times when service
would prove very costly indeed.

*After six days Jesus took Peter, James and John and led
them up a high mountain, where they were all alone.*

Three disciples are emerging as key figures in the gospel
stories. When Jesus went to the home of Jairus to heal his daughter it
was Peter, James and John who were allowed to go into the room
with him. Later in the Garden of Gethsemane the same three were
taken to one side with him. Here they are chosen for this special

experience, this revelation of the glory of Jesus. Peter was destined, after his failures, to be reinstated and to become a great leader and preacher; his was the responsibility of preaching the Pentecost sermon. James the brother of John would be the first of the apostles to become a martyr. John was the visionary who would write a mighty gospel. John would be allowed to look into heaven and write the wonderful book of Revelation. These three seem to form a special inner circle close to Jesus.

Jesus led them up a high mountain. We can only speculate concerning this, but Mount Hermon was not far from Caesarea Philippi. It is the only mountain in Israel which, being nine thousand feet high, maintains a snow clad peak throughout the year. At least for our imagination it would fit the bill. It is to be a place where they can be alone. It is somewhere where Jesus and his disciples can have a special meeting with God.

That is something we all need to learn – the need for a private place, a holy place where we can be alone with God. Jerry Vines says, "That place can become as sacred a spot for you as this mountain top, if you will take the time to allow it to be."

There he was transfigured before them. His clothes became dazzling white, whiter than anyone in the world could bleach them.

Luke in his account tells us they had gone up into the mountain to pray, and that this change took place as Jesus was praying. Both Matthew and Luke say that his face changed and shone. The Living Bible says:

suddenly his face began to shine with glory.

At the funeral last Tuesday I talked about the cabbage white butterfly; how from the pupa emerges at last the resplendent butterfly. I said it was an example of complete metamorphosis. That is exactly the word used in the original language here. Jesus metamorphosed before their very eyes.

What I believe happened was that the true glory of Jesus broke through. The amazing thing about Jesus was that he had put his glory to one side when he came to earth.

Who, being in very nature God, did not consider equality with God something to be grasped, but made himself nothing, taking the very nature of a servant, being made in human likeness. And

178

being found in appearance as a man he humbled himself and became obedient to death, even death on a cross! (Philippians 2.6-8)

Here on the Mountain of Transfiguration his glory was no longer contained, but shone through. The gospel writers struggle to describe it. It sounds just a little like the latest detergent advertisement:

his clothes became shining white, whiter than anyone in the world could bleach them.

I guess it was a frightening as well as an awesome sight – to catch a glimpse of the glory of God. But there is a verse in scripture where Paul says that others should be able to catch glimpses of that glory in us:

And we, who with unveiled faces all reflect the Lord's glory, are being transformed into his likeness with ever increasing glory, which comes from the Lord. (2 Corinthians 3.18)

Once again the word translated "transformed," is that word "metamorphosed." In other words, God wants people to see Jesus in our lives, not as a pale shadow, but as a true reflection of the glory of God. Remember that chorus:

> Let the beauty of Jesus be seen in me,
> All his wondrous compassion and purity,
> O Thou spirit divine, all my nature refine,
> Till the beauty of Jesus is seen in me.

Albert Orsborn

And there appeared before them Elijah and Moses who were talking with Jesus.

In Luke's account he tells us that the disciples were asleep and woke up to this sight.

Peter and his companions were very sleepy, but when they became fully awake, they saw his glory, and the two men standing with him.(Luke 9.32)

I was told this was in the Bible as an encouragement to preachers. "If the disciples can fall asleep when the transfiguration is happening – are you surprised some fall asleep during your sermon?"

Why were Moses and Elijah there? There is of course, all manner of speculation. Some say that Moses represented the Law and Elijah the Prophets. There are strange arguments concerning how they went to be with the Lord. Deuteronomy 34.6 says that the Lord himself buried Moses and no-one knows the exact place of his burial. Elijah as we know did not die but was taken to heaven in a chariot of fire.

For me, Moses represented the greatest leader that Israel had known. He had delivered his people from slavery and led them through the most arduous conditions for forty years through the wilderness. Elijah represented the greatest prophet of Israel who had defended God and his Word against overwhelming odds at perhaps the most apostate time in the whole of Israel's history.

Isn't this experience part of the preparation of Peter and James and John for the difficult task ahead? Wasn't this to strengthen them for the struggle against persecution; to fortify them when facing the need to die for the faith? Here at least for them is the assurance of life beyond death, of glory, of eternity with God.

Peter said to Jesus, "Rabbi it is good for us to be here. Let us put up three shelters – one for you, one for Moses and one for Elijah." (He did not know what to say, for they were so frightened.)

Poor Peter! He comes in for stick again. "Fancy him making an idiotic statement like that!" But what would you have said? What would I have said? I rather like Peter's statement, *"let's put up three shelters, and stay."* What is more precious than to spend time in the presence of the Lord? Where is there more peace? Where is there more sense of well-being, of being loved? O.K, so Peter and the others are frightened out of their wits – the glory is overwhelming – but Peter recognises that it is good.

Do you not sometimes get lost in wonder, love and praise? Are there not moments with the Lord when you would be quite happy if they went on for ever? If nothing else, this story tells us that these moments can and will happen. The time will come, when like Moses and Elijah, we too who have trusted, followed and obeyed Jesus, will share the bliss of eternity with him.

Then a cloud appeared and enveloped them, and a voice came from the cloud, "This is my Son, whom I love, listen to him!"

This, I suppose, is the hardest part of this miracle to comprehend – the appearance of the cloud. We are meant to

OXFAM

VAT 348 4542 38

Shop with us online at
www.oxfam.org.uk/shop

LIZ   SALES   F3410/POS1
FRIDAY 14 JUNE 2019   11:09 191909
1   NON FICTION   £1.99

                              1 Items
        TOTAL   **£1.99**
        £10   £10.00
        CHANGE   £8.01
        Oxfam Shop: F3410
        13 High Street
        Leighton Buzzard, LU7 1DN
        01525 854083
        oxfam.org.uk/shop

LIVES
FOR
GOOD | OXFAM

Reg charity in England and Wales No 202918 and Scotland SC039042
Oxfam GB is a member of Oxfam International.

WARM FUZZY
GLOW – TO GO

Every item you buy or donate helps
lift lives worldwide. Just £6 raised
could train a health volunteer,
helping communities in
Bangladesh prepare for disaster.

www.oxfam.org.uk

LIFT
LIVES
FOR
GOOD | OXFAM

Reg charity in England and Wales No 202918 and Scotland SC039042.
Oxfam GB is a member of Oxfam International.

TAKE HOME SOME
NECTAR POINTS

Donate your unwanted items to
Oxfam and you can collect Nectar

understand that God the Father is there too. In the Old Testament, the cloud that led the Israelites by day was the cloud of the presence of God. When Moses went into God's presence on Sinai, he went into the cloud. The cloud over the Tabernacle indicated that God was within his sanctuary. When Jesus ascended, he ascended into the cloud of the presence of God. Here again is the cloud, and as if they need any confirmation following the discourse at Caesarea Philippi, a voice from the cloud rings out:

"This is my Son whom I love, listen to him!"

Verse 8 makes me smile. It could be a reason to believe that Mark's gospel is Peter's account:

Suddenly, when they looked around, they no longer saw anyone with them except Jesus.

I suppose what we are meant to understand from this verse is that Moses and Elijah at that point were assimilated back into heaven – and something approaching normality resumed once more.

If I was Peter or James or John, I would be just itching to get back down the mountain to tell the other disciples, to tell anyone I met, of this mountain-top experience with the Lord. It must have been quite a blow when Jesus imposed a news blackout on them.

As they were coming down the mountain, Jesus gave them orders not to tell anyone what they had seen until the Son of Man had risen from the dead.

We saw a similar instruction last week when Peter stated boldly:

"You are the Christ." Jesus warned them not to tell anyone about him. (Mark 8.30)

Someone asked me then, and we may well ask again tonight, "Why was Jesus so anxious to have the news hushed up, at least until after the resurrection? In other situations in other gospels he was keen that people should tell of the miracles God had done for them."

I think we need to recognise again that Jesus' ministry is moving to a climax. God's purpose is that Jesus will die on a Roman cross, that we might be forgiven. God's intention is that it should take place at Passover time, so that there can be no excuse for failing to recognise him as the Lamb of God who takes away the sin of the world. Of course God could and would work those things out, but to be going round announcing that the Messiah had come was to invite early intervention by either the temple authorities, or by the Romans, who would have been quick to put a stop to what might be yet another Jewish uprising.

There is also the fact that what they had witnessed was so unbelievable. It would be risky to broadcast what had been said at Caesarea Philippi, but to broadcast what had transpired on the mountain would be to invite accusations of insanity and of delusions of grandeur. Later, when the resurrection occurred, when there was no body in the tomb, only the folded grave clothes; then it would help the disciples to understand why the tomb could not hold him. The glory of the Lord simply broke forth.

What are we going to take away tonight? Like the disciples we are to be encouraged, when the going is tough, when people refuse to believe concerning our Lord. We too are to hold on to our mountain top experiences and to say, "I know, for I too have glimpsed the Lord in all his glory."

Like Peter and James and John, we too are to listen anew to the words of the Father:

"This is my Son, whom I love. Listen to Him!"

Let us listen, obey, and walk in His ways!

PART 7

THE ROADS

LEADING TO

THE CROSS

Martha's Party

Kneading, pressing my knuckles into warm
dough,
brown with rye grains, springy with yeast,
I see in his eyes, behind his smile
sorrow like a storm brewing,
though we chuckle over the donkey he's
ordered from Samuel.
You'll look fine; regal as a King! I quip,
Lazarus shall lend you his Sabbath cloak.

Outside my brother is chopping wood;
sweat glistening on strong young arms,
so recently cold and stiff in the tomb.
Tonight we'll celebrate his rising from death, I say,
my heart feather-light, almost dancing.
But the Master looks away,
toward Jerusalem.

The lamb is nearly done; herbs, olives,
fresh cheese, the best wine.
As I pour, the wine darkens to blood-red.
Let me, he offers.
The loaves have risen well. Three of them,
cut with my knife, to try the proving dough,
bear crosses.
The Master nods,
This will be a celebration!

Romsey Baptist Church June 19th 1994, April 2nd 1995.

25. The Road through Jericho, where Bartimaeus sat
Luke 18.31-43

Jesus has already been travelling for several days. He has "set his face" to go to Jerusalem. Despite all the opposition to him there, despite the well intentioned advice of his disciples not to go, Jesus presses on towards the Holy City. Many will have been making the journey for the Feast of the Passover, for its celebrations and religious ceremonies were soon to begin. But Jesus is not going for the celebrations. He is going because, "His time has come."

Jesus took the twelve aside and told them, "We are going up to Jerusalem, and everything that is written by the prophets about the Son of Man will be fulfilled. He will be handed over to the Gentiles. They will mock him, insult him, spit on him, flog him and kill him. On the third day he will rise again." The disciples did not understand any of this. Its meaning was hidden from them, and they did not know what he was talking about.

You might well expect Jesus to be travelling with a heavy heart. He was on his way to his death, the cruellest death ever devised – death on a cross; and despite three years of teaching his followers just did not understand.

You might well expect too, that Jesus was very tired. He had been walking for several days. He had travelled all along the border between Samaria and Galilee and now is approaching Jericho. This is the last city in the valley of the Jordan, before making the steep ascent along the perilous, bandit infested road that wound up through the desert countryside to Jerusalem.

Jericho was a last stopping point for pilgrims on their way up to Jerusalem. The old Jericho had, of course, been destroyed by Joshua. Herod the Great had rebuilt it and re-established Jericho as a town of significance. It enjoyed a pleasant climate in winter and Herod used it as his winter base, but more than that, it was a prosperous area. It stood astride two great trade routes, which is undoubtedly why Zacchaeus, the tax collector, selected it as his base, that he might enjoy the rich pickings. Its name means, "The place of smells," yet not in any unpleasant sense: perhaps we should say, "The place of perfumes." Balsam and cypress were grown there, and it was especially famous for the vast rose gardens and the industry of extracting attar of roses, the most popular perfume of the day.

It will be good for Jesus to stop, to wash off the dust and sweat of the day, and to try to rest his mind from thoughts of the awful week which lies ahead.

The road was probably noisy, with bands of pilgrims making their way for the feast, travelling in groups because of the dangers of the way. Some would be telling stories to make the miles seem shorter, others singing songs, some laughing at ribald jokes. Probably a great deal of attention would be paid to the rabbi Jesus. What might he do? What might he say today?

If I were Jesus, I think the last thing I would want to do would be to give more of myself. I would have every excuse to withdraw, to take as low a profile as possible, and to try to shut myself away from the rest. But he is to meet Bartimaeus.

As Jesus approached Jericho, a blind man was sitting by the roadside begging. When he heard the crowd going by, he asked what was happening. They told him, "Jesus of Nazareth is passing by."

Mark identifies the blind man for us. *Then they came to Jericho – a blind man, Bartimaeus, (that is the son of Timaeus), was sitting by the roadside begging. (Mark 10.46)*

The Road through Jericho – Luke 18.31-43

We don't know why he was blind. He could have been born blind, in which case people in the streets would have attributed his blindness to the sins of his parents or ancestors. He may have become blind, for blindness was one of the commonest diseases in Palestine. Whichever it is, this poor man, Bartimaeus, is reduced to begging. He is an outcast of society. He cannot earn his living. He has lost his self-respect. He is counted as a sinner.

I don't like this link, for while we cannot deny that often there is a link between sinful behaviour and contracting a disease; sickness debases a person. It reduces their value in our eyes. Blind people were thought of as particularly helpless. Lepers were occasionally cured, the lame sometimes were healed, but the blind were lost. If you were blind no one would give you work, so even if you had some savings, you would very soon be bankrupt and reduced to the destitute status of a beggar. You would grope your way around and beg until your dying day. Because of this, it may be significant that there are more records of Jesus healing blind people than those with any other disease. Jesus can bring hope to the hopeless, light into darkness, joy to the outcast.

Our role as Christians is to affirm that everyone is important to God. God's plan of salvation included the dying thief on the cross. It included the adulteress. It includes today's alcoholic, today's heroin addict, and today's Aids sufferer. It includes me – it includes you.

But blindness is a useful illustration, for blindness is a handicap. Blindness deprives us of much that is beautiful. Blindness does prevent us living life as God intended. The sin, the wrong in our lives is like that too. The blind person can easily become lost, and the sinner is described as someone who is lost – lost from God and unable to see his wonderful plan of redemption, to enjoy his forgiveness, to rejoice in his salvation.

I wonder how this blind man came to have faith that he could be healed. What stories had Bartimaeus heard about Jesus? Had he heard how Jesus healed the blind man at Bethsaida? Had he heard about the day Jesus made mud with spittle and anointed a blind man's eyes and sent him to wash in the Pool of Siloam? What did he know of Jesus as prophet, as teacher, about his birth in Bethlehem and his descent from the line of David? Did he know people were asking, "Is he the Messiah, the promised one of God?" Today for him was there even an extra dimension – did the very nearness of Jesus cause his faith to increase?

Listen to his cry – *He called out, "Jesus, Son of David, have mercy on me!"*

Notice "Son of David." The great promise of God to the Jews was that one day he would raise up a Messiah who would be a King far greater than David, and who would trace his ancestry through the line of David. He would be known as "Great David's greater Son."

So the blind man, in effect, cries, "Jesus, Messiah, have mercy on me." On the surface this was a cry for alms. He was begging for a gift of money. For the beggar, *"have mercy on me,"* meant, "give me a gift." If a beggar could add a name it made the request much more powerful.

Do you easily walk by the beggar on the street today? Suppose he or she called out your name. What would be your reaction? What was the reaction here?

Those who led the way rebuked him and told him to be quiet, but he shouted all the more, "Son of David, have mercy on me!"

For a moment stop and look at the discouragement that exists for Bartimaeus. He cannot see what is going on. No one stops and says to him, "Look, here is your opportunity. Jesus the healer is passing by. Call out! Perhaps he will make you whole." No, the beggar is ignored, and has to ask for himself.

Then there is the discouragement of being told to hold his peace:

Many rebuked him and told him to be quiet, but he shouted all the more, "Son of David, have mercy on me!" (Mark 10.48)

You can imagine the comments. "Be quiet!" "Sit still." "You are interrupting a great teacher. Shut up!" But he shouted all the more, actually, "a great deal more." If it is possible he is determined to have an interview with Jesus.

Friend, are you spiritually blind? Do you suffer from sin, which will result in eternal spiritual death? Here is Jesus who can save sinners. Are you determined to be saved, or are you indifferent?

If Bartimaeus had been indifferent there was no way in which he could have received his sight. The greatest folly for the person who needs to find salvation is the folly of indifference.

Notice the discouragement. Jesus didn't immediately answer his cry. Bartimaeus called, and had to keep on calling. He had to shout all the more before Jesus responded to his cry. Sometimes Jesus does that. He seems to test us. Do we really want what we are asking of God? Do we really believe that he can meet our every need?

I would hate anyone to be discouraged tonight and say to me at the end of service, "I have given up calling to God because he doesn't hear me. He doesn't answer me."

Be like Bartimaeus. Go on calling. Jesus cannot and will not ignore the person who really seeks him.

You will seek me and find me when you seek me with all your heart. (Jeremiah 29.13)

There is a famous missionary account, though I forget the name of the missionary involved. It comes from China. The missionary doctor had been performing cataract operations. He operated on one Chinese peasant and was disappointed with the result, for whilst he restored a degree of vision, the outcome of the operation was far from perfect. The peasant was sent home and ordered to return to the clinic in six months to see if anything more could be done. He returned, but not alone. To his wrist was tied a long cord, and hanging on to the cord were seventy other blind men. With a smile he said, "I brought them to see the man who gave me back my sight. I believe you can do the same for them."

Do we encourage, or prevent, others from finding Jesus?

Jesus stopped and ordered the man to be brought to him.

Isn't that great? Doubtless Jesus was discussing with the other travellers as he walked along, but here is a soul in need. Jesus' first priority is clear. It is not a time for words; it is a time for deeds. How often we can be so full of words that deeds never happen!

Notice how the attitude of the crowd changes when Jesus commands:

"Call him."

189

They have been scathing in their rebuke. Now they encourage the man. "Cheer up!" they say, "On your feet." Or to put it in colloquial language, "It's your lucky day." But it is so much more than that; it is for Bartimaeus his day of Destiny. He is destined to be made whole and to become a follower of Jesus.

Throwing his cloak aside, he jumped to his feet and came to Jesus. (Mark 10.50)

Can you sense the urgency of this verse? Nothing is going to stop Bartimaeus coming to Jesus. He threw his cloak aside. Remember this man is a poor beggar. His cloak may well be his only possession of any value. It keeps him warm when there is too little money to buy food. It protects him when the cold winds blow, but it will be a hindrance in coming to Jesus. So he doesn't care what happens to it. It is cast on one side in order that he might get quickly to the Saviour.

He doesn't stagger up – "he jumped to his feet." Here is his opportunity. He has a hungry heart. He has inwardly glimpsed the possibility that he might see. He must come quickly and eagerly. He is not going to miss this. Can I say that of each of you? Would to God that I could. Are you are eager to know the Saviour, to find forgiveness, to serve the Lord, to receive salvation?

That is both my prayer and my heartbreak. I long for you to receive every good thing which Jesus has for your life, and I am distressed when I see how some neglect so great a salvation. "Tomorrow will do Lord, - not yet, I will come in my time."

Friends, it is not just me, it is God who longs that you should cast off your restraints, who longs that you take that step of faith.

What happens when the blind man gets to Jesus?

When he came near, Jesus asked him, "What do you want me to do for you?" "I want to see," he replied.

There is that lovely offer from Jesus, *"What do you want me to do for you?"*

Bartimaeus has no hang-ups. *"I want to see."* I believe Jesus is asking that question of some of you. "What do you want me to do for you?" It is another point where the devil gets in. I hear it in the form of excuses. "I'm not good enough to come to Jesus – I cannot pray." Friends, follow the example of Bartimaeus, come out with it, any language will do. "Lord the problem is: - my hard heart – my foul mouth – the way I lie – my problem with drink – the women - the pursuit of money – a sense of being lost – a deep-seated worry – a fear that grips me – a health problem that is not resolved. The problem is – that I need a relationship with you."

Come out with it. Tell it to Jesus. Give him your problem. That very act of faith will be the key to you receiving your answer.

For Bartimaeus Jesus simply says the word:

Jesus said to him, "Receive your sight; your faith has healed you." Immediately he received his sight and followed Jesus, praising God. When all the people saw it, they also praised God.

For Jesus, on this final journey to Jerusalem, when he is so anxious that his disciples will understand and believe in him, what a sign this is for them and for the pilgrims who knew the words of Isaiah concerning the Messiah:

"I will keep you and make you to be a covenant for the people and a light for the Gentiles, to open the eyes that are blind, to free captives from prison and to release from the dungeon those who sit in darkness." (Isaiah 42.6-7)

This incident affirms, yet again, one of the wonderful signs concerning Jesus. He can heal physical blindness – he is the Messiah. But it is much more far reaching than that. This miracle affirms that Jesus is on the side of the outcast, the oppressed and the underdog. There is no one outside the love of Jesus.

"Go," said Jesus, "your faith has healed you." Immediately he received his sight and followed Jesus along the road. (Mark 10.52)

One final and very precious thought. I suppose you could say that it is the one point of disobedience in the story. "Go," says Jesus, but this is the one thing which Bartimaeus will not do – he follows Jesus along the road.

Listen to Matthew's account of the healing of Bartimaeus.

Two blind men were sitting by the roadside, and when they heard that Jesus was going by, they shouted, "Lord, Son of David, have mercy on us!" (Matthew 20.30)

Matthew doesn't name either of the men, but he does tell us that both of them followed Jesus. Why then does Mark only tell us about one man, and how does he know his name is Bartimaeus? I can only assume it is because Bartimaeus became an avowed disciple of Christ. Many set out to follow Jesus. They seem full of such great promise; but as in the parable of the Sower, the cares of this world overtake them and they cease to be all that they could be.

I believe the call of Jesus today comes not just to those who have never found Jesus, but also to those who have let go. "Come back," he says, "whatever your problem. What do you want me to do for you?"

To have faith is to take a risk. It is to jump out of a plane for the first time, trusting the parachute will open. It is taking the warfarin tablets when you know that warfarin kills rats, because the doctor tells you they will do you good. It is stepping out with Jesus when the picture is far from complete, when there is so much you do not know.

For the beggar Bartimaeus who cried out, the result of exercising faith is so tremendous that he wants to join the crowd and follow Jesus. There is a wonderful knock-on effect too. The whole company rejoice and are caught up in praising God.

Jesus never again passed along the Jericho road. Bartimaeus had the one opportunity to cry out and he took it. His cry is still needed today.

He called out, "Jesus, Son of David, have mercy on me!"

26. From Bethany to Jerusalem
Luke 19.28-47

If you are ever privileged enough to visit the Holy Land you will discover the road from Bethany to Jerusalem. The buildings along it have changed, but the route is the same as in Jesus' day. It is less than three miles from the village of Bethany into the heart of Jerusalem, a steep and winding road, down past the Mount of Olives, past the garden of Gethsemane, across the Kidron valley, then sharply up and though the gate now known as St. Stephen's Gate into the city. It is still lined with olive plantations; gnarled trees that are old enough to have stood there in Jesus' time, though the olive trees of Gethsemane were almost certainly torn down in the destruction of Jerusalem in AD 70.

First come along the road with me on Palm Sunday. A little bit of background helps us to understand what is going on. Some two hundred years earlier Palestine had been conquered by the Greek King, Antiochus Ephiphanes. He commanded obedience to the Greek god Zeus. The reading of the Hebrew Scriptures was forbidden. The result was widespread rioting and open defiance by the Jews in Jerusalem. Antiochus decided on tough action. Determined to eradicate Judaism from the face of the earth, he marched his armies into Jerusalem in 168 B.C. and desecrated the temple, stripping it of all its gold, including that overlaying the stones. In three days forty thousand men, women, children, even babes in arms, were slaughtered and a further forty thousand were sold into slavery.

The king sent edicts by messengers to Jerusalem and the towns of Judah, directing them to adopt customs foreign to the country, banning burnt offerings, sacrifices and libations from the sanctuary, profaning Sabbaths and feasts, defiling the sanctuary and everything holy; building altars, shrines and temples for idols, sacrificing pigs and unclean beasts, leaving their sons uncircumcised and prostituting themselves to all kinds of impurity and abomination, so that they should forget the Law and revoke all observance of it. Anyone not obeying the king's command was put to death. (1 Maccabees 1.44-50)

Worst of all, on the temple altar itself, Antiochus set up an image dedicated to Zeus, but which in fact had his own face. On the altar he insisted pigs should be sacrificed. This was surely the abomination of desolation foretold by Daniel.

This is not the time to go into all the atrocities that were committed. Suffice it to say there were many brave and loyal Jews who refused to bow the knee, and eventually Judas Maccabeus led the Jews in rebellion and Jerusalem was recaptured. Maccabeus and his followers rode into Jerusalem on horseback, armed with swords and spears, along the Bethany road. His first task was to cleanse the temple.

Now Maccabeus and his followers, the Lord leading them on, recovered the temple and the city; and they tore down the altars which had been built in the public square by the foreigners, and also destroyed the sacred precincts. They purified the sanctuary, and made another altar of sacrifice. Then, striking fire out of flint, they offered sacrifices after a lapse of two years, and they burned incense and lighted lamps and set out the bread of the Presence.(2 Maccabees 10.1-3)

Listen to verse 7.

Therefore bearing ivy wreathed wands and beautiful branches and also fronds of palms, they offered hymns of thanksgiving to him who had given success to the purifying of his own holy place. (2 Maccabees 10.7)

Sadly this was not the end of troubles, and twenty years later there needed to be another freeing of Jerusalem, this time led by Simon Maccabeus. He had an almost identical reception.

The Jews entered Jerusalem with praise and palm branches, and with harps and cymbals and stringed instruments, and with hymns and songs, because a great enemy had been crushed and removed from Israel.

Apologies for the history lesson, but now can you sense the expectation of Palm Sunday? Zechariah prophesied judgment on Israel's enemies, and the Roman occupiers are enemies indeed. There had long been an expectation of a new Messiah, a new Maccabeus. There has been an expectation of the True, Long-promised Messiah. What did Zechariah say?

Rejoice greatly, O Daughter of Zion! Shout, Daughter of Jerusalem! See, your king comes to you, righteous and having salvation, gentle and riding on a donkey, on a colt, the foal of a donkey. (Zechariah 9.9)

Now recall the beginning of this story:

As he approached Bethpage and Bethany at the hill called the Mount of Olives, he sent two of his disciples, saying to them, "Go to the village ahead of you, and as you enter it, you will find a colt tied there, which no one has ever ridden. Untie it, and bring it here. If anyone asks you, 'Why are you untying it?' tell him, 'The Lord needs it.'"

The situation is electric. There has long been this question about Jesus. Now it seems clear – the King has come!

They brought it to Jesus, threw their cloaks on the colt and put Jesus on it. As he went along, people spread their cloaks on the road. When he came near the place where the road goes down the Mount of Olives, the whole crowd of disciples began joyfully to praise God in loud voices for all the miracles they had seen: "Blessed is the king who comes in the name of the Lord! Peace in heaven and glory in the highest!"

Of course the King had come. The King went on to cleanse the temple:

Then he entered the temple area and began driving out those who were selling. "It is written," he said to them, "My house will be a house of prayer; but you have made it a den of robbers."

The people had missed so much. They had not really taken in the prophecy of Zechariah – "Your king comes, gentle and riding on a donkey," not on a war-horse and with a mighty army. He doesn't come to cleanse the temple from Gentile defilement. Indeed it is not the sanctuary he has come to cleanse. Jesus has come to cleanse the Court of the Gentiles, the places of the Bazaars of Annas, from the Jewish fraud which offered pitiful rates of exchange for those who came to make an offering, and who condemned animals brought for sacrifice so that large profits could be made from the temple supply of lambs and doves.

Most of all, Jesus had come to effect righteousness and salvation. And salvation demanded sacrifice, not of a temple lamb, but of the Lamb of God – God's only beloved Son the Lord Jesus Christ.

I hope you have gained some new insight into the Palm Sunday story. I hope you have seen something of the power of the ride into Jerusalem as a sign that the prophecy of Zechariah was being fulfilled. The King, the Messiah, most certainly had come.

Before leaving the passage, can I take you back to one sentence?

As he went along, people spread their cloaks on the road.

Were you one of the honoured guests at the naming of the Oriana on Thursday? If you were there you will have seen the long stretch of red carpet laid out for the Queen. In our culture red carpet symbolises V.I.P. treatment. In the culture of Jesus' day a royal road was made by laying cloaks on the ground. It was not only a symbol for a V.I.P. acknowledging allegiance from those who laid down their cloaks. It was a symbol of submission to the king. You see, a man's cloak was his most valuable possession. It was his blanket at night, his protection by day. It was even a means of carrying loads. Jewish law forbade a man's cloak to be kept overnight when it had been taken as a pledge:

Return his cloak to him by sunset so that he may sleep in it. Then he will thank you, and it will be regarded as a righteous act in the sight of the Lord your God. (Deuteronomy 24.13)

The people in the crowd laid down their most valuable possession – in recognition and as a sign of allegiance to King Jesus.

When we follow Jesus he still requires that we put down what we consider to be valuable in submission to him, for he must be King. Nothing must come in the way of our allegiance to him. Often Jesus will give it straight back to us to use in his service.

Does Jesus have your full allegiance?

Betrayal

How silver birches weep as pale as widows
grieving in their lace on the heather hill,
hid from the grumbling road. A sky of swallows
sways in flight. Some other garden gave him shade,
a rock for prayer and friends before they fled.

Here leaves are yellow. There the olives trembled,
Oh my Father, take this cup from me!
Piercing the dark, with clashing swords and torches
the soldiers came; the betrayer strode towards
his prey. The rowan berries burn like flame.

I look away. Old gorse is harsh with sharp thorns.
Birches in this glade are prisoners,
whipped with winds, crushed for air, with quivering
fingers.
Clouds accumulate, the murmuring storm looms near.
The traitor greeted Jesus with a kiss.

What faith, who knew his death a Roman scaffold,
yet stood his ground despite the lonely hill!
What sadness to be sold by one his heart loved,
one who'd been his friend!
Now rain begins to fall.

27. From Simon's House to the Upper Room
Mark 14.1-31

Now the Passover and the Feast of Unleavened Bread were only two days away, and the chief priests and the teachers of the law were looking for some sly way to arrest Jesus and kill him. "But not during the Feast" they said, "or the people may riot."

Passover and Unleavened Bread were officially two separate feasts but because they followed each other without a break most families saw them as a single celebration. By Jesus' day the two had virtually become one. The Passover meal, if possible, would be eaten on the 14th evening of the first month of the Jewish year, known as the month of Nisan. Passover marked God's intervention when he delivered the Jews from slavery in Egypt after the final plague when God destroyed the firstborn of the Egyptians but spared those Israelites whose homes had the blood of a sacrificial lamb smeared on the doorposts.

Unleavened Bread was an older festival. It lasted for seven full days and marked the beginning of the grain harvest. During this feast special burnt offerings were sacrificed to give thanks to God, and a sheaf of newly harvested barley was brought and offered to

God. The only work that was allowed was the preparation of food. The rest of the time was to be spent in celebration with one's family.

The religious authorities, of course, were absolutely furious that Jesus had dared to overturn the tables of the money changers and those of the sacrificial dove sellers. They were determined that Jesus should die, but realised their need for caution remembering the victorious welcome Jesus had received as he rode into Jerusalem. So they had to wait for a suitable time.

The teachers of the law were looking for some sly way to arrest Jesus and kill him. "But not during the Feast," they said, "or the people may riot."

We often overlook that comment when considering the story of the crucifixion. We shouldn't for it helps us to remember that Jesus' death was God's plan coming to pass, not man's plan. It was something that the Father had determined from the very beginning of time – that at His appointed hour Jesus should die that we might be forgiven.

In the days immediately preceding the feasts Jesus and his disciples were staying in Bethany, a village just two or three miles outside Jerusalem. I imagine Jesus being put up by Mary and Martha and their brother Lazarus, whom Jesus had recently raised from the dead. There must have been tremendous interest in Jesus in Bethany. In a little community like that there would be no one who didn't know exactly what had happened to Lazarus. It is hardly surprising that while he was there, Simon the Pharisee invited Jesus and his disciples for a meal. Mark names him Simon the Leper and I cannot help but wonder if at some point Jesus had healed Simon.

While he was in Bethany, reclining at the table in the home of a man known as Simon the Leper, a woman came with an alabaster jar of very expensive perfume, made of pure nard. She broke the jar and poured the perfume on his head.

It is a fascinating study to put together all the gospel accounts of this incident, and to notice the different points that the different writers emphasise. But today we are simply looking at Mark, who emphasises the sheer extravagance of it all.

The woman broke an alabaster jar containing an expensive perfume; pure nard. As far as we know nard only grew in the mountainous regions of North India, now known as the Himalayas. The perfume was extracted from the roots and young spiky stems of the plant. It was normally concentrated until it was of ointment consistency. Merchants from the East would buy the ointment sealed in alabaster boxes in India. From here it would be brought to the wealthy women of Egypt, Israel, Greece and Rome. The ointment kept its perfume for many years and was seen as an investment. On special occasions the jar would be opened and the perfume allowed to fragrance the air. A bride might use just a little as she welcomed her husband on her wedding night. When a king or some very important person died, a little of the ointment might be used to perfume the body to drive away unpleasant odours.

The extravagance is that this woman breaks the jar and pours the ointment over the head of Jesus in one act of abandonment. At the very least her action said, "Jesus, you mean everything to me. I worship you, I adore you. I love you with all of my being."

Some of those present were saying indignantly to one another, "Why this waste of perfume? It could have been sold for more than a year's wages and the money given to the poor." And they rebuked her harshly. "Leave her alone," said Jesus. "Why are you bothering her? She has done a beautiful thing to me. The poor you will always have with you, and you can help them any time you want. But you will not always have me."

Listen to this next verse:

"She did what she could. She poured perfume on my body beforehand to prepare for my burial.

This is a situation where Jesus and his Father God, are in control. He knows what is about to happen – he knows that the perfume from that nard will still be about his body, even as they take it down from the cross and carry him to Joseph of Arimathea's tomb in the garden.

Now hear the lovely tribute from Jesus to this woman:

"I tell you the truth, wherever the gospel is preached throughout the world, what she has done will also be told in memory of her."

Wherever the gospel is preached, they will tell her story. Why? Jesus wants us to learn that extravagant love, for the gospel's sake, is never wasted. Have you been extravagant for Jesus? This woman could have held on to the ointment as her security. It could have been sold and it would have raised more than a year's wages, but she gave it away and instead aimed for treasure in heaven. It could have kept her from Jesus, but she loved him, and she knew he deserved everything she had. Oh, that we would learn to really love him!

John tells us that the chief complainer was Judas Iscariot; the one trusted to look after what monies Jesus and the disciples had; one who pretended to care for the poor, but who in practice cared far more for himself, and who was not beyond helping himself from the money bag if personal need arose. It is strange how people react when challenged, and this extravagance was clearly a challenge that Judas could not come to terms with. He must change sides. Instead of continuing to follow Jesus – he will collude with the priests and betray his master.

Then Judas Iscariot, one of the Twelve, went to the chief priests to betray Jesus to them. They were delighted to hear this and promised to give him money. So he watched for an opportunity to hand him over.

This is so sad, and we know how it ended for Judas:

With the reward he got for his wickedness, Judas bought a field; there he fell headlong, his body burst open and all his intestines spilled out. (Acts 1.18)

The saddest thing I know is to find someone who once walked with the Lord, but is now far away; against the Lord and against his people. Unfortunately it is not a rare occurrence, and it nearly always begins with criticism, grumbling. A friend or leader is doing their best, but the grumbler would have done it another way. Fellowship is broken. Satan gets in to destroy their faith. Do take care when tempted to grumble. Put yourself in the other person's shoes. Try to see a matter from his or her angle, and at that time remind yourself of Judas, and of the lady who poured perfume over Jesus at Bethany.

On the first day of the Feast of Unleavened Bread, when it was customary to sacrifice the Passover lamb, Jesus' disciples asked him, "Where do you want us to go and make preparations for you to eat the Passover?" So he sent two of his disciples, telling them, "Go into the city and a man carrying a jar of water will meet you. Follow him."

Yet again we see Jesus totally in control of the situation. "A man carrying a jar of water will meet you." He would have been so obvious – carrying water was women's work. Jesus has it all pre-arranged. Some suggest that it is John Mark, the author of the gospel, who carried the water, and that he led the disciples back to his parents' home.

"Say to the owner of the house he enters, 'The teacher asks; "Where is my guest room, where I may eat the Passover with my disciples?"' He will show you a large upper room, furnished and ready. Make preparations for us there." The disciples left; went into the city and found things just as Jesus had told them. So they prepared the Passover.

Large Jewish houses had a guest room. It would normally be an upper room built on the roof of the house and approached by its own independent staircase. Some Jews kept such rooms, not only for guests, but to let out for meetings and special events such as this.

They needed to make preparations. First the room would be thoroughly cleaned, and then they would perform the ritual search for leaven. When that was complete, the lamb had to be obtained, and the unleavened bread. They needed the bowl of salt water, which reminded them of the tears shed in slavery and the waters of the Red Sea through which their forebears had miraculously passed. There was the collection of bitter herbs – horse radish, chicory, endive, lettuce and horehound – to remind them of the bitterness of life in Egypt. There was the paste called Charoseth – a mixture of apples, dates, pomegranates and nuts – to remind them of the clay with which they made bricks in Egypt. Through it were sticks of cinnamon to remind them of the straw with which the bricks had been made. Then finally there were the four separate cups of wine. These would be shared at different stages in the meal to remind them of the promises of God:

Therefore, say to the Israelites: "I am the Lord, and I will bring you out from under the yoke of the Egyptians. I will free you from being slaves to them; I will redeem you with an outstretched arm and with mighty acts of judgment. I will take you as my own people, and I will be your God." (Exodus 6.6-7)

Each cup would be drunk as a toast, the final cup being the cup of Covenant.

Eventually all is made ready for the meal.

When evening came, Jesus arrived with the Twelve. While they were reclining at the table eating, he said, "I tell you the truth, one of you will betray me – one who is eating with me." They were saddened, and one by one they said to him, "Surely not I?" "It is one of the Twelve," he replied, "one who dips bread into the bowl with me. The Son of Man will go just as it is written about him. But woe to that man who betrays the Son of Man! It would be better for him if he had not been born."

It was at this meal that Jesus instituted what we now know as the Lord's Supper, or Communion.

While they were eating, Jesus took bread, gave thanks and broke it, and gave it to his disciples, saying, "Take it; this is my body."

As the meal drew to a close, the host would take any remaining unleavened bread and break it into pieces, one for each of the family or guests. Hands were washed and the bread was eaten. When Jesus was the host, his words were a little different: "Look, just as this bread is broken, so my body is broken for you. Look, just as there is one piece of bread for each of you, sufficient for all, so will my sacrifice be sufficient for all of you."

The most moving moment of all must have been as Jesus took that final cup:

Then he took the cup, gave thanks and offered it to them, and they all drank from it. "This is my blood of the covenant, which is poured out for many," he said to them. "I tell you the truth; I will not drink again of the fruit of the vine until that day when I drink it anew in the Kingdom of God."

The New Covenant is established – the covenant in the blood of Jesus. No longer is it the blood of a sacrificial lamb that will be remembered. No longer will salvation be deliverance from slavery. From now on, it is the blood of the sinless Son of God which will be remembered. From now on salvation is deliverance from sin.

When they had sung a hymn, they went out to the Mount of Olives.

Yes, at that point, amid all the drama, all the emotion, they had to stand to sing a hymn, and the hymn was Psalm 136 – the Great Hallel. Let me remind you how it begins:

Give thanks to the Lord, for he is good. His love endures forever. Give thanks to the God of gods. His love endures forever. Give thanks to the Lord of lords: His love endures forever. (Psalm 136.1-3)

From the upper room they make their way to the Mount of Olives and the Garden of Gethsemane. As they walk along, Jesus talks with the disciples, who will have hardly noticed that Judas is no longer with them:

"You will all fall away," Jesus told them, "for it is written: 'I will strike the shepherd and the sheep will be scattered.' But after I have risen, I will go ahead of you into Galilee." Peter declared, "Even if all fall away, I will not." "I tell you the truth," Jesus answered, "today, yes tonight; before the rooster crows twice, you yourself will disown me three times." But Peter insisted emphatically, "Even if I have to die with you, I will never disown you." And all the others said the same.

How often have we said that to Jesus, and then have failed him?

There is just one last lesson for today, and it is in the word which Jesus uses for "fall away." It was the term, "skandalizein" *from* which we get the word scandal. It actually meant, "you will all fall into the trap. You will all be tricked."

Peter's heart was that he would never fail his Lord, but Peter's failing was to forget his own human weakness, and the cunning of Satan's wiles. Let us take note, and take care, lest we become a scandal. Let us stay very close to Jesus, for His love endures for ever.

Romsey Baptist Church March 17th 1991 and April 9th 1995
Ferndown United Church. March 23rd 1997

28. From Gethsemane to Caiaphas' House
Matthew 26.57-75, Mark 14.32-41, Luke 22.41-51

There were no gardens within the city walls of Jerusalem, but many rich people owned plots on the slopes of the Mount of Olives. Some were olive groves, some more formal gardens. They were used as places of quiet retreat and rest. Perhaps Gethsemane belonged to the same family as owned the upper room. It seems to be a place where Jesus was in the habit of going, for Judas knew just where to find him.

On that Thursday night – the night of so many strange experiences – when Jesus had celebrated the last supper with his disciples, when he had initiated the Eucharist, when Simon Peter had pledged unfailing loyalty only to be told that before the cock crowed he would three times deny his master, when Judas had slunk out into the night, seemingly unnoticed by the other disciples; Jesus ends the day setting out, so it seems, back to Bethany, but stopping off as he often did at the Garden of Gethsemane, where the road begins to wind up the hill towards the Mount of Olives.

It was the end of the day. They were all desperately tired. They still didn't understand what was about to happen to their Lord.

Somewhere near the entrance of the garden, Jesus leaves eight of the disciples:

"Sit here while I pray."

He takes Peter, James and John along with him and begins to share some of the pain welling up in his heart.

"My soul is overwhelmed with sorrow to the point of death," he said to them. "Stay here and keep watch."

For Jesus the pressure is almost unbearable. Can you imagine the situation: the darkness; the sense of utter loneliness as Jesus takes leave of his disciples to be alone to pray? In front of him is the most terrible mission, his "cup of suffering." Crucifixion is awful in itself, but his most crushing burden is undertaking his divinely appointed task. As the spotless, sinless Lamb of God, he must bear the sins of all mankind.

> "We may not know, we cannot tell,
> What pains he had to bear,
> But we believe it was for us
> He hung and suffered there.
>
> There was no other good enough
> To pay the price of sin.
> He only could unlock the gate
> Of heaven and let us in."
>
> *(Cecil Frances Alexander)*

Jesus had almost certainly witnessed crucifixion. He had seen the agony suffered by its victims. The thought must have filled him with horror. Even though he knew what lay ahead: even though he had made his way purposefully to Jerusalem; even though he had shared the supper; and Judas had already gone to the temple authorities; for a moment Jesus considers. Could there be some other way?

He withdrew about a stone's throw beyond them, knelt down and prayed, "Father, if you are willing, take this cup from me; yet not my will, but yours be done."

What amazing grace, what commitment, what divine love! "Not my will but yours be done."

And being in anguish, he prayed more earnestly, and his sweat was like drops of blood falling to the ground.

My friend, Jesus had you in mind as he prayed in Gethsemane. It was for you he sweated those drops of blood. It was for your sins he went to the cross. It was for you he died.

Then he returned to his disciples and found them sleeping. "Simon," he said to Peter, "are you asleep? Could you not watch for one hour? Watch and pray so that you will not fall into temptation. The spirit is willing, but the body is weak." Once more he went away and prayed the same thing. When he came back, he again found them sleeping, because their eyes were heavy. They did not know what to say to him.

It is easy to criticise the disciples. In his hour of great need, they fail their Master. Sadly I would have done the same. Yet I can excuse them many times over: the busy day; the long walks; the work getting ready for the Passover; the food they have eaten; the late hour; the stress of the situation. What I think is important are those words of Jesus,

"Watch and pray so that you will not fall into temptation."

I remember that temptation is the Devil's trap. I remember that the Devil goes about like a roaring lion seeking whom he may devour.

This precious teaching of Jesus comes from his heart. "Watch and pray."

"Take time to be holy, let Him be thy guide:
And run not before Him, whatever betide;
In joy or in sorrow still follow thy Lord,
And looking to Jesus, still trust in his word."

(W. D. Longstaff)

Even as he rises from prayer there are flickering lights, the noise of a mob, and into the garden come marching the henchmen of Caiaphas. Jesus returns to his sleeping disciples once more.

"Rise, Let us go! Here comes my betrayer!" While he was still speaking a crowd came up, and the man who was called Judas, one of the Twelve, was leading them. He approached Jesus to kiss

Finding the Real Jesus

him, but Jesus asked him, "Judas, are you betraying the Son of Man with a kiss?"

William Barclay points out that when Judas says, *"The one I kiss is the man,"* the term he uses is "philein," *(Mark 14.44),* which is the normal word for the kiss of greeting. But in the following verse, when Judas actually kisses Jesus, the term used for kiss is "kataphilein," which was the kiss with which lovers greeted each other. Barclay says, "I find that the grimmest and most awful thing in the gospel story."

Yet I have seen it happen. Men and women, perhaps with arms raised high in worship and adoration, singing, "Jesus I adore you, lay my life before you." Yet on Monday with their tongue or in their actions they declare, "I never knew him."

Notice there is no attempt to run, no attempt to hide or escape.

"Rise, let us go. Here is my betrayer."

Jesus is back in control. As he set his face to go to Jerusalem, now he has set his face to go through with the cross.

Simon Peter, bless him, leaps forward, draws his sword, ready to defend Jesus and lashes out at Malchus, the High Priest's personal servant, cutting off his ear. Peter had not understood Jesus' way, but I admire his bravery. Even then Jesus refutes the way of power, the way of the sword.

Jesus answered, "No more of this!" and he touched the man's ear and healed him. (Luke 22.51)

"Am I leading a rebellion," said Jesus, "that you have come out with swords and clubs to capture me? Every day I was with you, teaching in the temple courts, and you did not arrest me. But the Scriptures must be fulfilled." Then everyone deserted him and fled.

For Jesus, the way is to accept the path to the cross. You see, the way of the cross is God's way. It still is, and God looks today for those who will follow; for those who will offer themselves in sacrifice, even walking the way of the cross, that they might be true disciples, that they might help build the kingdom of God.

Are you a cross bearer? It is easy to walk the road from Bethany when all is praise and hosanna and glory. But when the same road leads later to Gethsemane, to Golgotha and the Cross –

that takes commitment – that takes real men and women of God. And today Jesus calls you to follow him.

With his hands bound, Jesus is led up from the garden of Gethsemane, through the gate by the fortress into the city and so along several streets to the house of Caiaphas. The last part of this walk is so steep that stone steps were set into the narrow street leading to the house. Though the house is long gone and a memorial church is where it once stood, the steps are still there today and one cannot walk up them without that special feeling of reverence, for Jesus walked on these same well-worn stones.

Imagine a walled courtyard, a fire in the middle; soldiers warming themselves; people bustling about seeing what is going on. It's festival time. There are servant girls serving drinks. In the big room opening on the courtyard a kangaroo court has been convened.

Those who had arrested Jesus took him to Caiaphas, the high priest, where the teachers of the law and the elders had assembled. But Peter followed him at a distance, right up to the courtyard of the high priest. He entered and sat down with the guards to see the outcome.

Peter gets a bad press, and yet here he is, the only one, possibly with John, close to Jesus now. He wanted to know exactly where they were taking his Lord. I imagine Peter thinking, "I promised him, though all the others fall away, I will not." So Peter follows this rabble band, all the way to Caiaphas' house, and into the courtyard where a fire burns in a brazier. Because of the feast there are servant girls taking round mulled wine and small portions of food.

Jesus is standing, his wrists tied, in the doorway. The court, which shouldn't have assembled at this time of night, would have been inside the main room whose doors opened onto the courtyard.

The chief priests and the whole Sanhedrin were looking for false evidence against Jesus so that they could put him to death. But they did not find any, though many false witnesses came forward.

Various witnesses come forward, put up by the priests to make accusations against Jesus. At least three witnesses must agree if they are to sentence Jesus to death, but the witnesses cannot agree.

Legend says that a leper came forward and told how he was cleansed; a blind man testified that his sight was restored, and a paralytic said he now could walk. We cannot know if that is in any way authentic, but we know there was no agreement. So they brought in those who had been paid to give false witness.

Finally two came forward and declared, "This fellow said, "I am able to destroy the temple of God and rebuild it in three days.

To all this Jesus is silent. He will not answer the accusations. For him to die, his own words must condemn him. The court is reaching stalemate; time is ticking by. The atmosphere is tense and those outside are listening intently.

Then the high priest stood up and said to Jesus, "Are you not going to answer? What is this testimony that these men are bringing against you?" But Jesus remained silent.

In exasperation Caiaphas demands, *"I charge you under oath by the living God, tell us if you are the Christ, the Son of God."*

This time; the right time, Jesus speaks:

"Yes, it is as you say" Jesus replied. "In the future you will see the Son of Man sitting at the right hand of the Mighty One and coming on the clouds of heaven."

Caiaphas needed nothing else. Beside himself with anger he tore his clothes:

"He has spoken blasphemy! Why do we need any more witnesses? Look, now you have heard the blasphemy, what do you think?" "He is worthy of death," they answered.

It was over. These worthy dignitaries, priests and teachers now spat in the face of Jesus and struck him. Mark tells us that having blindfolded him, some struck him with their fists and said "Prophesy!" They allowed the guards to take Jesus and beat him. This would have taken place in the prison area below Caiaphas' house. You can still see the posts to which men were tied for flogging and the windowless dungeon below where Jesus would have been thrown for any rest he had that night.

Peter, of course, stood and watched all this. Now his time of trial had come. One of the servant girls of the high priest came by. When she saw Peter warming himself at the brazier she looked closely at him:

From Gethsemane to Caiaphas' House – Matthew 26.57-75

"You also were with the Galilean Jesus," she said. But he denied it. "I don't know or understand what you're talking about," he said, and went out into the entryway.

He must have been trying to escape the eyes of this prying girl. His heart was breaking for his Master. He did not want to be probed, but he couldn't leave.

When the servant girl saw him there, she said again to those standing around, "This fellow is one of them." Again he denied it.

We imagine Peter getting hot under the collar, but for all his discomfort, he doesn't leave his Lord.

After a while those standing near said to Peter:

"Surely you are one of them, for you are a Galilean."

Now Peter falls apart.

He began to call down curses on himself, and he swore to them, "I don't know this man you're talking about." Immediately the rooster crowed the second time. Then Peter remembered the word Jesus had spoken to him, "Before the rooster crows twice you will disown me three times." And he broke down and wept. (Mark 15.71-72)

Luke tells us:

The Lord turned and looked straight at Peter. Then Peter remembered.

Can you imagine how he felt? What was in the look? Was it: "I told you so – you've let me down again – Peter you are useless!" No, I think it was more like, "Peter despite all that, I love you, I love you, I love you."

Do you dare to look into the eyes of Jesus today?

I remember preaching about this incident in one of the Methodist chapels near my school in Oxfordshire. An old saint in the congregation said, "Yes, I know exactly how Peter felt, because I have denied him too. Satan always tries to remind me but I tell him that in the eyes of Jesus, both Peter and I saw forgiveness. So I go on to do my very best."

Scottish evangelist Brownlow North told of a similar experience. In his youth he had lived a wild life but had then turned to God. This particular Sunday he was due to preach in Aberdeen. Someone who knew of Brownlow North's life before he became a

Christian wrote to him and said that if he dared to preach, then he would stand up and tell the congregation all that Brownlow North had done. Brownlow North took the letter with him. He read it to the congregation and told them it was perfectly true. Then he recounted how Jesus had forgiven him and enabled him to overcome the past.

I believe that is true of every one of us here. We hurt him, we let him down, and we deny knowing him. Yet he still loves and forgives us. We must never stop telling others that he loves and will forgive them too.

When the Cock Crowed

When the cock crowed the earth split,
whirled, gushed in black;
thrust him spinning toward the pit;
though the fire still glowed
and no one laid hands on him.

The heat was too much
and, suddenly old,
with the soldiers' spears, the moon-bright
cackle of branches; voices heard; he shook
in his room of guilt.

Hidden in dark, his shame he saw
in the eyes that turned;
in the chains He bore; the Master's face
fallen in gloom; His love
in the depth of hell, undeserved;
when the earth split,
as the cock crowed.

AN ACT OF CONFESSION

Leader: Lord, forgive the sleep of the disciples.

All: And forgive me when I am too tired to pray.

Leader: Lord, forgive the change from welcoming you to attacking you.

All: Forgive me when I let Jesus down.

Leader: Lord, forgive the rage of the crowd.

All: And forgive me when I can't control my anger.

Leader: Lord, forgive the violence of the man with the sword.

All: And forgive me when I do things my way.

Leader: Lord, forgive the cowardice of those who deserted Jesus.

All: And forgive me when I miss the chance to stand up for you.

Leader: Thank you that you chose the cross so that we could be forgiven.

All: Have mercy on us Lord. Amen

Romsey Baptist Church October 24th 1994
Ferndown United Church March 23rd 1997

29. From the Gabbatha to Golgotha
Matthew 27.11-31, Mark 15.1-22,
Luke 23.1-23, John 19.1-22

The Gabbatha was the Hebrew name for the stone pavement immediately outside Pilate's palace. It was the place where he sentenced Jesus to be crucified. Golgotha means "the place of the skull." The hollow in an outcrop of limestone rocks just outside the city walls, about a mile from Pilate's palace, was reminiscent of a huge skull. Here Jesus was one of three men crucified.

It is easy to get a person's identity wrong. I liked the illustration concerning a lady who was walking down Regent Street in London when she saw two men of about her son's age walking towards her. She was sure she recognised one of them but couldn't think of his name. Assuming he must be one of her son's friends she gave a broad smile and they grinned back. As they passed she said, in her best cheery voice, "Sorry can't stop, got to rush to get the shopping done." About one hundred yards down the road it dawned on her. The man she recognised was Prince Charles, out with a bodyguard. She felt acutely embarrassed to have confused the next king with one of her son's friends. How could she have got it wrong?

When Bill Shankly was manager of Liverpool Football Club he once said, "Football isn't a matter of life and death, it's much more important than that."

Friends, failing to recognise Jesus as King, isn't a matter of life and death. Your decision will have eternal consequences. It is life – eternal life, or it is death – eternal death.

The Jews led Jesus from Caiaphas to the palace of the Roman governor. By now it was early morning, and to avoid ceremonial uncleanness, the Jews did not enter the palace; they wanted to be able to eat the Passover.

Notice how even now they put their needs first. However Pilate, most probably curious to meet this man of whom he must have heard so many tales, came out to question them:

"What charges are you bringing against this man?"

We need to remember that the Jewish day began at sunset, so this awful day had begun with Jesus sharing the Last Supper with his disciples. It was the day of Preparation for the Passover, the day that the sacrificial lambs would be killed in the temple. It was pressing for the religious community to get this sordid matter of Jesus dealt with a quickly as possible. In the few hours between dawn and the third hour, which to us is nine o'clock in the morning, Jesus is taken to Pilate, to Herod, and back to Pilate, and sentenced to die.

They reply to Pilate:

"If he were not a criminal, we would not have handed him over to you." Pilate said, "Take him yourselves and judge him by your own law." "But we have no right to execute anyone," the Jews objected.

This was not really true, but John explains:

This happened so that the words Jesus had spoken indicating the kind of death he was going to die would be fulfilled.

God is in control. His Son is not to be stoned, but is to give his life on a cross.

Doubtless a lot more was said than is recorded. Doubtless Pilate had heard all about the events surrounding the triumphal entry. Eventually the accusation is made,

"This Jesus is claiming to be king."

Luke's account tells us:

"We have found this man subverting our nation. He opposes payment of taxes to Caesar and claims to be Christ, a king. He stirs up the people all over Judea by his teaching. He started in Galilee and has come all the way here.

Jesus is represented as a troublesome, vociferous agitator. Yet in front of Pilate he shows himself to be serene and dignified. He is silent concerning all these accusations. So Pilate goes back inside the palace, summons Jesus and asks him the big question,

"Are you the king of the Jews?"

How could Jesus answer this question in a way that Pilate would understand? Suppose he told Pilate about the manifesto of his kingdom:

"Blessed are the poor in spirit, for theirs is the kingdom of heaven. Blessed are those who mourn, the meek, those who hunger and thirst for righteousness, for they will be filled. Blessed are the merciful, the pure in heart, the peacemakers. Blessed are those who are persecuted because of righteousness, for theirs is the kingdom of heaven." (Matthew 5.3-10)

Suppose he told Pilate about the prayer for the kingdom:

"This is how you should pray; Our Father in heaven, hallowed be your name."

Suppose he told Pilate about that passage he had read in the synagogue:

"The Spirit of the Lord is on me, because he has anointed me to preach good news to the poor. He has sent me to proclaim freedom for the prisoners and recovery of sight for the blind, to release the oppressed, to proclaim the year of God's favour." (Luke 4.18-19)

Suppose he told Pilate about washing his disciples' feet? What would Pilate make of it all? How could he, who knew so little of Jesus, possibly understand? So Jesus tells Pilate:

"My kingdom is not of this world. If it were, my servants would fight to prevent my arrest by the Jews. But now my kingdom is from another place." (John 18.36)

How will Pilate respond? His response in fact shows some understanding.

"You are a king, then!" said Pilate.

219

Pilate has realised – Jesus is truth. Jesus is a king. Jesus should at least be the spiritual king of the Jews.

Jesus answered, "You are right in saying I am a king. In fact, for this reason I was born, and for this I came into the world, to testify to the truth. Everyone on the side of truth listens to me."

Throughout this series I have continually made the point that Jesus is in charge. He gives his life voluntarily. Now he is teaching Pilate.

It is hard to seriously consider Jesus; his birth; his life; his teaching; his cross; and come to any conclusion other than that Jesus is a king, even if his kingdom is one we have not experienced, even if his kingdom seems a Utopia beyond our dreams.

But it is even harder to spend time in the presence of Jesus and not have your life-style, your priorities, your allegiance, your very purpose in living challenged to the very core, for Jesus promises a revolution, a radical way, so far removed from the tawdry life that is now. He promises a way of hope, a way of love, a way of purpose, a way of peace. Is our response to Jesus a matter of life and death? No! Jesus is far more important than that!

Pilate's response to Jesus is quite remarkable. Why should Jesus matter to him? Here is another insurrectionist, another megalomaniac, someone else to encourage the likes of Barabbas and all his Zealot friends. Why not please the Jews and do away with him?

But Pilate determines to release Jesus. First he invokes the old Passover custom – a single amnesty for the release of just one prisoner as a token to the Jews. They would always ask for a Zealot, someone fervently opposed to Rome, but this time Pilate would release their king.

Now it was the custom at the Feast to release a prisoner whom the people requested. A man called Barabbas was in prison with the insurrectionists who had committed murder in the uprising. The crowd came up and asked Pilate to do for them what he usually did. "Do you want me to release to you the king of the Jews? asked Pilate, knowing it was out of envy that the chief priests had handed Jesus over to him. But the chief priests stirred up the crowd to have Pilate release Barabbas instead.

From the Gabbatha to Golgotha – Matthew 27.11-31

Barabbas is described by Matthew as "a notorious prisoner." John calls him a robber. Mark says he was an insurrectionist who had committed murder in the uprising. Nevertheless he was probably a popular character with the Jewish people. It seems highly probable that he was a member of a Zealot group known as the Sicarii. They carried daggers under their cloaks; would lay ambushes and stab their victims to death. Rather like some of the fanatical terrorist groups today, they pledged their lives to free Palestine from Roman control. They saw murder and terrorism as a means of achieving their goals.

It is quite possible that many of the crowd outside Pilate's palace early that morning had come because they knew of the Passover custom to release one prisoner, and had come to shout for the release of Barabbas. If this is the case, they are a gift to the temple authorities.

"What shall I do then; with the one you call the King of the Jews?" Pilate asked them.

There is an angry reaction to Pilate's assumption that they see Jesus as a king.

"Crucify him!" they shouted. "Why? What crime has he committed?" asked Pilate. But they shouted the louder, "Crucify him!"

How could the crowd have changed so much since they cheered him into the city on Palm Sunday? Some go for the easy solution that they are not the same crowd; that those who cheered Jesus into Jerusalem were all Galilean pilgrims on their way up to the feast, and the crowd calling for his death were the inhabitants of Jerusalem, but I cannot believe this theory. Whilst I would concede some may have been different people, the Pharisees did not see this division after the triumphal entry. Their appraisal of the situation was:

"See, this is getting us nowhere. Look how the whole world has gone after him!"

I want to suggest three reasons for the crowd changing sides. Firstly the pressure brought to bear by the chief priests. Secondly the fact that Jesus did not turn out to be the sort of Messiah they wanted. Thirdly was their ignorance of the scripture.

Each of these should be a warning to us. We like to be one of the crowd – we don't like to stand out and to be different. We too are subject to the pressures to conform to the world and these pressures may turn us away from Jesus.

We too have our picture of the Messiah we would like Jesus to be. We are particularly reluctant to follow a path of suffering and find humble service difficult. The Jews wanted a glamorous Messiah. We must take care that we follow Christ – not our idea of what we feel he ought to be.

If they had known their scriptures the people should have recognised in Jesus the Suffering Servant of Isaiah. There were dozens of prophecies associating the Messiah with peace, pardon, healing, suffering on behalf of others and being an offering for sin. But as they cried, "Crucify!" the crowd chose to forget these prophecies.

The next phrase tells us about Pilate.

Wanting to satisfy the crowd, Pilate released Barabbas to them. He had Jesus flogged.

Pilate wants to be popular. He wants to please the crowd. Presumably he thought that flogging and public humiliation might satisfy the Jews. Some of the whips used in Roman floggings had pieces of metal or stone embedded in the leather thongs, so that the victim's back was lacerated. It was quite common for a prisoner to die from flogging even though it was not intended as a method of execution. The film makers, and there have been many films of the crucifixion, make much of the flogging. John does not go into the macabre details. He simply states the fact, wanting his readers to know that the scriptures are being fulfilled.

But he was wounded for our transgressions; he was bruised for our iniquities: the chastisement of our peace was upon him; and with his stripes we are healed. (Isaiah 53.5 KJV)

Pilate allows his soldiers to mock Jesus.

The soldiers twisted together a crown of thorns and put it on his head. They clothed him in a purple robe and went up to him again and again, saying, "Hail, king of the Jews!" And they struck him in the face.

From the Gabbatha to Golgotha – Matthew 27.11-31

I am not sure why, but the crown of thorns always seems to me to be one of the cruellest actions of the whole crucifixion story. But again John shows us that the prophecies are being fulfilled:

"I offered my back to those who beat me, my cheeks to those who pulled out my beard; I did not hide my face from mocking and spitting." (Isaiah 50.6)

Does it hurt you to think that they treated Jesus like that? How could they mock him, spit on him – Jesus the Rose of Sharon, the altogether lovely one? This morning we saw a crown of thorns. Can you imagine the situation – a whole posse of soldiers taking it in turns to debase our Lord – hitting him with the staff – driving the thorns afresh into his lacerated brow – pretending to bow down and worship – only rising to spit in his face? And no one intervened. No one said, "Enough is enough!" No one stood up on behalf of Jesus.

They still do it today: when they use his name as a curse; when he is mocked on the television; when an angry mother screams, "Christ Almighty!" at her children. And so often still, no one intervenes. No one raises their voice in protest and says, "Enough is enough – this is the precious Son of God!"

So Pilate takes Jesus out onto the pavement of Gabbatha and makes his second attempt to release him.

Once more Pilate came out and said to the Jews, "Look, I am bringing him out to you to let you know that I find no basis for a charge against him. Here is the man!"

"Ecce homo" – behold the man. The saying is now famous. Pilate clearly hoped that the sight of this beaten, bloody person would evoke pity from among the crowd. They would surely realise that there was no threat from this poor fellow. The words suggest that Pilate is saying, "How can you possibly believe this pitiful man's claim to be king?"

But the crowd are not so easily placated. Whipped up by the temple agitators, those who a week ago cried, "Hosanna," now shout "Crucify!"

But Pilate answered, "You take him and crucify him. As for me, I find no basis for a charge against him."

The Jews cannot crucify because it is illegal for them to do so and Pilate knows this. So is this a measure of desperation on the part of Pilate? He has before him an innocent man. He should have the courage to release him, but it is Passover. An uprising in Jerusalem now would be politically disastrous for him. Pilate had been reported to Rome on previous occasions. He had allowed the legions to parade through the temple courts carrying their eagle banners declaring Caesar to be God. This had brought him a reprimand. He had plundered the temple coffers to fund the building of an aqueduct, much needed to improve the water supply to Jerusalem, but had had to climb down and return the money. And now he thought he had sufficiently humiliated Jesus for the crowd to consent to his release; but still the chant of "Crucify," rings in his ears. Then things get worse.

The Jews insisted, "We have a law, and according to that law he must die, because he claimed to be the Son of God." When Pilate heard this, he was even more afraid.

Why does this cry make Pilate so afraid? In Roman mythology gods sometimes inhabited human bodies, so Pilate may well have thought for a moment, "Perhaps this Jesus is a god." And then there was the incident which only Matthew records. Pilate's wife had suffered a troublesome dream and had sent word to Pilate:

"Don't have anything to do with that innocent man, for I have suffered a great deal today in a dream because of him."

So he went back inside the palace, to think and to speak to Jesus once more.

"Where do you come from?" he asked Jesus, but Jesus gave no answer. "Do you refuse to speak to me?" Pilate said. "Don't you realise I have the power either to free you or to crucify you?" Jesus answered, "You would have no power over me, if it were not given to you from above. Therefore the one who handed me over to you is guilty of a greater sin."

John, I suspect, sees in Jesus' silence the fulfilment of Isaiah's prophecy:

He was oppressed and afflicted, yet he did not open his mouth. (Isaiah 53.7)

Jesus is not in the least intimidated by Pilate's claim to authority and power. Rather, Jesus seizes the initiative, and maybe even seeks to bring a measure of comfort to Pilate. Jesus knew that he was about to die. Jesus knew that it was the Father's will he should suffer. Jesus, I believe, realises that Pilate is an unfortunate pawn in all that is going on. "Pilate, it is not really you who has authority – it is my Father in heaven above. If he did not will it, you would not be in this position, and you certainly would not have the authority to pass sentence."

Do I read too much into the situation? I hope not. "Pilate, what you are about to do now, history will see as a terrible thing; but far, far worse, is the sin of the high priest who has handed me over to you, who has plotted this thing."

From then on Pilate tried to set Jesus free, but the Jews kept shouting, "If you let this man go, you are no friend of Caesar. Anyone who claims to be a king opposes Caesar."

Pilate gets a terribly bad press. He is described as weak, unjust, more concerned about his position than anything else. What would I have done in Pilate's shoes? What would you have done in his position? It is nice to think we would have acted differently, but I wonder if we would. I find it hard to condemn Pilate. I understand all the arguments about Pilate being responsible for his choices, but the outcome was what God intended. It was God who had planned in order that my sins, that your sins, might be forgiven. If Pilate is to be blamed, I must surely share in his blame, because it was for my sins that Jesus stood there accused.

Pilate makes one last attempt to set Jesus free:

When Pilate heard this, he brought Jesus out and sat down on the judge's seat at a place known as the Stone Pavement (which in Aramaic is Gabbatha). It was the day of preparation of Passover week, about the sixth hour. "Here is your king." Pilate said to the Jews. But they shouted, "Take him away! Take him away! Crucify him!" "Shall I crucify your king?" Pilate asked. "We have no king but Caesar," the chief priests answered. Finally Pilate handed him over to them to be crucified. So the soldiers took charge of Jesus.

Who would ever have dreamt that they would hear the Jews declare – "We have no king but Caesar!" They longed for a military leader who would rise up and free them from Caesar's grip, but when it came to choosing between Jesus and Caesar, they chose Caesar!

Just as countless thousands down through the ages have chosen the way of the world rather than the way of God.

This in a sense was the Jews' trump card. Pilate had been reported to Caesar before. To be reported again for having released a man who claimed to be king would have been certain to prompt his recall to Rome to face a court martial which was virtually certain to cost him his life. Pilate is left with no option, and he hands Jesus over to be crucified.

Yet there is one thought Pilate holds on to; his conviction that Jesus is king. When he writes the placard that will be displayed by the leading soldier in the execution party – the placard that will be nailed to the cross as the justification for the death, Pilate writes in Hebrew, Latin and in Greek – JESUS OF NAZARETH, THE KING OF THE JEWS.

There were some protests from the chief priests to Pilate when they read it.

"Do not write 'The King of the Jews.' But that this man claimed to be king of the Jews," they said. Pilate answered, *"What I have written, I have written."*

The outcome was inevitable, for it was God's way – the way of the cross. Yet our hearts are tinged with sadness for Pilate. What might have been, if he had been able to humble himself and stand for what was right? What might have been if he had let Jesus rule in his heart and life?

The world is full of "what might have been." Thousands have come to the point of realising that Jesus is King, yet have failed to surrender their lives to his kingship. There are those here for whom that is precisely true. You know he is truth, you know he is King, yet you have not humbled yourself. You have not let self off the throne and invited Jesus to be Saviour and Lord. Pilate had no other chance. Within a very short period he was recalled by Rome. There was no fame; only the infamy of being the one who sentenced Jesus to die.

What will be the story of your life? No! It is more important than that – what is the story of your future? Will it be eternity in heaven with the King – or eternity in Hell with the Prince of this world and all his angels?

Romsey Baptist Church October 23rd 1994
Ferndown United Church Good Friday April 18th 2003

30. The Road to the Cross
Mark 15.21-41, Luke 23.20-26

Roman government was stable, its justice tough but fair. In this highly civilised era Jewish religion was held in esteem throughout the known world. It recognised only one God. It had a code of divinely given law. In the eyes of most it stood for high morality and high ethical principals. Yet the Roman procurator, Pontius Pilate, allowed the execution of an innocent man. The priests, who should have had the closest relationship with God, used all manner of lies and political pressure to get their own way; to put to death Jesus, God's only Son, their Messiah.

David Gooding, commenting on our text, writes, "If these things happen, what kind of behaviour will prevail in a society that has lost all respect for justice, law, morality, religion and God? It may take a long while to turn a green tree into a dried-up trunk, a paradise into a desert; but bleed the moral life-sap of a nation, and the result, however long-delayed, is inevitable."

I am concerned that the tree that is Great Britain today, the church that is Romsey Baptist today, should be prevented from becoming dry. Only Christians can prevent spiritual and moral collapse in our nation. As part of that prevention we will look at how the cross affected Simon of Cyrene.

Finding the Real Jesus

A certain man from Cyrene, Simon, the father of Alexander and Rufus, was passing by on his way in from the country, and they forced him to carry the cross.

Try to imagine Simon. He comes from Cyrene, which is Tripoli today, on the Mediterranean coast of Libya. He may well be black. He has come fifteen hundred miles to Jerusalem to celebrate the Passover. It's quite probably "a once in a lifetime" pilgrimage, and Luke tells us that on this particular day he is on his way into the city from the country. That is quite normal. So many pilgrims went up to Jerusalem for the Passover that only the wealthy could afford to stay in the city. Many found lodgings in the villages around.

Just across from the temple mount is Pilate's house, and in front of it the tessellated Gabbatha, or Judgment Hall. A trial has just been concluded and the prisoner has been sentenced to death. What a sorry sight he is! Clearly he has been beaten. His bleeding back reveals the lashes of the lead weighted scourge. On his head is a crown of thorns. Loosely round his shoulders is a purple robe. Great crowds surround him and they are mocking him.

Simon can see the prisoner is on his way to die. He is guarded by five soldiers. Four of them form a square, one on each corner, and in the middle is the prisoner who carries a rough wooden cross that looks too heavy for him to bear. In front the fifth soldier carries a placard written in the handwriting of the presiding judge, Pontius Pilate. It details the crime. In this case it states, "JESUS OF NAZARETH, THE KING OF THE JEWS." When they get to the place of execution it will be nailed at the head of the cross to denote that justice is being done.

It hardly registers with Simon that the prisoner will never make it all the way along the Via Dolorosa to Calvary, when on his shoulder he feels the cold steel of the flat face of a Roman spear. A chill feeling runs down his spine. Simon knows he has been pressed into the service of the Roman Government. He is dismayed to find that his role will be to carry a criminal's cross.

We will never know what communication, if any, took place between Jesus and Simon, but there is enough in the scriptures to suggest that as a result of carrying the Lord's cross, Simon was wonderfully changed. What is remarkable in this passage is that

Mark names the sons of Simon – Alexander and Rufus. Mark wouldn't have done that out of some peculiar historical interest – he will have done it because the sons are, at the time when Mark wrote his gospel, well known in the community – they are Christians. Look at what Paul wrote in his letter to Christians in Rome:

"Greet Rufus, chosen in the Lord, and his mother, who has been a mother to me too." (Romans 16.13)

"Chosen" actually means "eminent" so Simon's son is an outstanding Christian. Simon's wife is such a wonderful Christian that Paul says she has been like a mother to him as well.

There are other verses too which cause one to wonder about Simon's witness on his return home to Cyrene –

Some of them, however, men from Cyprus and Cyrene, went to Antioch and began to speak to Greeks also, telling them the good news about the Lord Jesus. (Acts 11.20)

In the church at Antioch there were prophets and teachers; Barnabus, Simeon called Niger, Lucius of Cyrene, Manaen (who had been brought up with Herod the tetrarch) and Saul. (Acts 13.1)

All this was because he carried the cross of Jesus. Simon, of course, had no option but to carry the cross. It wasn't wise to argue with a Roman spear. How easy it would have been for him to be angry and bitter! He'd spent his money on the pilgrimage of a lifetime, and had to end up carrying a criminal's cross. Yet it seems that he was wonderfully converted.

His story speaks oceans to me. You see, I remember Jesus' call to me:

Then he said to them all: "If anyone would come after me, he must deny himself and take up his cross daily and follow me." (Luke 9.23):

And anyone who does not carry his cross and follow me cannot be my disciple. (Luke 14.27)

Jesus doesn't force me to carry a cross. I can refuse and take what seems to be the easy route; but he says that the basis of truly following is "cross bearing". If I will not take up a cross I cannot be his disciple.

That worries me, for I see so few examples of Christians bearing crosses. They want to take, but not to give. They want the triumph, but not the pain of the gospel. They want the rewards, but not the responsibility. They want things their way, and not the way of Jesus. Friend, if I am describing you, I implore you, look to Simon! See the wonderful results of identifying with Jesus and bearing a cross for him.

They brought Jesus to the place called Golgotha (which means The Place of the Skull). Then they offered him wine mixed with myrrh, but he did not take it.

The wine mixed with myrrh was intended to numb something of the agony of crucifixion. It would not have been offered by the soldiers, but by some of the bystanders, possibly the women who had followed Jesus. It was a practice allowed by the Roman authorities and we believe there was a group of women in Jerusalem who attended crucifixions to offer this kindness.

But Jesus refuses the cup of mercy. It might have eased his pain, but it would also have addled his mind. It might also lead to someone suggesting that he could not bear all the punishment that was being inflicted. So for our sakes, Jesus submits himself to crucifixion.

And they crucified him. Dividing up his clothes, they cast lots to see what each would get. It was the third hour when they crucified him. (This happened between six and nine in the morning.)

The written notice of the charge against him read: THE KING OF THE JEWS. They crucified two robbers with him, one on his right and one on his left. Those who passed by hurled insults at him, shaking their heads and saying, "So! You who are going to destroy the temple and build it in three days, come down from the cross and save yourself!"

This last verse shows the impact Jesus had made in Jerusalem, for these are passers-by. They are not part of the crowd who have been following events all morning, but those whose daily journey takes them past Calvary. They hurl insults.

In the same way the chief priests and the teachers of the law mocked him among themselves. "He saved others," they said, "but he can't save himself! Let this Christ, this King of Israel, come down now from the cross, that we may see and believe."

The Road to the Cross – Mark 15.21-41

They had hounded him by day and by night, had schemed and agitated the crowd. Now, when Jesus was cruelly nailed to the cross, they mocked him. "Now if you want us to believe, come down from the cross, King of Israel." And even worse:

Those crucified with him also heaped insults on him.

They rightly deserved to die and may both have been insurrectionists. Wonderfully one of the dying thieves came to repentance, yet their initial reaction was to join with those who taunted Jesus.

At the sixth hour darkness came over the whole land until the ninth hour.

What of the darkness from noon until 3 o'clock? How did it come about? It was not an eclipse, because Passover always took place at full moon. It was not a thunderstorm, for thunderstorms are localised and last only for a short time, and do not cover the whole land. There is a fascinating comment recorded concerning Diogenes, the Egyptian philosopher of barrel fame. He recorded the darkness away in Egypt and wrote, "Either the deity himself suffers at this moment, or he sympathises with one who does." The darkness was the hand of God. God the Creator caused the sun to refuse to shine. What fear must have gripped the land for full three hours, broken eventually by the haunting call of Christ from the cross:

And at the ninth hour Jesus cried out in a loud voice, "Eloi, Eloi, lama sabachthani?" – which means, "My God, my God, why have you forsaken me?"

When some of those standing near heard this, they said, "Listen, he's calling Elijah." One man ran, filled a sponge with wine vinegar, put it on a stick, and offered it to Jesus to drink. "Now leave him alone. Let's see if Elijah comes to take him down," he said.

With a loud cry, Jesus breathed his last. The curtain of the temple was torn in two from top to bottom.

And when the centurion, who stood there in front of Jesus, heard his cry and saw how he died, he said, "Surely this man was the Son of God!"

Let us allow St Peter the last word this evening:

"When they hurled their insults at him, he did not retaliate; when he suffered he made no threats. Instead, he entrusted himself to him who judges justly.

He himself bore our sins in his body on the tree, so that we might die to sins and live for righteousness; by his wounds you have been healed." (1 Peter 2.23-24)

PART 8

PEOPLE

WHO WERE

AT THE CROSS

The Centurion's Tale

I took charge of the blasphemer from Pilate's court;
a noble man who claimed to be a king.
I stripped and lashed him with the lead-tongued
whip;
ribboned his flesh till reddish blood ran black;
yet he submitted like a lamb, without a word.

We decked him out in purple robe and staff.
One wove a crown of thorns and crushed it on his
brow.
We spat on him and simpered, *Hail King Jesus!*
Yet still be would not curse like any man.

I nailed his hands and feet upon the cross.
We raised it up; stood back to watch him die.
He hung and twisted in the usual way,
but when he spoke his words shot me right through,
Father, forgive them, for they don't know what they do!

His eyes held mine, and I was struck with pain.
Could any man forgive what I had done?
The world grew dark, and yet he saw me still —
at last he cried, *It's finished!* And he died.
Then I knew I had killed the Son of God!

These cameos of people at the cross were given at Romsey Baptist Church October 23rd 1994 and at Ferndown on Good Friday 2000

31. People who were at the Cross

1. Daughters of Jerusalem – Luke 23.26-30

A large number of people followed him, including women who mourned and wailed for him.

The identity of the women is far from certain. They are probably not the faithful band of women who had ministered so much to Jesus through his life. They may be genuine followers who were utterly distraught at Jesus being sentenced to die, for whilst Jesus had often told his disciples he would be killed, they failed to believe it would really happen. Perhaps what is most likely is that these were the traditional wailing women who attended when there was a death. We still see this wailing at Middle Eastern funerals.

Remember when Jairus' daughter had died:

When they came to the home of the synagogue ruler, Jesus saw a commotion, with people crying and wailing loudly. (Mark 5.38)

I suspect that the wailing was not from the heart, but was an outward show, supposedly the right thing to do. Jesus turns to the women and pronounces a solemn warning:

"Daughters of Jerusalem, do not weep for me; weep for yourselves and for your children. For a time will come when you will

*say, 'Blessed are the barren women, the wombs that never bore and
the breasts that never nursed.'"*

In Judea there was no greater tragedy than to be childless. It
was sufficient grounds for a husband to divorce his wife. Jesus is
saying that such a terrible punishment will come upon Jerusalem,
that it would be better not to have children who would suffer through
the torment.

According to Luke, this is the seventh time that Jesus has
warned of a dreadful punishment that will involve the destruction of
Jerusalem. Two previous occasions were:

1. *The days will come upon you when your enemies will
build an embankment against you and encircle you and hew you in
on every side. They will dash you to the ground, you and the children
within your walls. They will not leave one stone on another, because
you did not recognise the time of God's coming to you. (Luke 19.43-
44)*

2. *When you see Jerusalem being surrounded by armies, you
will know that its desolation is near. Then let those who are in Judea
flee to the mountains, let those in the city get out, and let those in the
country not enter the city. For this is the time of punishment in
fulfilment of all that has been written. How dreadful it will be in
those days for pregnant women and nursing mothers! There will be
great distress in the land and wrath against this people. They will
fall by the sword and will be taken as prisoners to all the nations.
Jerusalem will be trampled on by the Gentiles until the times of the
Gentiles are fulfilled. (Luke 21.20-24)*

History tells us of the awful destruction which befell
Jerusalem in AD 70, the remnant fleeing to Masada and their final
destruction. Those who have made a study of the fall of Jerusalem
and the subsequent massacre say that the judgment was terrible
indeed. This punishment was foretold by Jesus to those who had the
opportunity to bow the knee in allegiance to the Messiah, but who
sought, actively or by their sheer indifference, to have him destroyed.

Jesus tells of judgment that is coming to each and every one
of us. It will either be judgment to eternal life for those who put their
trust in him, or a judgment to hell and damnation for those who tell

him to go away in this life: these people will be sent to the eternal company of the devil and his angels in hell in the life to come.

Rightly Jesus says, "Do not weep for me; weep for yourselves." How urgent it is that we come to the place of repentance.

Let me share with you the heart of Jesus:

"I tell you that in the same way there will be more rejoicing in heaven over one sinner who repents than over ninety-nine righteous person who do not need to repent. (Luke 15.7)

And in the beloved passage in John:

"For God so loved the world that he gave his one and only Son, that whoever believes in him shall not perish but have eternal life. For God did not send his Son into the world to condemn the world, but to save the world through him. "(John 3.16-17)

2. The Executing Soldiers – Luke 23.32-43

Can you imagine being at a crucifixion? The cross is laid on the ground. The crowd around are baying, hissing, shouting abuse. The victim is roughly pushed down. Thousands have been crucified by the Roman legions, mostly cursing and swearing, some protesting their innocence, many frantically struggling to get away – but failing at the hands of the soldiers. Often they are first roughly tied to the cross to restrict their struggling, and then the great cut nails are hammered through their wrists; the feet are crossed over and a third metal spike is nailed through to fasten them to the cross.

Then the cross is raised to the vertical and dropped into its socket, sending agony through every nerve in the body. Worse still is the prospect of hanging, bleeding, fighting for breath; slowly being dehydrated by the scorching sun, and dying principally from exposure.

But the crucifixion of Jesus is different. Just think of the impact – the man you are crucifying is praying for you!

Jesus said, "Father, forgive them, for they do not know what they are doing."

That must be just about the ultimate – to seek forgiveness for the men who crucify you! It became the mark of the Christians – a people who forgive. The first Christian to die for his faith in Jesus was Stephen. He died with this prayer as he was stoned to death:

Then he fell on his knees and cried out, "Lord, do not hold this sin against them." When he had said this, he fell asleep. (Acts 7.60)

Paul set it out as the standard for Christians when he wrote to the Ephesians:

"Be kind and compassionate to one another, forgiving each other, just as in Christ God forgave you." (Ephesians 4.32)

Let us notice the grounds on which Christ prayed for his executioners:

"They do not know what they are doing."

The soldiers did not realise the significance; who it was they were putting to death. To them he was just the third malefactor and rightly condemned to die.

Some think that the love of Christ is so far reaching, that in fact it is soft – wet. They think that in the last analysis everyone will be spared judgment. Friends, that is a lie! To have heard the gospel and to have consciously rejected Christ it is to be without excuse.

But because of your stubbornness and your unrepentant heart, you are storing up wrath against yourself for the day of God's wrath, when his righteous judgment will be revealed. (Romans 2.5)

May it be that each of us responds to the love of God while forgiveness is still open and available.

3. Caiaphas Reflects - Matthew 26.57-67

"It was the sad reality of religious politics. He had to go. How dare he claim that he was the fulfilment of the prophecies in the Scriptures – the Son of God? Arrogance! Blasphemy!

We tried to avoid this situation but he wouldn't listen to the warnings, the advice we gave him. What else could we do? This Jesus threatened the stability of the whole system! We've been maintaining God's law for longer than I can remember. We have to keep a good relationship with the Roman authorities. He was bringing our religion into disrepute. He even mixed with tax collectors and prostitutes and goodness knows who else!

When we questioned him in the council, at first I thought it was all going to go wrong. The witnesses we'd brought in couldn't get their stories straight, and Jesus wouldn't answer the questions we had carefully prepared.

Eventually I asked him if he was the Messiah, the Son of God. Even then he wouldn't answer directly but he said:

"In the future you will see the Son of Man sitting at the right hand of the Mighty One and coming on the clouds of heaven."

Well, if that wasn't a claim to be God, I don't know what is!

I was worried that some of the crowd might respond to Pilate's offer to free Jesus, but we had spread enough rumours and false reports, and once our own people started shouting: *"Crucify him!"* it was easy to sway the crowd. The fuss will all die down in a few days and he'll be forgotten."

4. A Woman in the Crowd - Mark 15.40-41, Luke 23.28

"I don't know how any of us coped with what happened! We'd heard about Judas' betrayal and that Jesus had been arrested. We couldn't believe our ears, though at the same time some of the things he had said to us suddenly began to make sense. We waited, desperate for news of the trial. I couldn't believe that he'd been condemned to die. He'd helped so many people and spoke with such authority and passion about a better future, and the coming of God's kingdom. We had such high hopes when he arrived in Jerusalem last week, with the crowds cheering and people singing praises to God. That was a wonderful time!

Now a few days later, it's been awful. Well …we didn't know what to do. We followed him on the journey through Jerusalem to the hill outside the city. Golgotha's a good name for it; the place of the skull! We got as near to the procession as we could, and I eventually found myself right next to Jesus and his guards. He saw the group of us crying and turned to us. I'll never forget his words:

'Daughters of Jerusalem, do not weep for me…."

As he was going out to die he was not worrying about himself, but was concerned for us. He seemed to be thinking with compassion of the effects his death would have on us all.

And the look he gave me – I can't really describe it – concern, love, gratitude that I was nearby. It was as if even in all the pain, he remembered the times we'd served him. Even when he was going to be crucified, he cared about me."

5. The Centurion's Thoughts - Mark 15.39

"At first it seemed like business as usual – well, I've seen violent death too many times to be squeamish about the miserable end of a few petty criminals.

But that Jesus character .... The others cursed and begged us to let them go, but he said nothing. He just seemed to accept what was going to happen, yet every now and again he would close his eyes and his mouth would move – praying to his God I suppose. One of my men said he heard him pray, "Father, forgive them," just at the time they drove in those coarse cut nails.

Everything seemed more difficult than usual. It took a long time to get the nails in, and one of the newer soldiers fainted. Once we'd done the business and put the crosses up I thought the worst was over, but the next few hours changed my life. I actually heard Jesus ask God to forgive us for what we were doing to him!

Lots of people shouted insults at him and I saw one of the criminals taunt him too. The other criminal stuck up for Jesus and Jesus promised that he would go to heaven. I found these words going round and round in my head.

I've seen more executions than most, but I've never suddenly felt so clearly that we killed an innocent man, a good man!

But things got even worse. It went dark in the middle of the day – everybody got really edgy. Then at about three 'clock in the afternoon this Jesus shouted out and died. At about the same time there was an earthquake and everyone was running for cover.

As I stood on that hill looking out over the city, I suddenly found something fitting into place and was able to say with complete conviction, 'Surely this man was the Son of God!'"

The Passion of Mary

Simeon once held you, saying to me,
Daughter, be strong, a sword will pierce your heart.
I pondered through the years how this might be,
not knowing then that I'd be torn apart.

You said you had to do your Father's will
when you were twelve. Yet I don't understand;
is this his path that you are walking still?
I can't believe that he would raise his hand

to strike his only son! You taught God's love
and caring. You raised cripples; healed the blind.
What sort of God the Father from above
allows his son to die like this? I find

it hard to watch; to stand beneath your cross.
Surely there was some other way, my son?
He turns his head, sensing my grief and loss
to whisper, *Only here is God's will done.*

And as he twists and gasps in agony,
I long to hold him in my arms again.
Nearby is Peter crying bitterly.
The world grows dark. I've never known such pain.

Now from the cross he speaks with tender voice,
Don't cry, dear mother. Here, behold your son.
It's finished! In a while you will rejoice.
I stumble into the strong arms of John.

And in the bleakness of this awful night
I hear again the words of Simeon,
A glory to his people, and a light
For all the world. Can this be true, my Son?

32. Mary, his Mother
Luke 2.41-52, John 19.25-27

I want this evening to take you to Golgotha, the place of the skull, and for you to stand alongside Mary, the mother of Jesus, and contemplate the cross.

You may say you don't want to do that. You want to think about Jesus rising, victorious, coming again. That is exactly why I want to take you to Calvary. I have been deeply moved by two books I have read recently; "Charismatic Renewal, the search for a Theology" by Tom Smail, Andrew Walker, and Nigel Wright; and "The Crown and the Fire" by Tom Wright. Both so clearly underline for me that the starting point of faith is the cross of Christ. In our attempts to be - charismatic, renewed, evangelical – we often turn our backs on the cross, and pretend a triumphalism that I believe Jesus would not own.

One example is the chorus, "We want to see Jesus lifted high, a banner that flies across the sky." What did Jesus say about being lifted high:

"Just as Moses lifted up the snake in the desert, so the Son of Man must be lifted up, that everyone who believes in him may have eternal life. For God so loved the world that he gave his one and only Son, that whoever believes in him shall not perish but have eternal life." (John 3.14-16)

"But I, when I am lifted up from the earth, will draw all men to myself". He said this to show the kind of death he was going to die. (John 12.32-33)

It is the preaching of the cross that will draw men and women to Jesus. So come and stand with Mary and contemplate the cross.

Carrying his own cross, he went out to the place of the Skull (which in Aramaic is called Golgotha). Here they crucified him, and with him two others – one on each side and Jesus in the middle. (John 19.17-18)

Mary is perhaps aged 50, maybe 53, and here is her first-born being savagely executed between two others. They are all declared to be Lestes – Insurgents, seeking to usurp and overthrow the rule and power of Rome.

To many a passer-by; there hangs Jesus, a defeated Messiah, just one of many.

What heartbreak there is at the cross! Think of the heartbreak of the disciples. Remember the enthusiasm with which they had followed Jesus:

The next day John was there again with two of his disciples. When he saw Jesus passing by he said, "Look, the Lamb of God!" (John 1.35-36).

Andrew, Simon Peter's brother, was one of the two who heard what John had said and who had followed Jesus. The first thing Andrew did was to find his brother Simon and tell him, "We have found the Messiah" (that is, the Christ). (John 1.40-41).

Philip found Nathanael and told him, "We have found the one Moses wrote about in the Law, and about whom the prophets also wrote – Jesus of Nazareth, the son of Joseph." (John 1.45).

So it had been with all the disciples. They had left everything to follow him. They had tramped the dusty roads of Galilee and Judea. They had seen so much, so many miracles, so many healings! They had heard great teaching and wonderful parables. Then there were those strange sayings they could not understand:

"For as Jonah was three days and three nights in the belly of a huge fish, so the Son of Man will be three days and three nights in the heart of the earth." (Matthew 12.40).

Mary, his Mother – John 19.25-27

When they came together in Galilee, he said to them, "The Son of Man is going to be betrayed into the hands of men. They will kill him, and on the third day he will be raised to life." And the disciples were filled with grief. (Matthew 17.22-23).

Now nearly all the disciples have fled. It is the women who are brave. Mary stays and contemplates the cross, agonising for her son, and recalling the memories and the mysteries of his birth. There was the day when the angel came:

But the angel said to her, "Do not be afraid, Mary, you have found favour with God. You will be with child and give birth to a son, and you are to give him the name Jesus, He will be great and will be called the Son of the Most High. The Lord God will give him the throne of his father David." (Luke 1.30-32).

Remembering those words as she watched her son suffer, she must have thought, "What kind of greatness is this? What sort of throne is a cross?"

She would remember her visit to the hill country, and Elizabeth, exclaiming when she met her:

"Blessed are you among women, and blessed is the child you will bear!" (Luke 1.42).

Where is the blessing in what is happening now?

We know Mary pondered deeply on her confinement in the stable in Bethlehem. There was the manger they used for a cradle; the lovely sound of the heavenly angel choir; the visits from the shepherds, and later the Magi with their gifts of gold, frankincense and myrrh. She could not forget the brutal savagery of Herod. Why did he seek to destroy her son?

There were those mysterious words of Simeon in the temple:

Then Simeon blessed them and said to Mary his mother: "This child is destined to cause the falling and rising of many in Israel, and to be a sign that will be spoken against, so that the thoughts of many hearts will be revealed. And a sword will pierce your own soul too." (Luke 2.34-35).

How hard those words were! She had never understood them. Yet now her heart is pierced, is bleeding for her son.

She remembers that Passover when they lost Jesus on their way home. Both she and Joseph had assumed he was with others in their party, but when they camped for the night no one had seen him. She recalled the fear she had, the panic she tried to push away. Didn't anyone know where he could be? There was the frantic rush back to Jerusalem. It was like losing a child in London. There were pilgrims, tourists, con-men, pickpockets, soldiers, whores, merchants, priests, drunks. It was like looking for a needle in a haystack. They searched for three days! Can you imagine how the parents felt? Their son was just twelve years old!

When they found him talking with the teachers of the law there was that mixture of relief and anger, "Jesus, the worry you have caused us!"

"Son, why have you treated us like this? Your father and I have been anxiously searching for you."(Luke 2.48) The Revised Standard Version reads, *"Son, we have sought you sorrowing."*

She remembers Jesus' look of innocent surprise at their distress:

"Why were you searching for me? Didn't you know I had to be in my Father's house? (Luke 2.49).

At the time they hadn't understood his reply. Now she did. She knew that a certain wonder had crept into her heart when she realised he had been confounding the wise men. He had come back to Nazareth with them and had been obedient to them from then on, while she had remembered and treasured these things in her heart.

It had been hard to be a loving mother, so many times.

Perhaps at this point Mary hears some of the taunts directed at her son.

The people stood watching, and the rulers even sneered at him. They said, "He saved others; let him save himself if he is the Christ of God, the Chosen One." (Luke 23.35)

Was there real doubt in the mind of Mary? Did she wonder if in fact he was just another idealist who had tried to lead his people against the Romans? Were all his sayings just delusions? Had she been mistaken all along?

I think of her memory going back again to the wedding in Cana, when she was responsible for the catering. She began to be concerned when the wine was running low. She couldn't think what to do, so she asked Jesus for help. She knew he would do something.

First he gave that strange answer that his time had not yet come; then he ordered that the stone water jars be re-filled. When these were poured out, and they each held twenty to thirty gallons, it was the very best wine they had ever tasted. No ordinary man could have done that.

What is it all about? What does it mean? She thought he was going to redeem the world. She thought he was to be the Messiah. To think she had once cried out:

"My soul glorifies the Lord and my spirit rejoices in God my Saviour." (Luke 1.46-47).

At that time she had been sure that she was called to bear the Son of God. Now all seems loss and shame. It is almost as if her son has been the prodigal. He could have stayed at home. At least with Joseph he could have been respected as a carpenter. This would never have happened. "Oh Jesus, to see you hanging there naked, nailed to the cross!"

Why have I painted this picture? It is because the way of Christ is the way of the cross. Jesus said:

"If anyone would come after me, he must deny himself and take up his cross daily and follow me." (Luke 9.23)

Things were about to change.

When Jesus saw his mother there, and the disciple whom he loved standing nearby, he said to his mother, "Dear woman, here is your son," and to the disciple, "Here is your mother." From that time on, this disciple took her into his home.

Here was a loving son comforting his mother even while he is dying. And this was not the end. Three days later when the women went to the tomb they saw angels:

In their fright the women bowed down with their faces to the ground, but the men said to them, "Why do you look for the living among the dead? He is not here; he has risen!" (Luke 24.5-6)

PART 9

EASTER

ROADS

Easter Dawn

Bleak midnight, dark as Hades, now is passing,
velvet mist lies purple over sand.
In distant Eastern sky, pink rose of Sharon
suffuses hope for lost and weary land.

The squirrels, still as statues, wait for daybreak;
foxes and deer are poised with listening ear;
skylarks hover, creation stands on tiptoe,
eager, hushed. His time is drawing near.

When dawning light glows golden in the garden,
God strikes the tomb one cataclysmic blast!
The stone is rolled,
hell's prison burst asunder.
The Christ is risen, death conquered at last!

Blackbird and thrush sing loud in celebration.
Iris and lily bloom along the way
where Mary ran with joyful proclamation,
He is alive! Rejoice this happy day!

33. The Road to the Tomb
Luke 23.35-56, 24.1-12: Matthew 27.51-66

Let us for a moment look back to the dreadful afternoon of Good Friday. What fear, what sense of desolation and despair filled the minds of those who loved Jesus! What a sad party made its way from the cross to the tomb in a garden. It was all over now. Jesus, for whom they had given up so much, was crucified, was dead and on his way to be buried.

It had been a terrible day. At dawn Peter had denied his Lord:

"Man, I don't know what you're talking about." Just as he was speaking, the rooster crowed. The Lord turned and looked straight at Peter. (Luke 22.60-61)

Jesus had been mocked and beaten:

They blindfolded him and demanded, "Prophesy! Who hit you?" And they said many other insulting things to him.

There had been trials before Pilate and Herod, and the heartless chanting of the crowd:

"Crucify him! Crucify him!"

The followers had watched the awful procession as Jesus was led out to Golgotha to be nailed to the cross. Even the board on the cross seemed to mock him:

There was a written notice above him, which read: THIS IS THE KING OF THE JEWS.

One of the two men crucified beside him jeered:

One of the criminals who hung there hurled insults at him: "Aren't you the Christ? Save yourself and us!"

The passers-by were scathing in their comments:

The people stood watching, and the rulers even sneered at him. They said, "He saved others: let him save himself if he is the Christ of God, the Chosen One."

Yet by midday things began to change. The watchers became subdued, fearful. Awe and mystery still surround these events:

It was now about the sixth hour, and darkness came over the whole land until the ninth hour.

Something unnatural was happening. Men have tried to put forward natural explanations: "It was an eclipse of the sun, or a mighty sand or dust storm." But we do well to remember the culture of the day which suggested that if the hand of God were withdrawn, then darkness would return to envelop the earth, as in the chaos before the creation.

And the curtain of the temple was torn in two.

According to Matthew the curtain was torn from top to bottom. Whatever could this mean? For generations the curtain had been used to veil off the Holy of Holies, which was the part of the temple to which only priests had access on behalf of the people. No one could have torn the curtain because it was very tall and thick. When Jesus died man gained free access into the presence of the Father. Because of the death of Jesus men and women can now be put right with God.

Jesus called out with a loud voice, "Father, into your hands I commit my spirit." When he had said this, he breathed his last.

Into this scene came a remarkably brave and generous man, Joseph of Arimathea:

Now there was a man named Joseph, a member of the Council, a good and upright man.

He is a member of the Sanhedrin, the fifty-two strong Council of leading Jews, mostly Pharisees, who have considerable power despite the Roman occupation. Luke not only tells us he is a good and upright man, but also explains that he had not consented to the decision to seek the crucifixion of Jesus. He is a brave man, for this will almost certainly be the end of his career. As far as we know the only other member of the Council ever to speak for Jesus was Nicodemus. Fifty of the fifty-two councillors were opposed to him.

In the light of the strange phenomena of the day he is bold to come forward. Most folk would rather keep away when events happen that they do not understand.

Joseph stands out against allowing the body of Jesus to be deposited on the city rubbish dump, Gehenna; where the bodies of most criminals were thrown onto the pile of burning refuse. At this time the Romans were exceedingly reluctant to release the bodies of criminals to family or friends, in case they became revered as martyrs, and shrines were set up in their honour. For this reason the disposal of traitors had to be ruthless.

As Joseph courageously made his request to Pilate there would have been three things in his favour. The governor was free to make his own decision at this point, despite advice from Rome, and Pilate would have wanted to re-assert his own authority. Making an unusual decision might well help him to do this. Secondly Joseph was a member of the Council and not a follower of Jesus. It is unlikely that Pilate would know that Joseph had spoken for Jesus. Thirdly Pilate would assess the risks as very low, for he had not been convinced that Jesus had stirred up the people. The followers of Jesus had fled, and Pilate knew that the people who had shouted for Jesus on Palm Sunday were largely the same crowd which had cried, "Crucify!" less than a week later.

Joseph is a generous man in offering his tomb. A tomb hewn in rock was very expensive. This is a new tomb never used before. He gives it to Jesus knowing full well that a tomb used by a criminal cannot be re-used by anyone else.

Having gained permission Joseph is joined by Nicodemus:

He was accompanied by Nicodemus, the man who earlier had visited Jesus at night. Nicodemus brought a mixture of myrrh and aloes, about seventy-five pounds. (John 19.39)

Myrrh was a resin exuded from the stems of an extremely thorny bush. It was difficult to collect and exceedingly costly. Prized by the Egyptians who burned it in their temples, it was also used in embalming. Aloes, powdered and dried were obtained from the almost rotting timber of the sandalwood tree and were very fragrant. The mixture was used, not to embalm or to fill the body cavity, but to disguise the smell of putrefaction.

So Joseph and Nicodemus made their way to Joseph's tomb. Following at a distance were the women folk; grieving and utterly bereft. The body is duly wrapped in strips of linen cloth and laid in the cool dark of the tomb:

Joseph took the body, wrapped it in a clean linen cloth, and placed it in his own new tomb that he had cut out of the rock. He rolled a big stone in front of the entrance to the tomb and went away.

There is a special agony for the women. Duty requires that they should anoint the body of the one they loved so much. This must be done within the next two days, but their grief is compounded because the next day is a Sabbath and a visit to the tomb is not allowed. There will be just the one little window, early on the Sunday morning, before the tomb is declared unclean and further visits are forbidden.

Then they went home and prepared spices and perfumes. But they rested on the Sabbath in obedience to the commandment.

Matthew gives us a glimpse of expectation that might be in the air.

The next day, the one after Preparation Day, the chief priests and the Pharisees went to Pilate.

Friday was the Preparation Day, as always happened before a special Sabbath. The Sabbath at the end of the feast of Unleavened Bread was a special Sabbath. So it was on a special Sabbath, of all days, that the chief priests and the Pharisees went to Pilate.

"Sir," they said, "we remember that while he was still alive that deceiver said, 'After three days I will rise again.' So give the order for the tomb to be made secure until the third day. Otherwise his disciples may come and steal the body and tell the people that he has been raised from the dead. This last deception will be worse than the first. "Take a guard," Pilate answered. "Go; make the tomb as secure as you know how." So they went and made the tomb secure by putting a seal on the stone and posting the guard.

The Road to the Tomb – Luke 23.35-56, 24.1-12

It seemed a very final end. The best man who ever lived had been cruelly put to death. For so many that is where the story ends; where their acceptance ends.

But on Easter Day you need to come with me again along the road to the tomb. It is very early in the morning. The women haven't really slept since Friday. They have turned events over and over in their minds – what might have been – what seemed to be promised.

Today they are up very early and in loyalty and love they make their way to the tomb to anoint the body of the one they once called Master and Lord.

We get various insights from the gospel writers:

When the Sabbath was over, Mary Magdalene, Mary the mother of James, and Salome bought spices so that they might go to anoint Jesus' body. Very early on the first day of the week, just after sunrise, they were on their way to the tomb. And they asked each other, "Who will roll the stone away from the entrance of the tomb?" (Mark 16.1-3)

There was a violent earthquake, for an angel of the Lord came down from heaven and, going to the tomb, rolled back the stone and sat on it. (Matthew 28.2)

They arrive at the tomb to find the stone rolled away. I imagine them creeping forward and peering into the tomb. When their eyes adjust to the gloom they realise the body has gone, but the grave clothes are still lying there. Fear grips the women. "The body has been stolen, or at least it has been moved," is Mary Magdalene's first thought.

The guards are still there but, seeing an angel on the stone, are petrified. However well-armed, they are totally incapable of stopping what is happening.

The guards were so afraid of him that they shook and became like dead men. (Matthew 28.4)

And as the women stand there perplexed:

While they were wondering about this, suddenly two men in clothes that gleamed like lightning stood beside them. In their fright the women bowed down with their faces to the ground, but the men said to them, "Why do you look for the living among the dead? He is not here; he has risen!"

Could they believe? Was it really true? There was the angel before them, reassuring them. "He has risen!" They hurry back to tell the Eleven and all the other disciples:

It was Mary Magdalene, Joanna, Mary the mother of James, and the others with them who told this to the apostles. But they did not believe the women, because their words seemed to them like nonsense.

So many are like this today. Yet there is all the evidence; not only of the bible, but of many who have met him since, over the years, in various different ways. Since his ascension, Jesus Christ still meets people today.

Paul met Jesus too. Here is his testimony:

For what I received I passed on to you as of first importance: that Christ died for our sins according to the Scriptures, that he was buried, that he was raised on the third day according to the Scriptures, and after that he appeared to Peter, and then to the Twelve. After that, he appeared to more than five hundred of the brothers at the same time, most of whom are still living, though some have fallen asleep. Then he appeared to James, then to all the apostles, and last of all he appeared to me also, as to one abnormally born. (1 Corinthians 15.3-8)

34. Coming to terms with the Resurrection
John 20.1-18

Jesus said to her, "Mary!" She turned toward him and cried out in Aramaic, "Rabboni!" (which means Teacher).

No one had slept much since Wednesday night. Thursday had been a busy day. The Master could have celebrated the Passover with the disciples on Friday, but, knowing his future, he had chosen the Thursday for his last supper in the upper room at John Mark's home.

Thursday night had been agonising for the disciples. After supper they had all failed him in the Garden of Gethsemane. Jesus often went there when he was in Jerusalem. It was a place where he could be quiet and pray. This night he asked them to watch with him but the disciples had eaten well, were tired and didn't understand. They had all fallen asleep. The rebuke from Jesus, however, was only the beginning of trouble.

The soldiers and temple guards had arrived and had seized Jesus. They bound him and dragged him off, first to Annas and then on to the house of Caiaphas the High Priest. There a mock trial was held before Jesus was taken to Pontius Pilate the Roman Governor.

In front of Pilate, the priests, with false witnesses to back their case, asked that Jesus should be put to death by crucifixion.

Peter had an especially bad time. He had promised Jesus that he would never let him down. Even if everyone else ran away, he would stay beside his master. But he had fallen asleep with the rest when Jesus asked him to pray; he had lost his temper and cut off the ear of the servant of the High Priest, which had resulted in another ticking off from Jesus; then horror of horrors, during that Thursday night, just as Jesus had said he would, he had denied three times, with cursing and swearing, that he even knew the prisoner Jesus!

Little wonder that no one had slept on Thursday. However Friday was worse: that sham trial; the crowd whipped up by the chief priests and temple guards baying to have Jesus crucified; the indescribable horror of seeing their Lord nailed to a cross, and his haunting cry:

"My God, My God, why have you forsaken me?" (Matthew 27.46)

There was the darkness and the great shout:

"It is finished!" (John 19.30)

Then, the way his head slumped forward on the cross; that spear they put into his side; the blood and water that flowed mingling down. It was an unbelievably dreadful day. The only help for them had been the actions of Joseph of Arimathea and Nicodemus who came forward to claim his body. They had given him an honourable burial in Joseph's tomb.

Have I conveyed to you the hopelessness of it all: their despair; the pointlessness; everything being lost? I hope I have, for while this picture is a particularly vivid one, I believe it is a valid picture of life for any person who does not have the Easter hope of the Risen Lord Jesus burning in his or her heart. If death is the end, then tell me – what is life all about? The writer of the book of Ecclesiastes reflected deeply on how short and contradictory human life is, with its injustices and frustrations, and came to the conclusion that life is useless.

"Meaningless! Meaningless!" says the Teacher. "Utterly meaningless! Everything is meaningless." (Ecc.1.2)

All things are wearisome, more than one can say. (Ecc.1.8)

Coming to terms with the Resurrection – John 20.1-18

For with much wisdom comes much sorrow; the more knowledge, the more grief. (Ecc.1.18)

All his day is work and pain and grief: even at night his mind does not rest. This too is meaningless. (Ecc.2.23)

No one has power over the day of his death. (Ecc.8.8)

So I commend the enjoyment of life, because nothing is better for a man under the sun than to eat and drink and to be glad. (Ecc.8.15)

Do you see what I am trying to get at? For countless of thousands, this is all life holds. Their gospel is: "when you are dead you are dead." No wonder so many antidepressant pills are dispensed; no wonder so many families fall apart; no wonder sinfulness and immorality abound; no wonder young people resort to drugs; no wonder people take their own lives. No wonder lives are empty, hurting and lost.

People I know experience this in varying degrees according to their circumstances, but friends, am I this Easter describing you? Come and look again at the events of the first Easter Sunday morning.

Mary Magdalene and Mary the mother of James and Joses, with Salome and Joanna, have met up before dawn, and have set off to anoint the body of Jesus. On the way they consider various problems. What about the guard of Roman soldiers that Pilate has set at the request of the Chief Priest? What about the great stone which seals the tomb? Who would have the strength to roll it away? Let us be clear – they are going to the tomb without the least expectation that Christ will have risen. They are expecting a body, and they are expecting problems in performing their last rites for that body.

Imagine the shock of the women when:

Early on the first day of the week, while it was still dark, Mary Magdalene went to the tomb and saw that the stone had been removed from the entrance. So she came running to Simon Peter and the other disciple, the one Jesus loved, and said, "They have taken the Lord out of the tomb, and we don't know where they have put him!"

Even though Jesus had patiently taught them that he would rise from death on the third day, it hadn't crossed their minds that this might have occurred! Theirs is the perfectly normal human reaction, panic! They expected a guard, a stone, and a body. All have gone. Someone must have raided the tomb and taken the body away.

There is a little part of the story that I love. Despite his failure and shame; the women still see Peter as the leader next to Jesus, and it is to him that they run.

Peter and John hardly stop to think. They must investigate. They need to verify the women's story for themselves, so they set out running to the tomb. John, the younger and fitter arrives first. He stoops down, peers in and realises it is just as the women had said, except that they hadn't noticed the grave clothes. These linen sheets which Nicodemus had supplied, and which had been wrapped round and round the body, enclosing the hundred pounds of myrrh and aloes, are still there. They are neatly folded as if they have never been used.

No wonder he is afraid to go in. No wonder he holds back, full of awe; something extraordinary has happened. If the body had been moved by the guards or stolen by the body snatchers, the grave clothes would have gone as well.

Peter catches up and arrives at the tomb. It is the same old Peter, the one who acts before he engages his brain. He is not afraid but goes straight in, and notices a piece of evidence which John has missed. There, separate from the main sheets, is the head cloth, rolled up by itself.

"The women were right. We have to believe them; the body has gone. Whatever has happened?" John and Peter stand there amazed, bewildered. It just doesn't make sense.

They still did not understand from scripture that Jesus had to rise from the dead.

I want to pause there, because I think this is a vital part of the Easter story. In our enthusiasm to emphasise the resurrection of Jesus we often fail to realise its importance. Mary and the other women have been to the tomb. They have found it empty but have not equated this fact with the possibility of resurrection. John and Peter have been to the tomb. They have seen inexplicable evidence but still do not understand. That Jesus should have risen from the dead defies logic. It is a totally unreasonable thing to believe. It's not a conclusion we arrive at by the application of our minds. We need something else to happen.

I understand those people who say, "I can't believe." No one can really believe unless God himself intervenes: unless God by the power of his Holy Spirit enables that person to see the truth; unless God convinces him or her, and convinces you concerning the risen Jesus.

Easter and Christmas both defy logic. A virgin conceives God incarnate. The Creator is laid in a manger. A dead man walks from a tomb. God in human form conquers death.

Peter and John make their way back into the city, to the safety of John Mark's home. But Mary Magdalene has made her way back to the tomb. She stands outside weeping inconsolably. The Lord who had done so much for her, her lovely Lord Jesus, has first been crucified, and now his body has been taken away.

At this point the graciousness of God takes over.

As she wept, she bent over to look into the tomb and saw two angels in white, seated where Jesus' body had been, one at the head and the other at the foot. They asked her, "Woman, why are you crying?" "They have taken my Lord away," she said, "and I don't know where they have put him."

It is then that Mary turns round, and sees who she believes to be the gardener. If anyone will know what has happened, perhaps the gardener will. She doesn't realise that it is Jesus, but notice that Jesus initiates the conversation.

"Woman," he said, "why are you crying? Who is it you are looking for?" Thinking he was the gardener, she said, "Sir, if you have carried him away, tell me where you have put him, and I will get him." Jesus said to her, "Mary." She turned toward him and cried out in Aramaic, "Rabboni!"

Do you see what has happened? In the midst of all the hurt, all the despair, all the pain, Mary goes on looking for Jesus. This is all Jesus needs. He calls Mary by her name. I can just imagine the thrill that gave her – the warm, tingling sensation that seeped through every fibre of her body. "It is the Lord! He has called me by name!"

How did you come to church this Easter morning? Perhaps you came full of expectation, but more likely you came with doubts and hurt and pain. I believe the Lord is here, just as he was in that Easter garden. He is longing to reveal himself to you, longing to call you by your name.

Do you sense his presence? To someone he wants to say, "You are forgiven." To someone else, "You are loved." To another he wants to say, "Understand now for the first time, Jesus is risen, is risen indeed!"

35. The Road to Emmaus
Luke 24.13-35

On the evening of May 24th 1738, William Holland was due to preach at a meeting in a house in Aldersgate Street in London. He had no special inspiration so chose as his message simply to read from the preface of Martin Luther's commentary on Paul's epistle to the Romans. In the congregation that evening was a virtually unknown Anglican cleric, John Wesley.

In his journal he later wrote:

"I went very unwillingly to a society in Aldersgate Street... at a quarter before nine, while one was reading, he was describing the change which God works in the heart through faith in Christ, I felt my heart strangely warmed. I felt I did trust in Christ, Christ alone, for salvation; and an assurance was given me that He had taken away my sins, even mine, and saved me from the law of sin and death."

John Wesley, of course, became one of the greatest evangelists history has known – the whole Methodist denomination owes its foundation to him.

I want to suggest that for John Wesley that evening was an "Emmaus Road" experience: an experience where the longing that there is a purpose to life; the longing that there is a God who can be found and known, suddenly became a certainty. He found a living hope, a faith to die for, because he realised the truth concerning the Living Lord Jesus.

My hope is that today's walk along the road that runs from Jerusalem to Emmaus will help us become more aware of the presence of Jesus in our lives, day by day.

We find real problems in identifying the road to Emmaus in Jesus' day. We know for certain of only one Emmaus and that was almost twenty miles north-west of Jerusalem; too far away to be the village referred to by Luke in his gospel. The name Emmaus means "The place of thermal springs or warm baths," and Luke tells us it is about seven miles, or sixty stadia distant, (sixty furlongs for the horse racing community). Josephus writes of Vespasian having settled a colony of soldiers in Emmaus, sixty stadia from Jerusalem. This village could fit the bill and was known at the end of the first century as Kolonieh, (colony), and has since been renamed Beit Mizza-Hammoza.

Alfred Edersheim describes leaving Jerusalem by the Western Gate and following the paved Roman road up onto the plateau and as far as Nephtoah on the border of Judah, following the description of the borders of Benjamin in Joshua:

"The southern side began at the outskirts of Kiriath Jearim on the west, and the boundary came out at the spring of the waters of Nephtoah." (Joshua 18.15)

"There one leaves the Roman road and heads up what is little more than a path into a lovely valley, which contrasts with the surrounding rocky region. Because of the stream it is a place of orange and lemon gardens and olive groves and at the head of the valley, with bright dwellings, the lovely village of Emmaus." He speaks of it still being a popular outing on a spring afternoon for residents of Jerusalem.

But it is not a pleasant Sunday afternoon stroll for Cleopas and his companion. It is a journey home with heavy hearts. Their expectations concerning Jesus have been shattered. They had gone up to Jerusalem, so they thought, to celebrate the Passover and to spend some time with Jesus. Perhaps they had hoped to see him really come into his own as Messiah. Instead he was arrested, tried and crucified. He died and was buried.

They can take no more. This morning the women going to anoint him at the tomb had found that his body had gone. Soldiers were telling a story that in the night some followers of Jesus had come, ambushed them and stolen the body away. The women were hysterical, saying they had seen angels and that the grave clothes were in the tomb but there was no body. The apostles had told the women they were talking nonsense. There was only one thing to do: to cut their losses; to go home and rebuild life all over again.

Naturally as they walk along with heavy steps, they keep going over again and again, what might have been.

Quietly a third person comes alongside them. It seems incredible that these disciples did not recognise Jesus. Perhaps they had not spent time with him like the twelve, though as the story unfolds it becomes clear that they were close followers. The Bible gives us a special insight:

But they were kept from recognising him.

Is this deliberate on the part of Jesus? If they had recognised him straight away what might have been their reaction? Fear, or an overwhelming emotional response, or might they have rushed straight back to Jerusalem to be accused of hysteria as the women had been?

What we see here is the true Jesus at work, dealing with individuals exactly as is appropriate for their need. He knows Cleopas and his companion need some good, solid teaching if their faith in the risen Christ is to be on a sure foundation. So watch the master at work:

He asked them, "What are you discussing together as you walk along? They stood still, their faces downcast.

They are stopped in their tracks. Their response to Jesus might be described as "open-mouthed."

One of them, named Cleopas, asked him, "Are you only a visitor to Jerusalem, and do not know the things that have happened there in these days?"

"How could you have been in Jerusalem and missed out on what was happening to Jesus?" Their hurt and disappointment simply floods out.

"What things?" he asked. "About Jesus of Nazareth," they replied, "He was a prophet, powerful in word and deed before God and all the people. The chief priests and our rulers handed him over to be sentenced to death, and they crucified him; but we had hoped that he was the one who was going to redeem Israel. And what is more, it is the third day since all this took place."

Then Cleopas feels he must tell the rest of the story:

"In addition, some of our women amazed us. They went to the tomb early this morning but didn't find his body. They came and told us that they had seen a vision of angels, who said he was alive. Then some of our companions went to the tomb and found it just as the women had said, but him they did not see."

All this time Jesus listens attentively to their story. When Cleopas has finished, Jesus responds with a rebuke. In modern parlance it might well have been, "You idiots, when will you learn?"

Jesus had tried so hard to forewarn his disciples. He had tried so hard to teach them about his forthcoming death, and about his resurrection; but it was as if they hadn't listened, or at least they hadn't understood.

A preacher asked his daughter when she returned home from morning service if she had understood the message. Like many teenagers she replied, "I heard him, but my mind was on something else, so I didn't really listen." Her father was discouraged. "If only you would really listen, you would understand."

How we must grieve the heart of God, who longs to show us good things, when we don't take time to listen for his voice.

The anxious travellers on the road to Emmaus were now ready to listen to Jesus; and he gave them a thorough lesson from the scriptures:

He said to them, "How foolish you are, and how slow of heart to believe all that the prophets have spoken! Did not the Christ have to suffer these things and then enter his glory?" And beginning with Moses and all the prophets, he explained to them what was said in all the scriptures concerning himself.

The Road to Emmaus – Luke 24.13-35

I wonder what was in the crash course Jesus gave them. Did he remind them of God's promises to Abraham, to Jacob, to David; the prophecies of Isaiah, Jeremiah, Micah, Zechariah and Malachi? It would be a good exercise to try to reconstruct the scriptural evidence Jesus used on the road to Emmaus. Could we do that, produce a coherent summary of the ground that Jesus must have covered? If not; might Jesus say to us, "How foolish you are!"

The party arrive at Emmaus still downcast, still not recognising Jesus; yet, I suspect, wiser in their knowledge and understanding of the scriptures. Jesus, it seems, bids them farewell as if he is travelling on further, but with true Eastern hospitality Cleopas and his companion will have none of it.

But they urged him strongly, "Stay with us, for it is nearly evening; the day is almost over." So he went in to stay with them.

I sometimes wonder what would have happened if they had let Jesus go. I suspect we would never have known. If they had let the Saviour pass them by, he may never have gone their way again. They might have missed their opportunity. But the joy of this account is that they didn't. Their hearts were warmed towards this stranger. If he would stay they could hear him further; they had so much to learn.

The meal is spread, and Jesus, as their guest, is invited to give thanks. Then it happened. As Jesus picked up the loaf, gave thanks, broke it and offered them pieces, they recognised him as the Saviour who had died on the cross.

Do we at this point make a mistake? Our natural reaction is to go back to the upper room. They would remember Jesus breaking the bread at the Last Supper and the significance of his words, "This is my body, broken for you," would suddenly become startlingly clear. But isn't it unlikely that Cleopas and his companion were there? They may of course have heard all about it in the conversations of Good Friday, and during the Sabbath, and perhaps early this very day, but it seems to me that it was when they saw what he did that they recognised him.

Perhaps they had been in Galilee when he took the lad's fishes and barley loaves:

And he directed the people to sit down on the grass. Taking the five loaves and the two fish and looking up to heaven, he gave thanks and broke the loaves. Then he gave them to the disciples, and the disciples gave them to the people. (Matthew 14.19)

It may have been that they saw the nail prints in his hands and were suddenly aware, and then everything he had said fell into place. Whatever it was, their eyes and minds were opened, and they recognised Jesus, the Risen Lord.

How they would have loved to have held on to him then! How many questions they had which they were longing to ask! But the Lord disappeared. He had revealed himself. He had convinced Cleopas and his companion. Now he required that they believe and act in faith in the certain knowledge that he had risen.

There is another journey to make along the Jerusalem to Emmaus road. Despite the late hour, despite the darkness, despite the danger from thieves and brigands to those who travel at night, here was news that could not wait, news that must be shared. The women were not hallucinating after all. The Master has risen, is alive!

They got up and returned at once to Jerusalem. There they found the Eleven and those with them, assembled together and saying, "It is true! The Lord has risen and has appeared to Simon."

How different the journey back to Jerusalem must have been. I envisage them half running, hurrying along full of joy; such wonderful news - such wonderful news!

When they reach Jerusalem they run through its darkened streets and bang on the door of the house where the Eleven have taken refuge. They expect to find a cowering band fearful of the priests and soldiers. As soon as the lock is turned and the door eased open they burst in with the news, "We've seen the Lord! We've talked with him! He broke bread with us!"

"That's wonderful! Simon Peter has seen him too. It all fits together. He has risen indeed!"

Have you met the risen Lord?

PART 10

RESURRECTION

AND

ETERNAL LIFE

Flying Towards Sunset

Is this like dying Lord, this long-haul flight
Between two continents, two worlds apart
Sailing on puff-balls tinged with rosy light;
Peach-orange spars, fantastic iceberg art;
Pink castles, curving harbours, midnight seas,
A fairy kingdom steeped in evening sun!
Far distant are the dry acacia trees,
White-sanded shores where dark-eyed children run
On spice isle Zanzibar. Now swiftly on
Through looming darkness, yearning soon to be
Within the warm embrace once more of one
Whose love through life has been a rock for me,
Whose arms reach out wherever I may roam.
Is dying like this Lord, like coming home?

36. How can we be sure concerning Eternal Life?
1 Corinthians 15.12-24

How can we be sure we will be raised from the dead? Christ's resurrection is the guarantee of ours.

But if it is preached that Christ has been raised from the dead, how can some of you say that there is no resurrection of the dead?

Some people like to think that death is the end, so they may as well eat, drink and be merry because this life is all they have. That is not just the philosophy of the present day. In Jesus' day the Sadducees taught that there is no resurrection of the dead. The idea was also popular in Greek philosophy, which at best suggested there might be some sort of spirit existence after death, but no bodily resurrection. Paul spoke to a sceptical audience on Mars hill in Athens:

*When they heard about the resurrection of the dead, some of them sneered. (*Acts *17.32)*

Writing to the people of Corinth Paul has already clearly stated that the resurrection of Christ is absolutely central to the faith, but now for a moment he runs with their teaching, and the implications if it is true:

If there is no resurrection of the dead, then not even Christ has been raised. And if Christ has not been raised, our preaching is useless and so is your faith.

It really does make nonsense of everything that Paul was about. All he taught – a crucified Christ – sins forgiven – a risen Christ – life eternal; is built on a monstrous lie if somewhere the body of Jesus lies mouldering in the earth. Worse than that, if the body of Christ can be produced, there is nothing left to believe. It is all blown away like chaff in the wind.

Then, says Paul, there is another serious factor. We would be shown, not just to be misguided, deluded, but simply to be well-intentioned buffoons. We would be discredited as the most gullible heretics:

More than that, we are then found to be false witnesses about God, for we have testified about God that he raised Christ from the dead.

To lie about anything is serious, but to lie about God, surely that deserves the most severe punishment! Ananias and Sapphira did not lie about God, but their lie to God cost them their lives. Paul realises that he needs to be careful in his testimony about God, and so do we!

Halfway through verse 15 we catch the second thread of Paul's argument. Suppose the false teachers in Corinth are right? Suppose the general philosophy of the day is correct:

But he did not raise him if in fact the dead are not raised. For if the dead are not raised, then Christ has not been raised either.

That is simple logic. You cannot have one without the other. If death is the end, then it is the end for Jesus, as well as for us. Paul follows through with his argument:

And if Christ has not been raised, your faith is futile; you are still in your sins.

One of the greatest, perhaps the very greatest fact about the Christian faith, is the promise of sins forgiven, or being put right with God. The Christian knows his faith is real because he experiences sins forgiven.

How can we be sure concerning Eternal Life? –
1 Corinthians 15.12-24

Something which is common to virtually every religion, short of Satan worship, is that they all teach that wrongdoing – sin – makes one dirty. It spoils and separates from God. Nearly all religions, as a core belief, seek to tackle the question of putting mankind right with their god. In most faiths this involves complex and arduous acts of penance. Many offer no real hope that this can be achieved. Some suggest it is a gradual improvement over several incarnations. The glorious message of Christianity is that Jesus died that we might be forgiven. The price that God has set concerning sin is death. Jesus died in our place, and through faith in him, by coming to him in repentance; we believe forgiveness is freely available.

A wag once challenged a preacher, "There must be a catch; there is nothing free in this life." The preacher replied, "There was a very great catch. Salvation is free for you, because someone else paid for you. Jesus, the only beloved Son of God hung in your place on Calvary's cross!"

The next part of Paul's argument is that if death is the end then the believers in Christ who have died are lost.

What a wonderful comfort it is to know that those who have died believing in Christ are at peace with Jesus. Pilgrim Homes, an organisation caring for elderly Christians, and which cared for my aunt towards the end of her life, publishes a quarterly magazine. Deaths are reported on the page which is headed, "With Christ, which is far better."

Recently I was asked to speak with a young mother who was terribly troubled. She went to a Spiritualist Meeting for help after hearing noises in the night. There she was told by a medium that it was the spirit of her little daughter who had died. Her daughter was not at rest and was trying to get back in touch with her. I was able to tell this lady about a Lord who loves little children and who took them in his arms. I prayed for her to experience the deep peace of Jesus in her heart; a peace which came to her.

Earlier in the year I was involved in counselling a lady looking to a "faith healer" for deliverance from physical pain. I discovered that she was being led into the worship of an Eastern mystic called Sai Baba. As I spent time with this lady and her husband I learned that the pain had developed following the death of her mother. Though she had cared wonderfully for her mother, she had been so upset at her death that she had not attended the funeral. She felt her mother was not at rest, and that she was unforgiven. In the name of Jesus I was able to pray for assurance concerning her mother, and for release from the pain, and that she might put her trust for salvation in Jesus. The first two parts of that prayer were wonderfully answered and I look forward to hearing of God's perfect work in her life being completed.

Paul says that if he is deluded, if his message is in vain:

Then those who have fallen asleep in Christ are lost.

The message going out in Corinth was that Jesus was a wonderful man, setting a wonderful example. If everyone tried to copy his life pattern the world would become a wonderful place. "Oh," says Paul, "the poverty of that message!"

If only for this life we have hope in Christ, we are to be pitied more than all men.

Yet in our churches today there are many for whom that is as far as it goes. They really do not have that assurance of sins forgiven, or of eternal life. Could that be you? If you are going through the motions only then Paul says you deserve pity.

Yet is there a wonderful alternative in God's purpose?

Christ has indeed been raised from the dead, the firstfruits of those who have fallen asleep. (v. 20)

The truth is that Christ has been raised as the guarantee that those who sleep in death will also be raised. (v. 20 Good News Bible)

I like the way that Alfred Martin puts it: "We can look forward to our resurrection because we can look back to his resurrection!"

I also like the thought that Christ's resurrection is the guarantee of our resurrection, for they say a guarantee is only as good as the company which backs it! Our guarantor owns the cattle on a thousand hills. He is the creator of everything that has been made. His company is not limited to this country, or to his world, or even to the universe!

Paul tells us why Christians can be so certain concerning the resurrection to eternal life:

"For since death came through a man, the resurrection of the dead comes also through a man. For as in Adam all die, so in Christ all will be made alive.

It is very important that we make sure we really understand verse 22. Paul makes a fuller exposition of this verse in Romans 5.12-21. Briefly today – when God created man he was sinless. Everything was good and death was not an issue. Yet God put one restriction on mankind: he must not eat of the tree of the knowledge of good and evil. Make what you will of that – was it an actual tree, or a parable? What is clear was that man should not seek to make himself equal with God his creator. God made the penalty quite clear. If he did this he would be punished and the punishment would be death. Satan, in the form of a serpent, came to bring temptation saying, "God has placed that restriction on you, not for your own good, but only so that you will not be his equal. Eat and be like God!" That is the root of all temptation. Why shouldn't you steal and enjoy the same benefits as the rightful owner? Why not take another man's wife and enjoy her body; destroy another woman's character by gossip in an attempt to enhance your own reputation; seek Nirvana by drinking yourself silly. It doesn't matter what the effects are on others as long as you can find some measure of satisfaction.

This disobedience to the limits which God has set, God calls Sin – and Sin pays its price – Death. Paul says, "It all began with Adam and has been handed down from generation to generation ever since, with a continuous disregard for God's standards and rules, and a continuing penalty of death."

But then God, because of his incomprehensible, amazing love; his heart broken by this continuing sin and death; intervened and sent his own son Jesus. Jesus not only set a new standard by living a perfect, sinless life; he offered himself as the perfect sacrifice for sin. By his death he enabled our forgiveness.

What incredible provision! There is a way for us to be forgiven. There is a way for us to escape the death penalty, to enter into newness of life. That way is to submit our lives to Christ.

Paul says that:

In Christ all will be made alive.

There is no other formula, no other way. We cannot clean up our own act and earn admission to heaven. God does not have scales; he doesn't put our sins in one pan and our good deeds in the other. God does not have league tables and allow the top half of the league into heaven. God has one simple standard – "What is your relationship to my Son Jesus Christ?

Have you come to him? Have you confessed your faults? Have you really put your faith in his atoning death at Calvary?"

I want us to look at one more verse in closing because it underlines and emphasises today's message.

In Christ all will be made alive. But each in his own turn: Christ, the firstfruits; then, when he comes, those who belong to him. Then the end will come.

Notice first that wonderful affirmation concerning those who have put their trust in Jesus. Each one will be raised. There are no doubts, no ifs or buts; just a certainty. It is guaranteed by God the Father. It is sure.

Secondly, *each in his turn* will be raised from death. There is a right order. God has already achieved the first step; Christ has been raised. The next step the scriptures teach is that:

Those who sleep in Christ will be raised. (1 Corinthians 15.20 GNB)

Notice the lovely phrase, *those who sleep in Christ*. Death, with all its fear, emptiness and hopelessness, is for the believer to fall asleep in Christ. It is the transition from this life to eternal life with the Father. It is the passing from spoiled earth to perfect heaven. It holds no fear, for we are safe in the arms of our Saviour.

Finally, at the Second Coming of Christ, those who are still alive will, like Enoch and Elijah, be translated and meet the Saviour in the air. This is wonderful, but there is a solemn warning also in this verse. We do not know the time of his coming. It could be today. Also we notice that he only comes for those who belong to him.

To be sure concerning eternal life you must be sure concerning your relationship to Jesus.

You can be sure today!

37. Recognisable, yet Transformed and Christ-Like
1 Corinthians 15.29-49

"What will life be like after death?" Chapter 15 of Paul's first letter to the Corinthian Christians is in answer to the questions that they have raised concerning life after death. Paul gives us some clues, but not clear-cut answers, to some of the great mysteries that occupied their minds and that occupy our minds from time to time.

We ask ourselves all manner of questions concerning life after death. What will my heavenly body look like? Will it resemble the body I had when I was in my prime, or will it be a slightly rejuvenated version of the failing body I had at the time of my death? Will I at last be handsome? Will I be beautiful? Will my body still show the scars I accumulated during my life? If I am handicapped or disabled, will I be free of these restraints? Those of us who have lost a child will ask if we will see our child in glory, and if we do, will he or she still be a child. Those who have lost a baby or had a miscarriage or a stillborn child may ask, "Will I recognise my child in glory?" Some are worried about how cremation will affect their heavenly body. Others ask, "If we are all going to be changed, how will we recognise our loved ones in heaven?"

The nutshell answer to all these questions is, "Don't worry." Our wonderful creator God has the whole matter in hand. It will not only be better than you expect, it will be better than anything you could possibly imagine!

But someone may ask, "How are the dead raised? With what kind of body will they come?" (1 Corinthians 15.35)

The questions mainly came from teachers opposed to Paul's messages who were challenging the claim that Jesus had been raised from the dead.

In last week's message we saw how Paul answered the challenge by referring to the witnesses, many of whom were still alive. These people could be approached and questioned personally and could witness from what they had seen and known. Now the issue is, "What sort of body will we have when we are raised from the dead?" Paul first tells them that it is a daft question, then he goes on to attempt an answer:

How foolish! What you sow does not come to life unless it dies.

Paul looks to the natural world and to things which people will understand, for his explanation:

When you sow, you do not plant the body that will be, but just a seed, perhaps of wheat or of something else.

Here is Paul's first illustration. I have here some runner bean seeds. They are quite attractive to look at: smooth, shiny and mottled purple and black. Just as they are, there is a lot to recommend them. But inside each one is the potential for something far greater, far more significant. However, unless the bean is planted, it will just remain an attractive bean and its value as a seed will cease to be. In the middle of the seed is the embryo with all the potential for life, but before the new plant can spring up, the food store in the cotyledons in the seed must be released. The shiny outer coat must soften and be prepared to rot away. It is as if the whole bean withers and dies in order that the new plant may grow. Then what?

But God gives it a body as he has determined, and to each kind of seed he gives its own body.

What Paul is saying is that the plant which comes up looks nothing like the seed that has been buried. Creator God gives the bean a totally new body. A stem appears, looking first a little bit like an umbrella handle, which protects a delicate bud as it pushes up through the rough soil. Then, as if by magic, the shoot uncurls, and as it uncurls the first two true leaves unfurl, and a plant which will climb, which will respond to the light, which will have attractive red flowers that summon bees from all around, which will bear a magnificent crop of runner beans, springs to life.

Resurrection is like that.

Now the fascinating point that I would share with you is this. The runner bean plant is totally unlike the seed which was sown, but we recognise it as a runner bean plant and have no doubts, because in all creation, even among the many beans and pulses, there is no other which is exactly like the runner bean. We can tell runner beans from weeds; we can distinguish them from French beans; we can tell them from broad beans. It will be like that with resurrection. Whatever new body God chooses to give us, it will be far better than the one we have now, but we will be recognisable.

It may well be similar to Mary's experience. At first she mistook the risen Lord for the gardener. There was something different about him. But when he called her by name, then she knew and was filled with joy.

It may well be as it was for Cleopas and his companion who failed to recognise the risen Jesus on the road to Emmaus, even though their hearts burned within them, until he took bread and gave thanks and broke it. Then they knew. But his body was different. He had walked a Sabbath day's journey with them that afternoon, yet in the evening his new body was able to disappear, as if it were the body of a spirit.

This same body is able to enter an upper room even though the door is locked. Yet the disciples do not talk about a ghost. They talk about the risen Lord. This same risen Lord is able to invite Thomas to put his finger into the nail prints and his hand into a wounded side! Amazing – this is beyond reason – beyond what we understand. Jesus' body was changed by the hand of Creator God.

All flesh is not the same: Men have one kind of flesh; animals have another, birds another and fish another. There are also heavenly bodies and there are earthly bodies; but the splendour of the heavenly bodies is one kind, and the splendour of the earthly bodies is another.

Paul has moved from the plant kingdom to the animal kingdom as he continues to develop his theme.

They tell me that you have missed the boat if you were planning to conceive a baby to be born on the first day of the new millennium. Friday was the best date to attempt to conceive; Saturday was OK, but a baby conceived today going to full term will probably be born too late! Now I can't show you a human egg and ask you what will develop, and it's too late in the season to show you some fresh frog spawn, but here is a hen's egg.

If it has been fertilised, which I admit is unlikely, and if it is incubated under exactly the right conditions: the surface temperature being kept at one hundred and three degrees Fahrenheit and the temperature in the centre of the egg being kept at one hundred degrees Fahrenheit; then after twenty-one days the egg will hatch. We know exactly what will emerge – a new baby chicken, which will develop white chicken flesh. It will not produce flaky flesh of fish, nor will it produce beef, or pork or lamb, or alligator steaks. It needs its own particular type of flesh for its own particular style of life, and the distribution of muscle will be just right for its life's activities.

"Ah," says Paul, "so it is with earthly and heavenly resurrection bodies. One kind of body is ideally suited to earthly life. It has grace and beauty all of its own. But yours is going to be heavenly life, and for that you need a heavenly body. It will still be magnificent, still perfectly suited to the role it will perform, but transformed."

Here is one final example from God's inanimate creation. Think about the sun and the moon and stars:

The sun has one kind of splendour, the moon another and the stars another; and star differs from star in splendour.

I never cease to find scripture amazing. To the vast majority of people in Paul's day the stars were lights that God had put in the sky, in a dome which covered the earth. Paul says every one is different, each has a splendour all of its own. It is like that with you and me. Here and now, each one of us is different, but each one of us is important to God. God has made us as individuals and he respects and honours us as individuals, though we may have wished God had made us differently. He knitted us together in our mother's womb and he cares for us and loves us as precious and unique persons in his creation. When I get my resurrection body; that too will be unique. It will not be the same as my body here. It will be splendid for it will be perfect, and exactly suited to my very own personal eternal life in the presence of the God who loves me and has redeemed me to be his own.

I think that is exciting, but there is even more good news concerning my new resurrection body.

So it will be with the resurrection of the dead. The body that is sown is perishable, it is raised imperishable.

I must have told you about old Mrs Lush. She used to ask me, "Pastor, have you got a recipe for knees?" She had worn hers out scrubbing the steps and stairs of the big house in Michelmersh. At weekends as an act of love she had been on the same knees to scrub the floor of the little parish church until the boards were white, and she had continued to do this for over sixty years. "Will I get new knees in heaven?" she would ask.

Do you know about aches and pains? Are there parts of you that refuse to work like they used to? Do you know what it is to be so tired you can scarcely drag yourself around? Listen:

The body that is sown is perishable, it is raised imperishable.

In the funeral prayer of committal we remember, "We are but dust; we are like the flowers of the field; the wind goes over it and they are gone." We use the words, "Earth to earth, ashes to ashes, dust to dust." We are sown as perishable mortals. We are raised imperishable and immortal. Put another way, Paul says of the body:

It is sown in dishonour, it is raised in glory: it is sown in weakness, it is raised in power.

We must not go home today without the best piece of news of all. When we are resurrected we will have spiritual bodies – and we will be like Him. We will be like Jesus our Saviour and Lord.

Paul introduces his final important issue in verse 44:

It is sown a natural body, it is raised a spiritual body. If there is a natural body, there is also a spiritual body.

The closing issue is this. If we are to have a natural body and an earthly life we need a natural birth. If we are to have a spiritual body and a heavenly life, we need to experience a spiritual birth.

So it is written: "The first man Adam became a living being;" the last Adam, a life-giving spirit.

The very fact that we are alive means that we are descendants of Adam, the first man; the man whom God intended should live in harmony with him and never die. But Adam was the man who sinned and became subject to corruption, sin and death. We cannot get away from that. We are all mortal. We have all sinned. We are all subject to the law of death.

But God who loved us so much did not leave the matter there. "A second Adam to the fight and to the rescue came." The Lord Jesus Christ, the Creator's only Son, came to die the death that should have been ours and to make possible new birth, spiritual birth, birth to eternal life.

The spiritual did not come first, but the natural, and after that the spiritual.

The first man was of the dust of the earth, the second man from heaven. As was the earthly man, so are those who are of the earth; and as is the man from heaven, so also are those who are of heaven.

We do not have time to develop those verses, but what we must take on board is that the second birth, the spiritual birth, is separate from natural physical birth and comes after it. It comes only because of what Jesus has done, and it comes only if we are born anew of him.

That is what it means to be a "born again" Christian. We know that we need new birth and we have come to Christ for sins to be forgiven and to receive that new life.

Here is the crowning glory of it all.

And just as we have borne the likeness of the earthly man, so shall we bear the likeness of the man from heaven.

38. Caterpillar and Robin
1 Corinthians 15.35-58

The caterpillar always thought that the robin was a cocky bird with his bright red breast. Caterpillar was afraid of Robin in case one day he decided that Caterpillar would make a juicy meal. But Robin was always telling Caterpillar about a bright and wonderful world where the sun shone, where there were waving trees, white clouds and blue skies. He described it as the heavens. "Caterpillar," Robin would say, "if only you could fly, instead of crawling about in those dark green stinging nettles in the ditch."

Most of the time Caterpillar was happy and content, but sometimes he would wonder about Robin's world. He saw glimpses of the sun and he felt its warmth. His muddy ditch wasn't very beautiful, but nettle leaves tasted good, and what more was there to life really? When Caterpillar was chewing a tasty leaf he thought, "What really is the difference between me and Robin?" After much pondering he decided that it must be wings. Wings enabled Robin to fly, and just sometimes he wished he had wings.

One day Caterpillar heard a fluttering noise. It wasn't Robin. The fluttering was much more delicate than Robin's wings. Looking up, Caterpillar saw a butterfly. "How lovely," he thought. I have never in all my life seen anything as beautiful as this butterfly!" It was light, it was wonderfully coloured, and it had wings. Caterpillar felt fat and round and heavy, and extremely ugly. He wanted to hide from something so lovely, but it was too late. Butterfly had landed on the very nettle that Caterpillar had munched half away.

"Where have you come from?" whispered Caterpillar. "You don't belong in this ditch; you are far too beautiful!"

"Neither do you," laughed Butterfly; you are only a visitor in the ditch. You too were born for the light, the sun, the air and the blue skies. You too were born for wings, and I have come to tell you the good news – you will be changed!"

"I don't know what you're talking about," said Caterpillar. He wanted to ask Butterfly lots of questions, but all she said was, "You will be changed, in an instant, in the twinkling of an eye!" With that she flew off, upwards towards the sunlight.

"I wish that was true," thought Caterpillar. "I really wish it was true," and he set about munching a few more nettle leaves.

But that very night, feeling strangely tired, Caterpillar fell into a deep sleep. In his sleep he dreamed about what Butterfly had said, "You too were born for wings – you will be changed." Caterpillar slept and slept and slept. He covered himself with a silken blanket, which by the morning had hardened into a stiff brown cocoon.

Caterpillar's neighbours in the ditch: the slug, the field mouse, the earthworm and the earwigs all thought that Caterpillar had died. They felt very sorry to see the hard brown cocoon. They would miss him. Caterpillar had been fun to talk with and a good friend too.

But Caterpillar wasn't dead. One day he woke from his deep, deep sleep. He thought he had heard a voice calling, or a trumpet sounding, but he was bound, bound in the blanket which had hardened into the brown cocoon.

The call kept on sounding. It was an order that had to be obeyed, and suddenly, in a moment, from somewhere Caterpillar discovered a strength he had never known before. He gave a tremendous heave and the cocoon, the blanket, split apart. Caterpillar looked down at himself and couldn't believe his eyes. He was different, completely different! He was no longer fat and green and round with short, fat hairy legs – he was slender, and he had wings!

Caterpillar looked up, and to his amazement, there was Butterfly. "You are one of us now," she exclaimed. "Come and fly with me to the Buddleia bush. There you can sip nectar and see all the beauty of the world. Caterpillar could hardly believe it but what she said was true. He had wings. He was changed. He was handsome. As he flew he caught sight of his reflection in the water in the bottom of the ditch. He was magnificent; he had dark wings with bright red spots. "This is wonderful," he thought, "This is heaven!"

The Bible says – when our earthly bodies are buried they are ugly and weak, but when we are raised from death our bodies will be beautiful and strong. We will be changed into what is immortal, in an instant, as quickly as the blinking of an eye.

What will it be like in the life beyond death?
This week we have been trying to clear up the vestry so that it looks a little bit less like an auction sale room. I was reminded of what happened at St Paul's Cathedral. Less than twenty years ago, when the authorities decided they needed to de-clutter; they sold very cheaply to a junk dealer, a number of statues and other artifacts that had been moved out of the main cathedral. More recently someone has realized that the items sold were of historical interest and should never have been removed from the cathedral. Not surprisingly the dealer, who still has them, is asking for a large amount of money to sell them back. Funds are being raised to pay for them. But fear not, your artifacts are hidden in the loft.

St. Paul's Cathedral is a wonderful building. Nearly everyone knows it was designed and built to plans drawn up by the famous architect Christopher Wren. It is not the first cathedral on the site. The original cathedral was burned to the ground in 1666 in the Great Fire of London. What most people don't know is that Christopher Wren was inspired to build the new cathedral when he was inspecting the ruins of the old cathedral. On the very first stone he turned over he found, inscribed in Latin, the words, "I shall rise again."

This has been the theme I have taken for these three sermons looking at 1 Corinthians 15. Our three questions are –
1. How can we be sure Jesus rose from the dead?
2. How can we be sure concerning eternal life?
3. What will it be like in the life beyond death?
Today I address the third question:

New and Splendid, Different Bodies
Firstly we will have a new, splendid, different body. Let us look at Genesis and the second account of creation in Chapter 2.

The Lord God formed the man from the dust of the ground and breathed into his nostrils the breath of life, and the man became a living being. (Genesis 2.7)

The miracle of life, surely, is that man is created from very basic ingredients. We know that when a body is cremated all that remains is a kilogramme or so of ashes. It has always been part of our understanding that when a person dies, that person's physical body returns to dust. But we know too that the person is not the body. Cut off an arm, cut off a leg, transplant a heart, liver, lungs and you do not change the person. The real person is spirit. The writer of Ecclesiastes was clear concerning this:

Man goes to his eternal home and mourners go about the streets. Remember him – before the silver cord is severed, or the golden bowl is broken; before the pitcher is shattered at the spring, or the wheel broken at the well, and the dust returns to the ground it came from. (Ecclesiastes 12.5b-7)

Here are two scriptural examples of the spirit returning to God. Firstly, when Jesus died Luke records:

Jesus called out with a loud voice, "Father, into your hands I commit my spirit!" (Luke 23.46)

Secondly when Stephen, the first Christian martyr, was being stoned to death, he called out:

"Lord Jesus, receive my spirit." (Acts 7.59)

The body returns to dust – the spirit returns to the Lord.

Some people were mocking the Christians, as indeed they do today. "Fancy you believing that you are going to enjoy life after death! However can you reconstitute a body that has rotted away, that the worms have eaten? How can you remake a body which has been consumed on a funeral pyre? What sort of body are you talking about?"

Someone may ask, "How are the dead raised? With what kind of body will they come?" (1 Corinthians 15.35)

Paul's response is that it is the very scoffers who are revealing their ignorance. He invites them to look at the examples around them in nature.

"How foolish! What you sow does not come to life unless it dies. When you sow, you do not plant the body that will be, but just a seed, perhaps of wheat or of something else.

The wheat plant bears no resemblance to the seed. Beautiful flowers bear no resemblance to their small seeds. It is only when the seed falls into the ground and dies that the life within it can be released and can come to full fruition. That, says Paul, is the potential in us.

God gives it a body as he has determined, and to each seed he gives its own body.

Having given one illustration from the plant world, Paul then gives another from the animal world.

All flesh is not the same: men have one kind of flesh; animals have another, birds another and fish another.

The point is this – if animals have different kinds of bodies for different natural environments, then we must expect heavenly bodies to be quite different from earthly bodies, to suit the heavenly environment.

There are also heavenly bodies and there are earthly bodies; but the splendour of the heavenly bodies is one kind and the splendour of the earthly bodies is another. The sun has one kind of splendour, the moon another and the stars another; and star differs from star in splendour.

This verse is a clever approach by Paul, because in the understanding of his day there was an ascending sequence of beauty. There was a wonderful radiance in the sun but the moon was even more beautiful; and compared with the beauty of the moon, the beauty of the stars was magnificent. Paul is building up to the truth about our resurrection bodies:

So it will be with the resurrection of the dead. The body that is sown is perishable, it is raised imperishable; it is sown in dishonour, it is raised in glory; it is sown in weakness, it is raised in power.

Pause for a moment and take this on board. The body which will be put into the ground or into the crematorium flames, wonderful creation as it is, is mortal; it is finite, limited; it wears out. Your new, heavenly body will be immortal; not subject to limitations, not subject to the fragility and decay of your present earthly body, and it will have no end. It will go on and on, perfectly. When it is buried it is ugly and weak; many of us would say we already have the wrinkles and the parts that don't perform like they used to and as we feel they should. God says, "Look forward, your new body will be beautiful and strong."

Do you remember when St. John was allowed that peep into heaven in his vision on the island of Patmos?

And I heard a loud voice from the throne saying, "Now the dwelling of God is with men, and he will live with them. They will be his people, and God himself will be with them and be their God. He will wipe every tear from their eyes. There will be no more death or mourning or crying or pain, for the old order of things has passed away." (Revelation 21.3-4)

Isn't that something to be thrilled about, something to which we can look forward? The old with all its pain and decay will be gone – everything will be new and good.

Paul has one more point to make before going into what I believe to be the best part of the passage.

It is sown a natural body, it is raised a spiritual body. If there is a natural body, there is also a spiritual body.

Finally, like Jesus

Let me explain why I feel the next part of the passage is really exciting. As I read the gospels and as I live the Christian life I find I am often comparing myself, measuring myself against the example of Jesus. It is a pretty devastating exercise. What do the scriptures say?

All our righteous acts are like filthy rags. (Isaiah 64.6)

"The good that I would, that I do not; the evil which I would not, that I do." (Romans 7.19 KJV)

Paul has the same problems here as I, and as I suspect, you have. Now look at these next few verses for encouragement:

So it is written: "The first Adam became a living being," the last Adam, a the life-giving Spirit.

My struggle and failure now is because of the old man in me, the Adam. As Adam was tempted and fell, and became susceptible to corruption and illness and hurt and pain and death, so do I. Strive as I may, I fall short of what I know I want to be, like Jesus. As I recognise this short-fall Satan comes and mocks me, tempts me to give up, tells me I will never be good enough for heaven. But this is Satan's temptation. Look at the scriptures – it is the common experience of all who have God's Spirit in them.

For we know that the whole creation has been groaning as in the pains of childbirth right up to the present time. Not only so, but we ourselves, who have the firstfruits of the Spirit, groan inwardly as we wait eagerly for our adoption as sons, the redemption of our bodies. (Romans 8.22-23)

In today's passage Paul shows me that my Saviour, the last Adam, is Jesus the life-giving Spirit.

Just as we have borne the likeness of the earthly man, so shall we bear the likeness of the Man from heaven.

We will be like Him.

We need to be ready
Let me for a moment take you back to verse 45.

The first man Adam became a living being, the last Adam, a life-giving Spirit.

If we are related to the first Adam, we are living beings like him. Living beings are earth-bound, corruptible, and finite. The vital phrase here is that we will be like him if his Spirit is in us. When we come to Jesus, God puts his Spirit into us. This Spirit is heaven-bound and incorruptible.

Remember Nicodemus who came to Jesus by night. Jesus answered his question about being born again with:

Jesus answered, "I tell you the truth, no one can enter the Kingdom of God unless he is born of water and the Spirit. Flesh gives birth to flesh, but the Spirit gives birth to spirit. You should not be surprised at my saying, 'You must be born again.'" (John 3.5-7)

Jesus is explaining exactly the same thing as Paul explains. The only way to share in glory is if we have the life-producing Spirit of Christ in our lives.

I declare to you, brothers, that flesh and blood cannot inherit the kingdom of God, nor does the perishable inherit the imperishable.

PART 11

THE ASCENSION

Ascending

Touch heaven with your hands,
Stretch through the clouds where He ascended.
Reach with grace; like summer daisies
Turn your face towards the Son.

He is there, beyond the trees,
Beyond the planes, beyond the stars,
And yet not far.
Within a room a mother prays
And Christ is there.

39. Taken up to Heaven
Acts 1.9-11, Luke 24.50-52

While he was blessing them, he left them and was taken up into heaven. (Luke 24.51)
We non-conformists make little if anything of Ascension Day. This is a great pity. We are all the poorer for ignoring it. We tend to think only about God raising up Jesus from the dead on Easter Day. That is supremely important. That is how we know that sin and death have been conquered. That is what adds substance to our hope of eternal life. At virtually every funeral service we hear the words of Jesus:
Jesus said, "I am the resurrection and the life. Those who believe in me will live, even though they die. And all those who live and believe in me will never die. (John 11.25-26)
The other raising up of Jesus was on Ascension Day. For forty days following his resurrection Jesus remained here on earth, in human likeness, yet with his new resurrection body. He appeared to his disciples giving them many infallible proofs that he really was alive – he who had died that vicious death on the cross.
Then on Ascension Day he gathered his disciples together on the slopes of the Mount of Olives not far from Bethany. There he taught them about the power they would receive when he was taken

from them. God would put his power in the form of the Holy Spirit into their individual hearts and lives.

"You will receive power when the Holy Spirit comes on you; and you will be my witnesses in Jerusalem, and in all Judea and Samaria, and to the ends of the earth."

This is the same promise which Jesus made before his crucifixion. He knew about his death on the cross, his resurrection, and how he would in his physical body finally leave his disciples. He promised to be with them.

"I will not leave you as orphans; I will come to you. Before long, the world will not see me any more, but you will see me.

I will ask the Father, and he will give you another Counsellor to be with you forever – the Spirit of Truth..

The Counsellor, the Holy Spirit, whom the Father will send in my name, will teach you all things and remind you of everything I have said to you." (John 14.18, 16, 26)

We sometimes think of Jesus as a human being. That is both right and wrong. Jesus is God. He always has been. He was involved in the creation of the universe. He is beyond our understanding, but he chose to become a man so that he could show us more of what God is like; and most importantly, to die for our sins.

When Jesus rose from the dead, something about him was changed. His friends could still recognise him. He still did human actions; eating and drinking, but he could also act in ways which humans cannot.

Jesus hasn't got a grave, because he didn't die again. He left earth in a completely different way. He ascended:

After he had said this, he was taken up before their very eyes, and a cloud hid him from their sight. They were looking intently up into the sky as he was going, when suddenly two men dressed in white stood beside them. "Men of Galilee," they said, "why do you stand here looking into the sky? This same Jesus, who has been taken from you into heaven, will come back in the same way you have seen him go into heaven."

Jesus was taken back. He ascended into heaven. He was raised up into glory, to be back with the Father. He returned to the place that is rightly his.

Taken up to Heaven – Acts 1.9-11

In his gospel Luke added:

When he had led them out to the vicinity of Bethany, he lifted up his hands and blessed them. While he was blessing them, he left them and was taken up into heaven. Then they worshipped him and returned to Jerusalem with great joy. And they stayed continually at the temple praising God.

I like the thought that Jesus left them with a blessing. And they are not lost or unhappy although he has gone from them. When he died on the cross they were desolate. Now they have seen him resurrected – alive! They believe his promises. This time they worship and joyfully wait for his promised Holy Spirit.

Do you remember what Jesus said when he had calmed the storm?

"You of little faith, why are you so afraid?"(Matthew 8.26), "Where is your faith? (Luke 8.25)

Why do we have doubts about Jesus the Son of God? We have the story of his life; his teaching; his promises. There are many proofs that he died and rose again. His disciples saw him ascend into heaven and a few days later were filled with his Spirit and remarkably changed. They were changed in a way they could not have engineered.

Many can witness today to knowing Jesus; to recognising the transforming power of his Spirit in their lives. Over the years many have died rather than deny their faith, others have been great preachers for him; John Wesley, Charles Haddon Spurgeon; Billy Graham; hundreds have gone into far countries to be missionaries, suffering hardships for the satisfaction of following him. Others live quiet lives of humble service around us.

It is a privilege to follow the Master, to be a servant of the King, whose service is perfect freedom, whose love is everlasting.

Do you know him? Do you talk with him? Have you felt his presence in your life? If you don't you are missing the purpose of life. You could find him today.

PART 12

WHO IS

THE HOLY SPIRIT?

Pentecost

It was a time of sharp-penned ogres,
vixens wailing in the night, the coal-black fear
which blew my early years; Grimm's tales,
Dan Dare's exploits in alien wars
and air-raid sirens louder than my ears,

when I first felt the hand,
and glimpsed a country where I might grow
green;
a place to go on living without pain.
There came a rainbow shining in my world,
which proved the promise of the Gentleman.

In that black book was strength
taller than forests and the eagle's eye,
a sky of loving in an upper room;
for them a hurricane of joy which spread
the Presence over all Jerusalem.

For me, a summer beach in Wales,
my back against the grassy dunes; the ocean's
dashing, slackening foam. Through passing clouds
I touched the hand that held my being;
I heard His calm voice in the wind.

40. Who Dares Speaks Out
Acts 2.1-21, 36-47

But you will receive power when the Holy Spirit comes on you; and you will be my witnesses in Jerusalem, and in all Judea and Samaria, and to the ends of the earth.

Do you remember the sense of fear in the fellowship when about three years ago I suggested that we should knock on every door to the north of the Wimborne Road and offer every home a free copy of the Jesus video, on condition that we could go back and get the folk to complete a short questionnaire?

A few spoke out, but looks on faces didn't require words – "I couldn't possibly do that," – "don't think I'm going," – "I'm not prepared to stick my neck out and actually tell people that Jesus is important to me!"

The aim was to complete the task by the end of the millennium year, 2000. It has taken us about six months longer than that, but now the task is complete and some homes have in fact been approached twice. In every fifth or sixth home a copy of the video has been placed. What is amazing is how many of you have been involved. About a third of the membership has been from door to door. More have been addressing and delivering introductory letters. A few people have come into fellowship. Many contacts have been established. Very importantly, all of you who have been involved have grown much bolder concerning Jesus. You have experienced something of the power of the Holy Spirit enabling you to witness. You have not only been a delight and joy to your pastor's heart; you have pleased God, and God is pleased with you. Well done!

Now I wonder what reactions are all around church this morning? Many of you feel good, for you have been part of the outreach. Some of you are eager to know: What can we do next? What is going to be the next opportunity to reach out for Jesus? Some of you, of course, had very good reasons for not being able to take part in the outreach. A few are feeling deprived. You have joined us in recent months and the task was virtually complete. You feel you have missed out. Another few, and maybe this is you, feel a bit down, - "I muffed it again, I failed to seize the chance which was there. How does God feel about me?"

That is why I am glad that today we remember Pentecost or Whitsun, for today is about Christians coming alive, receiving the power of God's Holy Spirit; doing great things for God.

I wonder what would be your response if I asked you to name the exciting days in your year. Would you say your birthday, your wedding anniversary, the day you go on holiday? Those should be exciting days, but it is sad if they are the top days on your list.

I hope that at the top of your list are these exciting days: Christmas, because that was when Jesus, your Saviour, came into the world; Easter, because that is the day you remember Jesus' victory over sin and death; and Pentecost – today; because you remember God sending his Holy Spirit upon the disciples in Jerusalem. This is a good day to remember when you invited him into your heart and life. You celebrate your baptismal day, when Jesus washed your sins away, and you know your life was filled with the Holy Spirit.

If birthdays, holidays, anniversaries and Christmas are "Wow!" days for folk in the street, then for the Christian today should be one of the greatest 'Wow!' days of all. Because at Pentecost, every one of you can experience the truth of our text:

You can receive power, as the Holy Spirit comes on you, and enables you to witness.

Let me remind you of a very challenging verse, one of the clear statements made by Jesus. He has been talking about his death and about returning to his Father, and in the midst of it all he says:

I tell you the truth, anyone who has faith in me will do what I have been doing. He will do even greater things than these, because I am going to the Father. (John 14.12)

A few verses further on he explains how this will be possible:

And I will ask the Father, and he will give you another Counsellor to be with you for ever, the Spirit of truth. The world cannot accept him, because it neither sees him nor knows him. But you know him, for he lives with you and will be in you. (John 14.16-17)

Do you know; have you experienced the truth of those words of Jesus? The disciples hadn't. When Jesus, their leader, was arrested they all fled. Peter, who earlier had boasted of his boldness, was as weak as any. He cursed and swore as he denied the Lord three times.

After the crucifixion the disciples hid in an upper room, the shutters closed and the door locked for fear of arrest by the Jews. Nothing could have been further from their minds than the thought of witnessing for Jesus. They were in despair; they were terrified; they were totally without power until the Holy Spirit came. Even after the resurrection they did not know what to do next.

What a change occurred that first Pentecost! There were dramatic manifestations!

Suddenly a sound like the blowing of a violent wind came from heaven and filled the whole house where they were sitting. They saw what seemed to be tongues of fire that separated and came to rest on each of them. All of them were filled with the Holy Spirit and began to speak in other tongues (languages) as the Spirit enabled them.

This was God at work in a new way, for the first time, and the reaction was amazing. Every one of them was a changed person. They were given a holy boldness which made them long to share their faith, to talk about Jesus, to work for Jesus, to go anywhere for Jesus, to die for Jesus. The Holy Spirit made Jesus the most important part of their lives.

Some people still receive the Holy Spirit with dramatic manifestations, but for the vast majority of us he comes quietly and in response to our prayers. But whether the Spirit comes in a dramatic way or quietly it is unmistakable that he has come, for we are changed. We receive an inward power and an inward confidence in Jesus. We are enabled to be witnesses for him. We are able to do the things Jesus would have us do for him and in his name.

You will know if this has happened. It is not really something you can be in doubt about. You know if you have confronted the sin in your life, whether you have confessed your sin and received Christ's forgiveness. You know if you have asked Jesus to be your Saviour and Lord. You should not be in doubt. Either you have addressed these issues or they still wait to be addressed. I propose that you know too if you have asked him for the gracious gift of the Holy Spirit, a gift which he promises to all who have believed and are baptised.

If you then, though you are evil, know how to give good gifts to your children, how much more will your Father in heaven give the Holy Spirit to those who ask him! (Luke 11.13)

I have noticed in our passage five factors which are vital if you really want the Father to give you the gift of the power of the Holy Spirit.

The first is the sense of unity which prevailed. The believers were together in one place. They had a unity of purpose and the deepest respect for one another. Sadly some people today have petty jealousies and rivalries. They hold things against one another. They want their own way rather than the Lord's way. Such problems prevent the infilling activity of the Holy Spirit.

Secondly I notice the persevering prayer of the disciples. They had been told to wait in that upper room, where they had cowered in fear, until the gift of the Holy Spirit came. As they waited together, they prayed together. Acts 1.12 tells me that this was a constant activity, men and women alike, doubtless beseeching the Lord that his promised gift would come soon.

Thirdly I notice that their hearts were open to God and to what God wanted. This was particularly evident in the way they set about choosing Matthias to replace Judas.

Fourthly I see an expectancy that God would keep his promise. They believed the Holy Spirit promised by Jesus would come soon.

Fifthly and finally I notice they believed that God would keep his word. They believed his promise was for each one of them.

My friend John Perry for many years ran an organisation called "Partnership Missions." It took teams of people on mission both in this country and in the United States. It was built around people sharing their testimonies, telling what God had done in their lives. In the preparation meetings John would always say, "Everyone who claims to be a Christian is a witness. You cannot help but be a witness, to your neighbours, to your friends, to those with whom you work. The question is, 'What kind of a witness are you?' Are you a witness to the living power of the Holy Spirit who has made you new; or are you a witness who has never been filled with the Holy Spirit, whose life suggests that God is dead and that belonging to him makes no difference to you?"

Listen to the words of Jesus:

How much more will your Father in heaven give the Holy Spirit to those who ask him!

Listen to the words of the prophet Joel:

And afterward, I will pour out my Spirit on all people. (Joel 2.28)

Listen to the words of Peter at Pentecost:

Repent and be baptised every one of you, in the name of Jesus Christ for the forgiveness of your sins. And you will receive the gift of the Holy Spirit. The promise is for you. (Acts 2.38)

Finally listen to the words of Jesus:

You will receive power when the Holy Spirit comes on you; and you will be my witnesses. (Acts 1.8)

> Holy Spirit, we welcome You.
> Holy Spirit, we welcome You
> Please accomplish in me today
> Some new work of loving grace, I pray;
> Unreservedly have Your way;
> Holy Spirit, Holy Spirit,
> Holy Spirit, we welcome you.
>
> *Chris Bowater: Sovereign Lifestyle Music 1986*

41. Like a Dove, like Wind, like Fire
Acts 2.1-4, Matthew 3.13-17

Suddenly a sound like the blowing of a violent wind came from heaven and filled the whole house where they were sitting. They saw what seemed to be tongues of fire that separated and came to rest on each of them. All of them were filled with the Holy Spirit and began to speak in other tongues as the Spirit enabled them.

Many find the concept of the Holy Spirit difficult to understand. We have no problem in relating to Jesus as a man, human as we are, and somewhere out there we realise there is a creator whom we call God. He is far beyond our understanding, wonderfully powerful, unaccountably merciful and amazingly loving and we are reassured that he allows us to call him Father.

However the idea of the Holy Spirit, referred to in the past as the Holy Ghost, is harder to imagine. There is no tangible form we can visualise, yet Jesus teaches that without him we will fail and be powerless in our discipleship.

This morning I want us to try to understand the Holy Spirit in a better way. For a moment think about yourself. What or where is the real you?

You have a body of course, which is exceedingly important. It enables you to function and helps other people to recognise you. I was amazed recently to be recognised by a dinner lady I hadn't seen for over twenty years. She remembered how I looked and how I walked – but did she really know me? Is my body me? Is your body the real you?

The Bible teaches that we should honour our bodies and that is right. Now all sorts of things can go wrong with our bodies. Does that change the person inside? I think not. You can have an arm, a leg, a kidney, a gall bladder or other parts removed without losing any of the essential you, without diminishing the real person. Nowadays we can even swap pieces with other people. Do you remember the reverence which used to be paid to the heart? Now you can have a heart transplant and you are still yourself, not someone else. The real you is intangible, something which cannot be put on a table or in a glass jar and displayed. The real you is spirit.

Some people think of the mind as being the real you. Again it is extraordinarily important, but is it you? What your mind can do depends on the educational opportunities you have received. To an extent memory depends on application and training, and, as some of us know, when we become older our memory deteriorates. The real me, the real you remains vital and alive and as young as ever. It's just that the mind and body don't function as well as once they used to. What about someone who becomes mentally ill or is brain damaged? Those who care for such people will testify that whilst the afflicted person's responses are affected; underneath there remains the real person: important, precious and warranting full esteem. The person God intended, the person God will redeem is still there and indeed is eternal. The spirit has not changed.

If we have grasped that, we have begun to grasp something of the Holy Spirit of God. There are many ways in which the Holy Spirit is utterly intangible, yet the Holy Spirit too is Person, the third person of the Trinity. He is the very life of God. When we talk of the believer having the life of God in him, we literally mean that he or she has the Holy Spirit living in him or her.

Don't you know that you yourselves are God's temple and that God's Spirit lives in you? (1 Corinthians 3.16)

Do you not know that your body is a temple of the Holy Spirit, who is in you, whom you have received from God? You are not your own. (1 Corinthians 6.19)

(God) set his seal of ownership on us, and put his Spirit in our hearts as a deposit, guaranteeing what is to come. (2 Corinthians 1.22)

Because you are sons, God sent the Spirit of his Son into our hearts, the Spirit who calls out, "Abba, Father." (Galatians 4.6)

Those who obey his commands live in him, and he in them. And this is how we know that he lives in us: We know it by the Spirit he gave us. (1 John 3.24)

So what is the Holy Spirit like? God knows that we have difficulty in understanding the Holy Spirit so in scripture he gives us various pictures to help us understand. We have time today to look at just three of them;:Wind, Fire, and Dove.

The Holy Spirit is like Wind

In the Old Testament the best example comes from Ezekiel:

Then he said to me, "Prophesy to the breath; prophesy, son of man, and say to it, 'This is what the Sovereign Lord says: Come from the four winds, O breath, and breathe into these slain, that they may live'" (Ezekiel 37.9)

You may remember that strange experience of Ezekiel when God showed him a valley of dry bones:

He asked me, "Son of man, can these bones live?" I said, "O Sovereign Lord, you alone know." (Ezekiel 37.3)

In his vision Ezekiel is told to prophesy to the bones.

Then he said to me, "Prophesy to these bones and say to them, 'Dry bones, hear the word of the Lord! This is what the Sovereign Lord says to these bones: I will make breath enter you, and you will come to life'".. So I prophesied as I was commanded. And as I was prophesying there was a noise, a rattling sound, and the bones came together, bone to bone. (Ezekiel 37.4-7)

At this point there is no life, so Ezekiel is told to prophesy, or preach, again:

So I prophesied as he commanded me, and breath entered them; they came to life and stood up on their feet – a vast army. (Ezekiel 37.10)

What God is promising Ezekiel is a day when he will restore Israel's people, and that he will put his Spirit into their hearts.

Like a Dove, like Wind, like Fire – Acts 2.1-4, Matthew 3.13-17

What a wonderful picture this is for us. To be without the Holy Spirit dwelling in our lives, actively filling us day by day, is to be like a bag of dry bones. Even if you could join the bones together, even if you could put on sinews and flesh, you could not make them live without breath, without the Holy Spirit of God. We need the Holy Spirit of Christ day by day giving us a new heart; a new direction; a new purpose; a new joy and life.

In the New Testament Jesus says:

The wind blows wherever it pleases. You hear its sound, but you cannot tell where it comes from or where it is going. So it is with everyone born of the Spirit. (John 3.8)

The Spirit can't be pinned down and its effects are powerful. In a gentle or moderate breeze the sailor is delighted as his boat skims along, but in high winds or storms the sailor becomes fearful that his boat may sink.

A lack of wind means the sailor cannot sail at all. Some will know the rhyme of the Ancient Mariner who is becalmed in the ocean. Dreadful things happen because he cannot make any progress. Millers used to dread the still days when their windmills could not be used to grind corn. How awful if God should withdraw his Holy Spirit from us because of our sinful disobedience!

If the Holy Spirit is in our lives he will gently encourage us, giving us his power to fulfil all God's commands. If we have backslidden; if we have strayed from God's path for us; he may in mercy blow like a mighty storm of his Holy Spirit, filling us with fear and causing us to turn back to him.

I remember the great storm which blew down a great many trees a few years ago. I journeyed to Brighton the day following the storm. In Patcham Place and Preston Park I saw huge old trees which had stood since these parks were established; uprooted and lying on the ground. I talked with a friend who is wise concerning country matters, expressing my sadness at such destruction of beautiful trees. "Yes," he agreed, "it is sad, but in the long run there will be a good outcome. People assume that trees will go on for ever, but trees grow old, they weaken and some become hollow. We needed a storm like this to make people think about conservation and replanting."

Do we need a storm of the Holy Spirit blowing through our lives to bring us to our senses concerning the things of God?

The Holy Spirit is like Fire.

Fire is a source of power. The magnificent steam trains built years ago consumed vast quantities of coal. As the fire burned the water boiled, producing steam which sent the great engines surging forward.

In the Old Testament God appeared to Moses in fire. The burning bush was a sign of the very presence and power of God.

There the angel of the Lord appeared to him in flames of fire from within a bush. Moses saw that though the bush was on fire it did not burn up. (Exodus 3.2)

The Spirit came at Pentecost in fire as a sign of power. This was almost like an anointing for the disciples in the upper room.

They saw what seemed to be tongues of fire that separated and came to rest on each of them.

Every single one of us needs an inner power over and above ourselves so that we too might be witnesses for the Lord Jesus Christ.

The Spirit as fire can lead and guide. God led his people out of Egypt with a cloud and fire.

By day the Lord went ahead of them in a pillar of cloud to guide them on their way and by night in a pillar of fire to give them light, so that they could travel by day or night. (Exodus.13.21)

The pillar of fire was a sign to the people that the Lord was with them, going ahead of them, guiding them. It was the tangible sign of the real presence of the Spirit of God.

Isaiah wrote of the guiding presence of the Spirit of God:

I will lead the blind by ways they have not known, along unfamiliar paths I will guide them; I will turn the darkness into light before them and make the rough places smooth. These are the things I will do; I will not forsake them. (Isaiah 42.16)

The Lord will guide you always; he will satisfy your needs in a sun-scorched land and will strengthen your frame. You will be like a well watered garden, like a spring whose waters never fail. (Isaiah 58.11)

Like a Dove, like Wind, like Fire – Acts 2.1-4, Matthew 3.13-17

Jesus explained to his disciples how his Spirit would act as a guide.

But when he, the Spirit of truth comes, he will guide you into all truth. He will not speak on his own; he will speak only what he hears, and he will tell you what is yet to come. (John 16.13)

The Spirit as Fire can be a source of cleansing and purifying. John the Baptist was baptising with water as a sign of repentance. The baptism of the Holy Spirit is a cleansing, purifying baptism to holy living:

"I baptise you with water for repentance. But after me will come one who is more powerful than I, whose sandals I am not fit to carry. He will baptise you with the Holy Spirit and with fire." (Matthew 3.11)

Malachi prophesied concerning the days of Christ's coming in power:

But who can endure the day of his coming? Who can stand when he appears? For he will be like a refiner's fire or a launderer's soap. He will sit as a refiner and purifier of silver; he will purify the Levites and refine them like gold and silver. Then the Lord will have men who will bring offerings in righteousness. (Malachi 3.2-3)

We too need the purifying work of the Holy Spirit.

The Holy Spirit is like a Dove.
While both wind and fire can be threatening, the dove is a gentle image. A white dove is the symbol of peace and purity:

As soon as Jesus was baptised, he went up out of the water. At that moment heaven was opened, and he saw the Spirit of God descending like a dove and lighting upon him. (Matthew 3.16)

The dove is able to travel for long distances and has a strong homing instinct. After the ark had rested for a while on Mount Ararat, Noah sent out a dove.

When the dove returned to him in the evening, there in its beak was a freshly plucked olive leaf! Then Noah knew that the water had receded from the earth. (Genesis 8.11)

It is the Holy Spirit who searches us out, who finds us, who convicts us of sin and who brings the olive branch from God. This tells us that the Father loves us and seeks that we should be reconciled with him.

When King Hezekiah became very ill and was near death, he turned his face to the wall and prayed to the Lord:

"I cried like a swift or thrush; I moaned like a mourning dove. My eyes grew weak as I looked to the heavens. I am troubled; O Lord, come to my aid!" (Isaiah 38.14)

When the Lord promises to be with us, even through the valley of the shadow of death, it is by his Holy Spirit.

Listen to the words of Jesus when he was teaching his disciples just prior to his own death:

"And I will ask the Father, and he will send you another Counsellor to be with you forever – the Spirit of truth. The world cannot accept him, because it neither sees him nor knows him. But you know him, for he lives with you and will be in you." (John 14.16-17)

This is the promise of Jesus to everyone who believes and knows him.

"Dear Lord, may we this Pentecost feel the presence of your Spirit. Send down your Spirit upon us!"

42. Can we be transformed by God's Holy Spirit?
Acts 2.14-42

For the past few weeks we have been learning from the life of Simon Peter. First we considered his call and how he responded unreservedly to Jesus' words, "Follow me." Then we thought about how he came to realise Jesus was far more than a wonderful man – that he was, and is, God. We spoke a little about the retreat at Caesarea Philippi, but dwelt mainly on the Transfiguration. Peter who acknowledged to his Lord, "You are the Christ," was one of the disciples to witness that amazing event.

Peter was so sure of his Master that he boasted he would never let him down, only to fail miserably when put to the test. Then last week we were quiet and serious as we considered his need of forgiveness and of re-establishing his relationship with Jesus. Only through his failure did he learn his deep need of forgiveness. All these were vital lessons for him, as they are for us, lessons on growing into really mature Christians. Today comes the climax, for we are going to see how the Power, the very Power of God, came into Peter's life, transforming him. God will extend to us the invitation to receive his power into our own lives.

Today is Pentecost or Whit Sunday. Pentecost is the fiftieth day. Originally it was the fiftieth day after Passover, when the Jews celebrated the Feast of Weeks. Pentecost for them marked the completion of the wheat harvest. The day was observed as a Sabbath day. All labour was suspended and the people went to Jerusalem, if at all possible, to worship in the temple to express their gratitude. The central ceremony of the day was the presentation of two loaves of leavened, salted bread to the Lord. It was a festival of good cheer, a day of joy. Free Will offerings were to be made to the Lord (Deuteronomy 16.10), and it was to be marked by making generous gifts to the Levites, and to orphans and widows.

But God was to make it a special day for Christians too. Jesus was crucified at Passover and on the fiftieth day following the crucifixion God sent his Spirit. God put his power into the very hearts of the followers of Jesus.

It was the day when Peter, newly empowered, spoke with such amazing conviction concerning his Lord that three thousand committed their lives to Jesus and were baptised in order that their sins might be cancelled and that they too might receive the gift of the Holy Spirit. It became a traditional day for new Christians to be baptised, and as they were baptised in white robes, it became known as Whit or White Sunday.

As an aside, you may be interested to know that the Christian festival threatened to sideline the old Jewish feast, so in order to "beef up" the Jewish feast, the Jews decided to make it the occasion when they also celebrated the giving of the law to Moses.

The Holy Spirit, the very power of God, came quite dramatically to these twelve men. At his ascension Jesus had sent them back to Jerusalem and had told them to wait for in just a few days following his return to glory they would be overwhelmed, immersed, baptised with his new power, The Holy Spirit.

They waited and prayed, and then suddenly it happened. It was not private, but obvious for all to see. First there was the noise, strangely localised on the house where they were gathered. It was like a mighty rushing wind, like a storm, perhaps like a whirlwind. It seemed to fill the house. Then there was that strange phenomenon, flames like tongues of fire, which came like a fireball, but then separated and hovered above the head of each disciple.

There must have been a tremendous presence of power. But most amazing of all was the change which came over these men.

Then Peter stood up with the Eleven, raised his voice and addressed the crowd: "Fellow Jews and all of you who live in Jerusalem, let me explain this to you; listen carefully to what I say."

Clearly the commotion had caused quite a crowd to gather – nothing unusual in that. It happens when a fire engine or a police car arrives, its siren wailing down your street. You look up, eager to know what is going on.

That is how it was in Jerusalem that morning. People came to find why there was the noise of the wind and the flames and they found these men, all speaking in languages they had not learned.

The immediate reaction is that the men have been celebrating too hard. "They are all drunk. They are as bad as a crowd of England football supporters at an away match! It shouldn't be allowed, letting a group of men get together to celebrate Pentecost, and Galileans at that! It's widely known; no good thing ever came out of Galilee. They have a reputation for drunk and disorderly behaviour. Here it is happening again. Soon the authorities will be along to haul them off and put them inside until they sober up."

But Peter says, "Whoa, that's not the case at all. Let me explain. Listen to what I have to say." Can this be the same Peter, the one who told a servant girl that he had never seen Jesus before now; the one who became angry when he was accused of being a disciple; the one who cursed and swore that he'd never known Jesus?

"These men are not drunk, as you suppose. It's only nine in the morning!"

I imagine someone in the crowd saying to his mate, "So what! I bet they've been boozing all night!"

Peter, with new found authority raises his voice and asserts:

"No, this is what was spoken by the prophet Joel: 'In the last days God says, I will pour out my Spirit on all people. Your sons and daughters will prophesy, your young men will see visions, your old men will dream dreams.'"(Joel 2.28)

Some of the better educated ones stop and think. Yes they could remember that being read out in the synagogue. They could remember some of the rabbis talking about it as a day to look for. It was something God would do when the Messiah came. It had been written down in their scriptures. Hey! Perhaps this Galilean fisherman is on to something important. Perhaps he really has something to say. Before you know it the wags in the crowd have been told to shut up and listen. The crowd is growing by the moment. You know how a crowd draws a crowd. Soon they are all listening intently to Peter.

And Peter the fisherman, with more skill than they have ever heard from the teachers of the law, unfolds and explains the Old Testament scriptures to them in a masterly manner. What Joel foretold, what the other prophets related with regard to the Messiah: he shows how all this has been fulfilled in Jesus: Jesus, the man whose miracles, wonders and signs they have witnessed.

It is the Jesus they had chanted against fifty days ago; and had consented, had shouted for his crucifixion. They had watched him being nailed to the cross.

Peter, with his new found wisdom and courage takes them first to Psalm 16 and then to Psalm 110 and shows them how it had been foretold, how his body would not know corruption – how God would raise him from the dead – how God would bring him honour and glory – how he would reign as Lord and King – how his enemies would be put beneath his feet. This, explains Peter, has all been fulfilled in Jesus.

He speaks for some time – the crowd in rapt attention. Finally he reaches his conclusion:

"Therefore let all Israel be assured of this: God has made this Jesus, whom you crucified, both Lord and Christ."

I suspect that Peter himself was amazed. He had never spoken like that before. He had a big mouth, yes and had occasionally said something wise, but he had said far more that was stupid. He had never imagined himself standing up in front of a great crowd and preaching a sermon, and what is more, the crowd listening!

Can we be transformed by God's Holy Spirit? – Acts 2.14-42

Feeling somewhat stunned and drained Peter is all for stepping down from his position, but he senses something is happening. There is a quiet murmuring among the people, not of dissent, but of consulting with each other. "This is amazing! What is God doing? What should we do?" A startling change has come over the people. Some are quietly weeping. All are giving serious consideration to what they have heard. After a few minutes one man stands forward as a spokesman for the assembled crowd:

When the people heard this, they were cut to the heart and said to Peter and the other apostles, "Brothers, what shall we do?"

What shall they do indeed? They have agitated for the Messiah to be slain. Could God ever forgive them? Previous generations had persecuted and even killed prophets; that was bad enough, but to be a party to the crucifixion of God's only son, the Messiah; could that ever be forgiven?

I came across this powerful statement by C.S. Lewis, which I feel you ought to hear. "Christianity tells people to repent and promises forgiveness. It therefore has nothing to say to people who do not know they have done anything to repent of, and who do not feel that they need any forgiveness. It is after you have realised that there is a real Moral Law, and a power behind the law, and that you have broken that law and put yourself wrong with that Power – it is after all this, and not a moment sooner, that Christianity begins to talk. When you know you are sick, you will listen to the doctor."

It wasn't Peter really who had got through to the crowd. It was the Holy Spirit in Peter who gave his words power. And it won't be Goff who gets through to you, though in his grace God might allow me to be the instrument through which the Holy Spirit speaks to you and similarly convicts you, "Lord, what must I do?" What Peter tells the crowd that first Pentecost, God would tell you this Pentecost Sunday.

Peter replied, "Repent and be baptised, every one of you, in the name of Jesus Christ for the forgiveness of your sins. And you will receive the gift of the Holy Spirit."

In answer to the question put by the people, Peter presented a fourfold challenge:

1. *"Repent!"*

The Greek word means, "Change your outlook" or "change your mind." "Turn around and change your way of living"' Repentance is not just sorrow or even sorrow for sin but an actual change in the way a person thinks and lives. It is a fundamental and wholehearted change of mind which results in a change of purpose, direction and values. *"Every one of you"* reminds us that this message is for all. Everyone needs to make a decision about Christ. His offer is the only effective solution for the sin problem that plagues every one who has ever lived.

2. *"Turn to God."*

Turning from your sins is not enough. In addition to turning from sin, people must turn to God. It does no good to turn from sin without turning then to the one who can solve the sin problem. By ourselves, without God's power, without the Spirit of God in our lives, we will slip back, albeit little by little, until we are in a worse state than we were at the beginning. Satan will mock us for our lack of power and we will be more tightly held in his snare. But Peter says that turning from sin and turning to God is not enough to ensure that we will receive the Holy Spirit. He continues:

3. *"Be baptised in the name of Jesus Christ for the forgiveness of your sins."*

We believe that baptism was already being used for Jewish converts as a sign of their conversion to Judaism. John the Baptist had called for baptism as a sign of repentance and a changed heart. Now for believers, baptism is proof of repentance and commitment to follow Jesus, the Messiah. Baptism is an act of obedience to Jesus, who was himself baptised by immersion. Jesus said that in doing so we do all that the Father requires. Baptism is a mark of future intent for our lives. Repentance, not baptism, brings about forgiveness, but baptism is an outward display that Jesus asks you to undergo, a demonstration of an inner change which has taken place in your heart. Have you been baptised as a believer?

4. *"Receive the gift of the Holy Spirit."*

Only through the coming of the Holy Spirit into believers' hearts can they truly experience the forgiveness of sin. Only the Holy Spirit can fill your life with God's power. The Holy Spirit is a gift from God, and God promises the Holy Spirit to all who turn from their sins, to all who turn to God and are baptised.

Does this mean me? Does this mean you?

"The promise is for you and your children and for all who are far off – for all whom the Lord our God will call."

Luke doesn't tell us any more about what Peter said that day, but he does tell us that the matter was so important that Peter spoke for a long time:

With many other words he warned them; and he pleaded with them, "Save yourselves from this corrupt generation."

People must be prepared to step out from the world, not caring what the world says or thinks. People must be prepared to turn to Christ. There is no other way to be saved. There is no other way by which God can transform us by His Spirit.

What a remarkable response there was to the message Peter gave:

Those who accepted his message were baptised, and about three thousand were added to their number that day.

Just imagine the scene. That very day, there and then in Jerusalem, three thousand people believed and took the step of faith in Christ! Those who believed were baptised. That must have kept the apostles busy. Three thousand took their first step of obedience and publicly identified with Christ. These folk were added to the church; they immediately joined the fellowship of believers:

They devoted themselves to the apostles' teaching and to the fellowship, to the breaking of bread and to prayer.

I wonder how Peter felt as he went to bed that Pentecost evening. Tired I'm sure, but I would be surprised if he could sleep. I think the excitement of it all kept him awake, praising God, thrilled to bits. After all that was past he had really done something effective for the Kingdom of God.

It wasn't that Peter hadn't tried before. He had given up a lot to follow the Lord; his business, his home, his security. He had made some fantastic discoveries about Jesus, but nothing had prepared him for this. What a difference the Holy Spirit had already made in his life. It had given him the power to be what God wanted him to be.

Ah, you say, that must have been great for Peter, but I don't suppose anything like that will ever happen to me. Listen:

"Repent and be baptised, every one of you, in the name of Jesus Christ for the forgiveness of your sins. And you will receive the gift of the Holy Spirit. The promise is for you and your children and for all who are far off – for all whom the Lord our God will call"

If you then, though you are evil, know how to give good gifts to your children, how much more will your Father in heaven give the Holy Spirit to those who ask him!" (Luke 11.13)

Contact Details

Kathy would be pleased to know if this book has helped you in any way.

More copies of this book may be obtained from Amazon, Keith Jones Christian Bookshop in Bournemouth, other Christian Bookshops or from Kathy.

Kathy Butler,
Rosebush Publishing,
12 Southern Avenue,
West Moors,
Ferndown, Dorset. BH22 0BL
www.kathybutler.net
kathybutler@aol.com